FLIGHT OF THE ANGELS

Twelve Adventure Stories in Tracking with Angels

Barton R Thom

All Rights Reserved
Copyright 2014 by Dancing Hawk Press
223 East Maxan St # 107, Port Isabel, Texas 78578

Tracking With Angels   ISBN 9780991347735
Flight of the Angels   ISBN 9780991347704
Path of the Angels   ISBN 9780991347766
Justice of the Angels   ISBN 9780991347780

Dedication:

TO ALL THE GUARDIAN ANGELS

CERTAINLY THEY ARE THE HARDEST WORKING ANGELS I KNOW!

With a special thanks to the men and women of (and working with) The 2nd Battalion; 75 Infantry; the pilots and the men aboard the eight Black Hawk helicopters (you know whom you are and why I am not allowed to say whom you are); whose actions prevented the largest terrorist attack in United States history. And to the teenager and her Chesapeake Bay Retriever whom were literally first in on the ground leading the way. And to the Angels whom were truly behind:
THE FLIGHT OF THE ANGELS

I have asked GOD for a Special Blessing;
To those of you who make the effort,
And take the time needed;
So you too can Track the Trails
With your Guardian Angel

Table of Contents

Introduction

Angels are a unique Gift from GOD. These stories intended to help you connect with your Guardian Angel. Numerous sections are written so as to allow your Guardian Angel to give you your personal recognition signal as the Angels show you which sections are true or important lessons for you to understand. **These stories are designed to be a bridge helping you to begin the biggest adventure in your life: Interacting with the Angels!** These twelve adventure stories let you accompany Dancing Wind, a teenage Native American Indian girl as she learns from a Lakota Indian Medicine man how to spirit track. Come along with Dancing Wind as she follows the path of the Angels from Alaska to the Mediterranean Sea. Travel with Dancing Wind as she travels into the high mountain peaks of Cañada del Oro, north of Tucson, Arizona. Walk along the beaches of Padre Island, Texas as she follows the guidance of her Guardian Angel. For you too will experience the adventures she encounters as she travels with the Angels. Travel through time with her as she encounters: Mexican bandits, men of honor and integrity like Arturio, Indians, Spaniards, Jews fleeing the Spanish Inquisition, women whom have been kidnapped, ghost, cattle rustlers, women treasure hunters, fishermen, priest and even a Flight of Angels all working to set things right.

The same methods Dancing Wind uses as she interacts with Angels are explained in detail, so you too can unleash the adventures that are awaiting you. You may cry, tingle, shake, vibrate or even begin hearing your own personal Guardian Angel communicate with you as the Angels use these stories to teach you to recognize when your Guardian Angel who watches over you, is trying to communicate with you! Open your heart to Love and let these stories bring you closer to your spiritual side.

The Angels in our life are a unique gift from GOD. Like all gifts, we can accept the gift or ignore the Gift. Certainly few individuals take the time and make the effort to connect to their own Guardian Angel. **To those who do interact with their Guardian Angel; a world a wonder and delight can unfold in their life. Certainly my Angel has warned me of danger, had me rolling on the ground in laughter, as well as crying like Noah's flood.**

With an Angel at my side, we have had adventures I never envisioned possible. Not ever trail one tracks in life turns out the way you wish. Many of the trails I have tracked with Dancing Wind have been sad trails, not every time I look for a treasure do I recover a treasure. Yet on ever Trail that I have tracked, she (my Guardian Angel) had a lesson for me to learn.

Many of the trails I have tracked with my Guardian Angel, Dancing Wind have had a purpose in life far beyond my immediate self interest. For frequently my Guardian Angel will want me to assist a spirit who needs help / assistance. Helping those spirits that one can; goes with the territory. Never have I ever regretted the actions I have taken under my Guardian Angels direction!

You may never want to spend a day among the mountain peaks of Cañada Del Oro, track a trail as in the account of *Flight of the Angels* or stand beside a men like Wild Buffalo and Arturio whom I do call my Friends. *I would hope these stories do work as a bridge or a path to help you connect to YOUR GUARDIAN ANGEL.* Some individuals will read these stories and say they are impossible. Some individuals will read these stories and be amazed at the possibilities. I would hope that as you read these adventure stories that you open your self to your Guardian Angel and allow him or her to show you their personal recognition signals for you. Each time you sit down to read these stories ask GOD to place a White Light of Protection around you and then ask your

Guardian Angel to sit beside you as you read these stories. She / He (your Guardian Angel) may begin opening you up to begin your adventure with the Angels by causing you to vibrate, shake, tingle, cry, get hot, or many other forms as they open the bridge to communicate with you. The very fortunate individuals may begin communicating directly with their Guardian Angel. If you wish; you may ask your Guardian Angel to give you your personal recognition signal every time that the Angels feels there is an important lesson for you to understand, or that story or account is true. This will rapidly get you on the path to communicating with your own Guardian Angel. Always insist upon this recognition signal when communicating with your Angel to be sure the information you receive is authentic.

I hope you enjoy these adventures with Guardian Angels and I sincerely hope that they help you connect with your own Guardian Angel. GOD Speed; and enjoy!

These stories were written months to years after I tracked these trails. As I wrote down my adventures; sometimes in my mind the events became alive and I recalled the exact conversation of what was said, when that occurred, I put it in italics, I hope that this does not detract from the story but enhances it for the reader - -every name of in individual, every company name and ship name is from my imagination—while every place or terrain description is as accurate as I recall.
Dancing Wind

Kisses of Love
Kisses of Grace
Kisses of Angels
On Your Face
Show to You
GOD's Divine Grace

The Cattle Rustler's Treasure

S amuel Jackson was used to hard work. Often his day began in the early predawn morning when the ground was frozen and he was so cold he just could not sleep. His fingers would be numb from the cold as he built a fire and warmed his fingers and body trying to get some circulation back into them. If he was lucky enough to have any remaining he would try and heat some coffee. As he held the hot coffee he would warm his fingers with the cup. If he had any jerky he would dip it in his hot coffee to try and soften it a little. As he chewed the hard, dry meat, he placed the horse's metal bit on a log near the fire to warm it slightly so the horse would not begin the day mad at him for putting a frozen piece of metal in his mouth. If Samuel put a frozen metal bit in the horse's mouth she would show her displeasure by trying to buck Samuel off her back. In a few minutes he would put the reins, a saddle blanket and then saddle his horse. He had a long day ahead of him.

Samuel put in another fourteen hour day as he moved the longhorn cattle towards the silver mining town of Creede. Samuel was driving the cattle to Creede, as he felt that he could sell them in a quick sale for hard cash money As he moved northwest from Del Norte, he followed the wagon road--where it existed. Frequently he moved the cattle in the river bed of the Rio Grande, as it literally was the best road. .

Samuel put his faith in his six-gun and hard cash money; gold and silver. You could not trust paper money; the wind coming suddenly in a strong gust could blow it away. Counterfeiters could make fake money, and if one had drunk a few too many beers, they would not realize until they sobered up that their pockets were full of the worthless money. Everyone knew, with the fall of the Confederacy to the Union Forces in the Civil War fifteen years ago, that instantly all Confederate currency had become worthless. There was a certain weight to gold and silver, so you knew the money was valuable. You could bury gold and silver in the ground and come back later when you needed it and it was always good. Samuel kept his extra money buried in three wooden cigar boxes. Inside three wooden boxes, was just a little bit over one thousand dollars in gold and silver coins, which it had taken him thirty years to save up. Samuel thought that one day, when he was too old to work, he would buy himself a small ranch, retire to the front porch, and enjoy a rocking chair. Maybe he would have a partner he could trust and they would sit there together telling stories of their adventures and the hard winters that they had gone through. Samuel knew that a good partner, one he could trust with his life, would be very hard to come by.

The twenty head of beef he had with him were destined to be sold to feed the hungry, hard working miners at the new silver mining camp called Creede. In the fall of 1890 it was a booming city with over a thousand people living there. He was pushing west from Alamosa for two days until he hit Del Norte. A day later he would reach South Fork. From South Fork, he would follow the river northwest to Creede. For twelve to fourteen hours a day he rode in the saddle, moving the cattle towards Creede at approximately two miles per hour. He had about 30 miles to go once he reached South Fork. He was sure he could cover the thirty miles in three days.

Upon arriving in Creede, Samuel Jackson wanted to meet up with some saloon owners and the butchers to sell the beef to. Normally beef on the hoof sells at 2.5 cents a pound, meaning a 1,200 pound steer sold for $20. After butchering you could figure two thirds of the steer's weight was actual meat. So on a 1,200 pound steer there would be about 800 pounds of good useable beef worth 2.5 cents per pound.

Samuel stopped at the first business he saw, a butcher shop where he sold ten head of cattle for a hundred dollars in gold. Counting his out his gold pieces Samuel walked out of the butcher shop happy with his sale.

The butcher was about to tell Samuel he did not need any beef cattle until next week, but when Samuel told him he needed cash money now for the beef, and he would sell twenty-dollar steers for ten dollars the butcher could not resist a bargain. The butcher knew that by only paying ten dollars a head, instead of the fifty dollars he hoped to make this month, he would instead triple his income and make a hundred and fifty dollars.

Samuel stopped next at the Creede Miners Kitchen where hungry miners came to eat their fill after a hard day of work. In talking to the owner, Samuel realized the owner was desperate for some good beef at a bargain price so instead of selling the ten steers for a hundred dollars, Samuel insisted that the owner also throw in a week's worth of meals to the deal. The owner's counter offer was ten dollars a head and ten meals to boot. Samuel immediately agreed to the counteroffer. The owner then went into his kitchen and got out one hundred dollars in silver dollars. With so many heavy silver dollars, Samuel put the coins in his saddle bag since Samuel did not want to walk around with over eight pounds of silver dollars bulging out of his pockets, clinking and jingling with every step he took. Walking out of the Creede Miners Kitchen with his saddle bag over his left shoulder, containing eight large fists full of silver dollars Samuel looked for a bank. There, Samuel was able to exchange most of his silver dollars for a few gold coins. In five minutes he had exchanged eight pounds of silver coins for about four ounces of gold coins. The gold coins were very compact, light weight and would not attract the attention of dishonest men bent upon robbing him like all the jingling silver dollars would.

Samuel was not a man any robber with common sense would chose to rob, or at least the robber would not choose him twice. Samuel was strong and his fist hit like rock. The last two men who had tried to steal his horse had died trying to do something very foolish. Samuel had an awareness of who was approaching or following him, so seldom was it possible to approach him without his full awareness of your presence. He was also skilled in the use of his .44 caliber revolver. Samuel never went looking to start trouble; he was a quiet man who kept mostly to himself.

Samuel intended to enjoy his arrival in town so he planned to get a shave and a haircut, he felt he was looking a little rough as he had not had one or the other in over two months. Samuel sat down at the Creed Barber shop, but all the prices seemed high to him they wanted five cents for a shave and five cents for a haircut. Samuel could recall that back east he only paid five cents for both. No wonder he only went to the barber shop every two to three months with these kinds of prices.

Next on Samuel's list was to get some clean clothes from the Creede Clothing Emporium which he would change into after he took a bath. Samuel felt that after five weeks of hard work pushing these cattle up the trail to Creede, maybe he should change his clothes and take a bath whether he needed to or not.

At the Creed Clothing Emporium Samuel spent his money freely, buying a pair of blue jeans, a flannel shirt, two pair of socks and two neckerchiefs. He also picked up a box of "Lucifer's." The Lucifer's always came in handy for building a fire to keep warm or cook on when he was out riding on the trail. The prices were high in mining camps so the jeans cost a dollar, the flannel shirt was ninety cents, the two pair of thick, woolen socks were fifteen cents and the two neckerchiefs cost him a dime. The matches cost a nickel. Samuel had just spent two dollars and twenty cents. Two and a quarter days' worth of pay for a hard-working man, he thought to himself. He knew that had the same clothing been purchased back east of the Mississippi River, the same clothing would have cost about a dollar. All the goods in mining camps were very expensive!

When he asked where he could get a bath, he was directed to a street where there was a Chinese Laundry and bath house, along Willow Creek. It would cost him ten cents to have all his dirty clothes washed. He could pick up his clean clothes tomorrow afternoon. The baths were four cents for a bath with cold water. A hot bath cost six cents more. Samuel spent his hard earned money freely; he decided to have a hot bath. When Samuel took a bath he kept his six- gun handy, placing it between a fold in the towels where he could instantly grab his revolver. Samuel tried to be a careful man, so he wanted to be prepared for trouble should it arise.

Once Samuel had a haircut, a shave, a bath, and all new clothes, he felt like a new man. He decided he would go over to the saloon and have himself a drink of whiskey, but his real purpose in going to the saloon was not to drink, but to catch up on the news. For it was by listening in the saloon that one could find out all the latest news of what is happening.

Samuel went into the saloon and ordered a whiskey. As he listened to the people talk about the news, he learned what was going on in Creede. He saw miners selling their stolen high grade gold and silver ore to a man down at one end of the bar, and he also learned the Commodore and the Holy Moses mines were hiring. He declined to join in a friendly poker game in which none of the men looked very friendly. He did not intend to lose his hard-earned money gambling.

Then out of the corner of his eye he saw Charlene. Now that was a pretty lady. Several women were in the saloon making their living. Dancing was three cents for a short dance of about three minutes, or one song, and five cents for two dances. Samuel decided he wanted to dance with Charlene. Samuel did not know how to dance. In fact, he had never danced before but he wanted to dance and talk with Charlene. He really liked her, so after two dances, Samuel paid for another two dances. He really liked her. So he did what came to mind but seldom actually happens to a woman like her. He asked her if she would like to join him for a steak dinner; of course he would buy. Charlene was surprised by the offer but she was more surprised when she heard herself say,

"Yes, I would like that."

Samuel and Charlene walked over to the Creede Miners Kitchen and Samuel looked at the menu on the wall. He asked Charlene what she would like to eat and she quietly asked him what he could afford. Not replying to her question, he instead asked her another: how she liked her steaks and when she replied medium, he told the cook to bring two medium steaks, two potatoes, and a bottle of wine. Samuel sat at the corner table with his back to the wall where he could see anyone coming in or out of the doors as well as anyone approaching him. Charlene had been around enough to realize that Samuel always sat in a defensive position, so she knew he must have enemies.

Charlene really enjoyed her steak and potato as she drank the wine with Samuel. She had been a little short of cash lately and she could not recall how many years had passed since she had enjoyed a steak dinner. On what Charlene made, she simply could not afford the fifteen cents for the steak dinner, or the ten cents for the bottle of wine. She certainly would not forget this night for months to come. Usually she danced with miners who had not had a bath in months and she could smell their approach from ten feet away; that, or the men reeked of alcohol. They would put their hands in inappropriate places and try to steal kisses from her. Many men she danced with were crude, rude, and said despicable things to her. Samuel was the first person who had treated her with dignity and courtesy since she had arrived in Colorado three years earlier.

When dinner ended Charlene invited Samuel up to her room above the saloon. Charlene apologized to Samuel but she had to charge him a silver dollar, which she handed to the bartender, for the saloon charged the women a dollar for each customer they took up to their rooms. That was the saloon's cut of the money the women made. Over the course of an average week the saloon ended up with two thirds of the money the women made from dancing and entertaining men in their rooms.

In the morning Samuel invited Charlene to go with him to the Clothing Emporium so he could buy her a new dress. Samuel had noticed that Charlene's dresses were really worn and had numerous patches where she had repaired them. All the cuffs and hemlines were becoming tattered and frayed. Charlene wanted to go in the worst way, but she had no money for a dress and she told Samuel that. Samuel told her it was a gift from him, so together they walked over to the Clothing Emporium.

At the Clothing Emporium Charlene began looking at dresses. Just as Charlene found a red dress she really liked, the wife of the store owner came over and told Charlene she had to leave her store at once.

Samuel asked "why?",

The woman replied, "We cannot have her kind in our store."

Samuel's face got stone cold and he replied, "And what kind is that?"

Then Henry, the store owner who was standing behind the counter, spoke up, "You know what kind of woman she is! I won't have a woman like that in my store!"

Charlene put down the dress and started to leave, but Samuel stopped her with his tone of voice when he told Charlene, "No, we are not leaving until you get your dress."

The store owner's wife told Samuel, "I want you both out of the store NOW!"

Samuel replied, "We are getting the red dress or you will be wearing a black dress after I kill your husband!"

"That will be murder, with all these witnesses you will hang for it," she replied

"No I won't, as all these witnesses will testify your husband drew first. When I kill him I will simply be defending myself. You see, your husband intends to back your play, Mama. He is working up the courage to go for that pistol behind the counter, and as soon as he grabs that gun I will kill him. You see, Mama, your husband has more grit than you give him credit for, and in a minute he will go for that gun he is staring at now. It is your call, Mama: are you selling us the dress or are you going to be wearing black?"

Henry's wife saw the gunman slide the leather thong off the hammer of his revolver. She knew the gunman facing her husband and herself was now prepared to draw his weapon. Suddenly a cold fear struck her; she knew in moments she would be a widow wearing black. She knew her husband Henry had no chance going up against a professional gunman.

"Henry, step back away from that counter now! Don't you dare touch that gun Henry! I changed my mind and I am going to sell her that dress now!"

He paid two dollars for the red dress and Charlene picked up her dress and walked out of the store with Samuel. As they walked out of the store, they heard the store owner's wife saying,

"Can you imagine the nerve of a woman like that--coming in here with good Christian folk."

That night Samuel and Charlene had dinner again. Again, they ate at the Creede Miners Kitchen. Just as the night before, Samuel sat in the corner with his back to the wall. Even while he and Charlene talked, he always kept an eye on the doorway, glancing to see who was coming in and out of the diner as they ate their steak dinner and drank red wine. Charlene was in a very good mood; no one had ever given her a dress before except her mother when she was a little girl, and Samuel had asked for nothing in return; she had never met such a nice man.

That night Henry, of the Clothing Emporium, was taking his wife out to dinner. By chance, he happened to pick the Creede Miners Kitchen, as he liked their big bowls of beef stew. Samuel saw them enter and when they saw him with that woman they sat on the opposite side of the restaurant. Charlene saw Samuel's eyes follow them across the room so she, too, turned to see who he was looking at. Samuel saw the tension in Charlene's eyes and he placed his hand upon hers.

As she looked down he told her, "Forget about it. You can never change some people. Some people grow up fast, while some people never grow up."

The butcher came into the Creed Miners Kitchen looking for Samuel.

He told Samuel, "I could use some more beef. If you get me those white-face cattle called Herefords I will pay you twenty dollars a head, as they have more meat on them than the longhorn cattle." Samuel told the butcher he would try to find him some, but they were a lot harder to find than the longhorns.

That night Charlene wanted to do something special for Samuel because he had purchased her the dress and asked nothing in return. She knew that Samuel enjoyed her company. So she asked Samuel if she could give him a hot bath and massage his shoulders. Samuel thought that sounded nice and he told her so. So Charlene went down stairs to heat water on the pot belly wood stove for the bath.

When she left the room Samuel went over to his saddlebag and removed ten silver dollars. He went over to Charlene's purse and placed the ten coins inside. When he had opened Charlene's purse to place the ten silver dollars inside, he noticed she had sixty cents inside her purse.

He did not want Charlene to know he had given her a gift to help her out, until he was gone. Samuel enjoyed the hot bath and having Charlene massage his shoulders. Yes, Samuel thought, he had enjoyed the time he had spent with Charlene, but tomorrow he had to get back to work.

Samuel slipped out of Charlene's bed at the crack of dawn. He quietly got dressed and took his saddle bag with his clothing and slipped out the door. Charlene was still asleep. Down at the Creede Miners Kitchen Samuel ate breakfast with the miners who were getting ready for another backbreaking day working in the mines. Samuel asked the cook to make him up a bag of food for the trail. The cook gave him four sandwiches, two made of leftover ham and fried eggs from breakfast and two made from leftover steaks from the night before. The cook wrapped up the sandwiches in some old newspapers and handed them to Samuel, who put them in his saddle bag. These would hold him until he reached the road house at South Fork in two days.

He walked down the street three blocks to the livery stable and paid the owner the stabling fee of twenty five cents a day for stabling his horse. The owner brought Samuel's horse out of the stable already bridled. Samuel saddled his horse, tied his equipment to the saddle, and rode out of town. His mind was already focused on the trail ahead.

As he rode to the southeast alongside the Rio Grande, Samuel reflected back on the two days he had spent in Creede. He had sold two hundred dollars' worth of cattle. He thought he would have to control his wild spending. He had spent eighteen dollars for his two days on the town! Samuel knew that represented over half a months' pay. He told himself he would have to watch is spending. Of course he told himself the same thing after every trip to town, and yet in the last ten years nothing had really changed. There was always someone he felt just needed a little help, it was Charlene this time, there were other woman in other mining camps, or some orphan he met in town just begging for a meal that he would try and help out.

Often he would help out the nuns or padres he encountered with a two dollar gift as he knew they were always trying to help sick people and those who were in need and they were always in need of an extra dollar. To him it seemed most people had become hard and bitter and did not take the time to help their fellow man, even when they had extra money in both their wallet and the bank.

Samuel always remembered the time he had not eaten in days and an old man fed him and shared all his food with him. This one simple act of kindness had been at a time when Samuel had been desperate for help, as he had fallen upon hard times. While he had never seen the old man who shared the last of his food with him again, by helping others he had been showing himself that he remembered the lesson of kindness the old man had shown him and he was trying in his own manner to repay that help by helping others.

When Charlene awoke in the morning, Samuel was gone. She

asked at the livery stable and learned he had saddled his horse and rode out at dawn.

Sometimes in life we have friends whose company we enjoy. Occasionally in life we meet someone who gives us a helping hand. A person who is both a friend and gives us a helping hand when we need it is truly a treasure beyond price. So, when you have the chance to be a friend or to help one in need, you, too have the choice, to turn your head away and pass on by, or be a treasure beyond price. For indeed GOD has given you free will to choose your path. So choose wisely.

★★★★

Two days later Samuel rode into South Fork. Samuel stopped at a road house which fed travelers on their way to Creed to the northwest or Durango to the west. Before tackling the pass he wanted a hot meal under his belt for it would likely be the last time he ate until he reached Pagosa Hot Springs, two and a half days ride to the west. He was headed west for Durango and he had to cross Wolf Creek Pass. The pass worried him, as it was already October and one heavy winter snow could close the pass to travel until spring.

Samuel ate stew at the road house. Stew was the only item on the menu, had there been a menu. Frequently, when one ate at a road house every one sat down at one or two tables. Customers had a choice of whatever the cook had decided to fix that day or you could do without eating. At the South Fork Road House the dinner consisted of the left over stew from lunch. The stew consisted of potatoes, carrots, onions and elk meat. The waitress said you could also have one biscuit and your choice of drinks: water or coffee. The meals were priced at six cents per bowl of stew and two cents for coffee.

After eating Samuel looked the cook up and told her he enjoyed the meal. It was very good and filling. Then he asked her if she could make him several sandwiches to carry him over on his ride through Wolf Creek Pass. Twenty minutes later Samuel got his three elk meat sandwiches wrapped up in an old newspaper. He packed his sandwiches in his saddlebags and rode out for the pass. He just figured he could make a couple miles before dark and somewhere along Wolf Creek he would camp for the night.

The next morning at daybreak Samuel was up and riding, but he did not like the look of the clouds rolling in from the west. The gray color reminded him of snow. Throughout the day Samuel passed several wagons also trying to get across these mountains before the incoming storm broke. No one was taking a break or stopping to rest. They were pushing hard to get across the pass. The men coming from Durango heading east did not stop to rest either, even though they had successfully crossed the high mountain pass, because they wanted to drop down in elevation to where the coming storm would be less intense. Everyone knew the snow storm was coming. With the buildup of clouds, the temperature had dropped twenty degrees in the last two hours.

The snow began in the afternoon. The cold wind from the west was blowing large, cold, white snowflakes into his face. Samuel got down to walk his horse in order to give her a rest. He knew he was pushing her hard and he would push her harder as he wanted to be over the mountain pass before dark. Slowly the snow began to whiten the ground and the surrounding forest. Late in the afternoon the snow storm was unleashing her full fury. Visibility had dropped to a hundred feet and about four inches of snow had accumulated on the ground. Samuel knew he could not stop to camp for the day until he had crossed the pass and dropped in elevation one or two thousand feet where the fury of the snow storm would not be as intense and the snowfall accumulation come daybreak would be a lot less.

About an hour before dark Samuel reached the top of Wolf Creek Pass. He had been told the elevation was about two miles above sea level. There were gray snow clouds shrouding the top of the mountains. He began descending the west side of the mountain. Samuel pushed on until just before dark when he looked for campsite with some protection from the wind and plenty of firewood. Opening his saddle bag, he noticed that blowing snow had gotten into his box of matches and the body heat of his horse was enough to melt the snow, resulting in water getting his matches wet. Until thoroughly dried out, they could not be used to start a fire.

Samuel used an axe he carried to gather up as much fire wood as possible to carry him through the night. From his saddle bag Samuel removed a pair of fencing pliers he used when cutting a barbed-wire fence. He removed two of the lead bullet heads from two .44 shells with the fencing pliers. Taking fine dry wood shavings, he poured the gun power from the two shell casings into his fine tender. He held his revolver close to the ground and took aim, not at the gun powder, but at the ground. His tinder and gun powder were three inches away from his pistol barrel. Samuel fired his revolver, the muzzle flash setting off the gun powder in his tinder. The gun powder in turn started the tinder of wood shavings on fire. Samuel had used his revolver to start a small fire. Twenty minutes later he had a good, warm fire going. He would keep it burning all night to keep from freezing to death. As night fell the full intensity of the snow storm could be felt as the temperature kept dropping.

Later, another wagon pulled up and the driver asked Samuel if he could join him at the fire. The driver was mighty grateful for the company and the warm fire on a cold and snowy night like tonight. Before morning seven men and two boys were enjoying the warmth of the fire Samuel had built. Every year there were men who were not as lucky as those who found Samuel that night. They had pushed on until the point where they were too cold to work or lacked the skills to build a fire under adverse winter conditions and they froze to death. Samuel had eaten one of his sandwiches during the afternoon. That night he shared his remaining food with those who had none.

A day and a half later, Samuel rode into Pagosa Hot Springs. He was dead tired so he decided to take a warm relaxing bath in the hot springs located along the river. Near the river he would camp where Native American Indians had been camping for centuries. Everyone enjoyed the relaxing hot sulfur mineral waters.

Traveling west, Samuel rode past Chimney Rock and made camp beside the Piedra River. The Piedra River was about fifty feet wide and two feet deep where he crossed. Looking towards the north, he though a man could lose himself, or if necessary, a posse, in those rugged San Juan Mountains. Had Samuel been a prospector, he thought that the San Juan's looked good for finding mineral deposits.

Two days later around dark, Samuel rode into Durango. At the mercantile store he purchased some food. He bought a twenty five pound bag of dry pinto beans, a twenty pound bag of flour, a ten pound ham, two pounds of coffee. Lard, salt, baking powder, and some jam and honey for his biscuits finished up his grocery shopping. The month's supply of food cost four dollars and fifty cents. The store owner gave him four burlap sacks and Samuel put the ham and the flour in one burlap bag. In the second burlap bag went the rest of his food, a bag of pinto beans and he double bagged both the burlap sacks. Samuel tied the burlap bags together with a strip of leather and hung the load over opposite sides of the saddle horn so the load would balance out on his saddle. Samuel spent the night in the livery stable. The next morning he got up at day break and was riding south towards his cabin.

Nine days after having left Creede, Samuel rode up to his cabin located approximately thirty miles south of Durango, Colorado. It is good to be home, he thought. Someday Samuel hoped to own a nice ranch with good water, good pasture, good Hereford cattle and some forest land to supply him with logs to build a home and firewood for heating and cooking.

To make that plan happen, Samuel had been saving money for the last thirty years. At fifty five years of age his dream had more substance than most, as he had amassed three small boxes of treasure. There was almost a thousand dollars in gold and silver coins in those three cigar boxes. Two were hidden in his root cellar. It was the third one, to which he added one hundred and seventy dollars in gold coins. Samuel kept seven dollars in his pocket, so he had a little spending money until he could make some more money. Samuel was thinking of a good spot to hide his treasure when he walked out to the outhouse to use the bathroom. He heard a horse ride up, and not knowing who it was, he simply dropped one cigar box of his treasure down the outhouse hole, hiding his box. Then he went out to see who had ridden up. It was just a neighbor boy looking for a lost cow. Samuel told the boy he had not seen it but he would keep an eye open for the cow and if he saw it he would let him know.

★★★★

Samuel tried to be a careful man when he worked. Whenever he worked he was always careful to be sure he had two ways in and out. This was a rule that had saved his life more than once. Over near Las Vegas, New Mexico he had been working with seven men rustling cattle and horses. He had gotten up early that morning to check on the horses when he heard the crack of a rifle. Three hundred yards down the valley he saw one of his fellow rustlers stumble, drop his bucket of water, then fall forward dead. A posse rode into the valley, pouring their rifle fire into the log cabin where the gang had been hiding. He grabbed a horse and rode out of there. Never after that did he forget to consider his need for a second way out of where ever he worked.

★★★★

Samuel had been scouting the remote ranch in southern New Mexico for a week where the only remote herd of white face cattle he knew of was down in a box canyon. When he saw the men ride out of the canyon, he rode in to steal the thirty-five head of Herefords. He came in quick and started the herd moving towards the only exit of the box canyon. He heard the wife of the rancher fire a shotgun at him, but he knew that he was too far ahead of her to be hurt by a shot gun.

★★★★

Oh, she was mad. That cattle thief had just stolen all the cattle they depended upon to make a living! When she looked out of the kitchen window and saw the cattle rustler stealing their herd of cattle, she grabbed the shotgun and fired at the man.

Her husband had told her the shot gun was only for short ranges of about a hundred feet. That was when it was most effective. Already the man was six hundred feet away from her when she fired her shot gun. The sound of the shotgun echoed down the box canyon. She was simply doing her best with the only weapon her husband had left her in the house. GOD, she prayed, send her husband and sons home now to catch this cattle rustler robbing them.

★★★★

Samuel quickly moved the cattle down the canyon.

"Let's see," he thought, "if I make it to Creede with thirty head at twenty dollars a head that will be six hundred dollars." He expected to lose about five of the thirty five head along the trail as he pushed these cattle as hard as possible. That is two years' pay to an honest, hard-workingman. He was rich; one more job like this and he would retire and buy a ranch, he thought. He figured that if he had one thousand two hundred dollars saved that he would have plenty of money to live out the rest of his life. Yup, with one thousand two hundred dollars he could buy a small ranch and a home and still have plenty of money for retirement. Very few men had that kind of money saved to retire on.

Suddenly Samuel's thoughts were interrupted by the presence of danger ahead, for into the box canyon rode the owner of the cattle and his two sons. The father and his two sons had heard the sound of the shotgun firing, as the sound echoed down the box canyon. They knew some emergency must be occurring at their house. The rancher and his sons were riding hard for the ranch house when they spotted a cattle rustler stealing their cattle. Samuel put the spurs to his horse to ensure a burst of speed as he saw the father and his two sons' Winchester rifles come up to their shoulders. The three rifles cracked as one and he flew off his saddle backwards.

★★★★

The father and sons immediately headed for their cabin to check on the man's wife when they heard the shotgun go off. They were just happy they could kill the cattle rustler who was trying to steal their cattle. The husband had his sons bury the cattle rustler. He would not report it to the sheriff, as he would be expected to turn over the rifle, six gun and horse to the sheriff.

The husband rode up to check on his wife. They were so happy that both of them were fine.

The husband hugged his wife and told her, "Tomorrow I am going to take the day off work as we are spending it together. You can pack us a picnic basket and we will go on a picnic. It is time I took some time to teach you how to shoot a rifle and a revolver. I just could never afford them before. Well it looks like you have your own set of weapons now, as well as your own horse."

★★★★

Samuel Johnson's spirit returned to his small ranch where he stayed at his old adobe to watch over his money. Sometimes the neighbors talked about the light they saw at night where the old homestead adobe used to be. For a hundred and twenty years Samuel Johnson watched over his three treasures. And suddenly he saw all the money he had worked and saved over a period of thirty years, all in danger of disappearing!

★★★★

Sarah Williams had been told stories about the strange lights on her family's ranch when she was a little girl. There was a story that a cattle rustler used to live on the land that they now owned. She knew the ruins were out there against the reddish sandstone cliffs where there was a small spring. When Sarah was nineteen she recalled the stories she was told as a little girl. She had also heard there may be a treasure where one sees a glowing light at night or during or after a storm.

Sarah had once seen the glowing lights herself and so she decided to purchase a Garrett Infinium LS Pulse Induction metal detector to look for the treasure that might be under the lights. It took Sarah six months to save the $1,250 for her metal detector. Out of each of her pay checks she set aside a hundred and five dollars until she had reached her goal. Finally, after six months of saving up her money, she had enough money to purchase her new metal detector. She first tried out her metal detector in her yard. Under the clothesline she found some small change. Sarah was excited now, as she knew the metal detector could find coins.

On the first weekend she had off work from Wal-Mart, she went out excitedly and began her search of the old adobe ruins. Her father and brothers made fun of Sarah for wasting one thousand two hundred and fifty dollars to chasing a fool's dream. All of her family told her she was wasting her time even trying to find anything by the old adobe ruins.

For three days she searched the land around the old adobe ruins. Sarah was finding odd bits of metal, cinch rings, old, square, handmade nails, a broken skillet, and numerous rusted cans. Every night over supper or when her brothers saw her, they made fun of Sarah's search, calling it "A fool's dream." When she invited them to help her, even their refusals were delivered with sarcasm.

Sarah's brother Jake told his sister, "It just would not be fair to you Sarah! At three cents a pound for scrap metal you are going to need every rusty nail you find to pay for your treasure machine."

Her brother Silas told Sarah, "You are always full of these crazy ideas which never amount to anything. You need to be looking at the end of the rainbow for your pot of gold, not in some run down adobe!"

★★★★

At first, Samuel was curious about this woman and what she was doing. He liked watching the pretty lady. But as he watched he heard the machine beat faster every time metal was detected. Suddenly his enjoyment of watching Sarah turned to alarm. He realized that her metal detector would enable this woman to find his treasures. This woman, this thief, had come to rob him of his treasure!

It was on the third day of searching, for Sarah would just not give up, that she decided to clean out the old root cellar of what had been the old adobe. With a shovel and pick she removed the dirt that had fallen in over the last century. She had invited all her family to come help search the site but they had one excuse or another as to why they would be unable to help her. Yet her brothers were curious, so they looked to see what she found each day. They made fun of her recovery of old cinch rings, broken frying pans and old square nails. Each night they made fun of Sarah and asked her for their share of the treasure, and she invited her stronger brothers Jake and Silas to help her dig out the old root cellar so she could search it properly. Every night they had lame excuses for why they were too busy. They had to drive the car to town to have the oil on the car changed; they were going to the dance that night so they could not be getting dirty; they could not miss their favorite TV show and so on.

As Sarah searched the area, she found many small bits of metal which had fallen into the root cellar when the walls had fallen in. Sarah was determined she would find what caused the glow in the old adobe ruins at night, for Sarah thought there must be a treasure here. After an hour of digging Sarah would stop to rest and drink water, then she would stop and search the area she had cleared with her Garrett Pulse Induction metal detector. It was hard, dirty work and she was covered in dust and sweat. Sweat ran down her arms, back, and chest as she worked.

The pictures of the smiling men, woman and children using the metal detectors on the magazine cover of the metal detector magazines did not show what it was really like.

She was dirty, tired, her muscles ached and she wanted a bath in the worst way. As she looked at how much digging was left to clear the rest of the root cellar, she wanted to quit but her pride and her stubborn persistent nature would not let her give up. Only the big horse flies kept her company and they were constantly trying to bite her. The horse flies reminded Sarah of the last man she dated, and then dumped after the first date. He could not keep his hands to himself and leave her alone.

"Good riddance," she thought.

Sarah dug and threw out the shovels full of dirt. Then she stopped to drink her water and use the metal detector. The metal detector beeped faster again--another piece of metal that her family would have to make fun of her tonight, she thought. She dug down with the shovel and up came the remains of a small rotten wooden cigar box. The dirt in her shovel was filled with old silver dollars, now tarnished black, and she saw one small, bright-yellow ten dollar gold piece.

Sarah just sat down on the dirt floor and looked at the single gold coin and she saw nine black silver dollars!

After a few moments looking at them she thought to herself, "I knew it was here, I knew it was here!"

She turned over the shovel, spilling its contents on top of the ground. More gold coins and black silver dollars appeared! She carefully picked up four of the gold coins and looked at them. She had two five-dollar gold pieces and a ten-dollar gold piece. She guessed the three coins were worth at least a thousand dollars! As she picked up and looked at the three-dollar gold coin, she studied it with a perplexing look, for she had never heard of a three-dollar gold coin. For forty-five minutes she carefully dug around the dirt with her bare hands to carefully remove the coins, so that she did not damage the coins with her shovel. She also wanted to be sure she recovered every coin in her treasure hole. When Sarah finished, she counted forty-one gold coins and forty-one silver dollars. With a smile on her face she sat there on the ground and slowly counted her coins three times. Twice she savored every moment as she scooped up handfuls of coins and then she deliberately let the gold and silver coins spilled through her fingers.

Sarah went to her car and got out her small knapsack and she carefully placed the coins in it. She caved some dirt from the remaining part of the root cellar she had not searched into her hole, removing all trace of the small treasure hole.

As Sarah filled her knapsack with Samuel's treasure, Samuel jumped into the cellar beside Sarah and yelled at her to put his money back, but she did not hear a word the ghost said. When Samuel realized that Sarah was simply ignoring him, he reached down to grab the knapsack and snatch his treasure away from the woman. Samuel's hand passed right through the knapsack. No matter how many times he went to grab his money from the knapsack, his hand simply passed right on through it. As a ghost he was unable to move a single coin.

Sarah then picked up her knapsack full of treasure and walked to the rear of her car to place the treasure into the trunk. Again, Samuel attempted to stop the woman from taking his treasure. This time he stood directly in her path; there was no way a hundred and twenty pound woman was going to get by a two hundred pound man of solid muscle like Samuel, he thought. Instead of stopping Sarah like he'd planned, to his astonishment Sarah simply walked through him like he was not even there!

Sarah opened the trunk of her car and placed her knapsack inside where no one would see it. On top of her knapsack Sarah placed her shovels, the empty water bottles, and the trash from her lunch. Then Sarah walked over to the adobe ruins and picked up a large handful of the scraps of metal she had found searching the ruins. She placed these on the front seat of her car. This was what she would show her family.

Sarah drove home. She took a shower and changed her clothes. Over dinner her family made fun of the all the trash and junk she had recovered.

"I tried; I did my best," Was her only response.

Throughout the evening, Sarah's brothers and parents made fun of their daughter and scolded her for wasting good money chasing ghosts in the old ruins of the adobe cabin. It was all Sarah could do to restrain herself and not tell her brothers what she really thought of them. Inside Sarah's mind she was ecstatic--her hunch had been right, and shortly she would reap the rewards of her following it through with action. Sarah thought to herself that she had always wanted to see England, Buckingham Palace, visit the old museums, be a tourist and see the English countryside. Tonight she would go to the library so she could use the internet; she had a trip to plan.

★★★★

It was a dark day for Samuel. That woman had come and stolen his gold and silver coins and he had been unable to stop her! He replayed the day's events in his mind over and over. He could think of nothing else. He had yelled at her to put his treasure back, but it was like she could not hear a word Samuel told her. As Sarah had walked back to her horseless carriage with his treasure, Samuel stepped in front of Sarah, blocking her path, but to his total surprise, Sarah simply walked right though him like he was not even there! In three days she had taken away what it had taken him ten years to earn and save. What was he to do if she returned and took his remaining treasures?

"GOD" he thought, as a deep depression came over him, "What am I to do?" Everything he had saved in ten years from rustling cattle had disappeared in three days!

It was in his deepest, darkest depression that he thought of his worst fears, that woman returning and stealing his other two treasure boxes. Each box represented ten years of his life's work saving every dollar he could. Had she cleared another two feet of the root cellar, she would have uncovered his second box of treasure. Samuel was in a deep, black depression as he prayed to GOD for help.

"What in GOD's name am I supposed to do?"

Then he heard the creak of saddle leather and heard the sound of an approaching horse. He did not know it yet, but his partner who he could trust rode in that night. Samuel watched the approaching horse and rider. The horse was white, the same color as the large, loose robe the man wore that made him look like a shepherd. The man appeared dark and weathered like he, too, had spent a lot of time in the outdoors. The man approached and asked if he could share supper and the fire with Samuel.

Samuel nodded yes.

Suddenly, a fire with a pot of stew cooking appeared. It may be surprising, but a spirit can often create, in the spirit realm, whatever they are thinking of. As fast as the spirit can think of something, it then appears in the spirit realm. After a hot supper Samuel's new friend invited him to go riding with him. Samuel was not interested in a ride but he went because he enjoyed the company after so many years alone. So at night when the moon was full, Samuel and his friend would go riding. As Samuel's only interest outside of his treasure was horses and cattle, that is what they would check out on the nightly rides.

Occasionally Samuel's friend would stop to help a cow deliver her calf or to deliver a mare's foal. Samuel's friend was very good at delivering animals. Even when a calf came out wrong his partner could turn the calf or mare so it would not kill the mother and her young foal. Then he would help the cow deliver her calf or the mare to deliver her young colt.

Over the months they broadened the range they would ride, as they become accustomed to riding the range at night. Sometimes Samuel would talk of his cattle rustling, his mistake in not having two ways out of the canyon on the day he was shot out of his saddle. As time went on, Samuel's partner took him to observe a disabled young girl or an old woman who lived alone on Social Security. At first Samuel just went along with his partner for the company. Over time, he began to take an interest in the welfare of the disabled girl and the old woman who had no one to help her. Neither woman had much food in the house. Samuel had often gone without eating for days at a time, so he knew what hunger was like. The disabled young girl lived in a house, but she was unable to pay her bills for fuel to heat her house, so often in winter she went without heat. Samuel knew that the winters in Durango, Colorado were cold!

One night as they rode their rounds, Samuel told his partner he would like to give 40% of his gold and silver to the disabled young girl and the old woman.

His partner told him, "You know what you ask is not easy. As a Spirit or Ghost you cannot move the money from where you buried it in the ground. Neither one of those women you want to help has the ability to get over here, but I will see what kind of solution I can come up with to help the two women. There might be a way that it can all work out."

★★★★

Sarah Williams had some decisions to make; she had always dreamed of going to England. If she played her cards right, her wish might just come true. She checked on the internet and read the different coin dealers' advertisements, but most gave her a bad feeling in her stomach. Sarah would not go to a coin dealer who she had a bad feeling about. One coin dealer in Dallas, Texas seemed like he might give her a fair price, so she called and made an appointment then drove down to meet him in person. Sarah hoped her car would make the round trip to Dallas and back to Durango. Her car had 315,000 miles on it and her engine was sounding awfully loud so she was a little worried about how much longer her car would last.

On a sudden impulse Sarah Williams removed twenty of her gold coins from her back pack and set these aside, hiding them in the ground in her flower garden. Though she did not know it, her sudden impulse to set aside twenty of her gold coins was prompted by her Spirit Guide (Guardian Angel) trying her best to help Sarah. She took the remaining twenty-one gold coins and forty-one silver dollars to Dallas, Texas.

The coin dealer promised her she was getting the highest possible price by dealing with him. For each silver dollar, he paid her fifteen dollars. The coin dealer had arrived at that price by examining the date and condition of each of the silver coins. Most of the coins were only worth about fifteen dollars, but one of the silver dollars was in excellent condition and because of its rarity was worth $1,230! So the coin dealer thought if I cut that amount in half, say $615, that is what I will offer her for all the silver dollars. As the dealer looked at the twenty gold coins, he decided that on their face, they were worth a hundred and fifty one dollars. For the coin dealer, this was always the hardest part. If he offered too little money, his coins--and after looking at the collections he was already thinking of them as "His Collection"--might walk out the door. So he had to offer her enough money that she would not leave his store.

Properly displayed, he was sure the collection would bring sixteen- to twenty thousand dollars. So he offered her $615 for the silver dollars and $8385 for the gold coins, for a total of $ 9,000! As he started to write her a check, the coin dealer noticed that Sarah had suddenly gone from an agreeable customer to a clear display of anger in her body language, eyes and posture.

The coin dealer did not want to lose "His Coin Collection," so he paused to talk to the woman and see if he could salvage his deal. He asked Sarah what the problem was.

"The check," she told him.

He assured her the check would be good, but no matter how much he tried to reassure Sarah, she absolutely refused to accept a check. He realized the check was the deal-killer.

So he offered to go to the bank with her while she cashed the check.

She told him, "No! If you go get the cash and hand it to me, we have a deal, but if there is a check involved I leave with my coins."

In the end, the coin dealer left the coin shop and personally walked over to the bank and obtained the nine thousand dollars. When he returned and handed Sarah the money, she handed him the coin collection. Sarah did not want any legal documents tying her to the money she just made. She wanted her side income to be tax-free. She was also dubious about accepting the check and it being worthless. Often in the past people had paid her with worthless checks and she was certainly not going to let those gold and silver coins leave her possession unless she had the cash in hand.

★★★★

Samuel asked his partner what that thief Sarah had done with his one box of treasure. Samuel's partner told him, if you really want to know we will go and find out. Most people do not realize spirits can travel at the speed of thought. As fast as they can think of someplace, they can instantly be there. As Samuel and his partner looked down into the room from above, they watched the entire exchange between Sarah and the Dallas, Texas coin dealer. But unlike Sarah, Samuel and his partner could read and hear every thought of the man and the woman. Samuel instantly realized that one of the silver dollars Sarah was selling was worth $1,230 dollars and if Sarah had negotiated the coin prices more effectively or started out the door, the coin dealer would have raised his price to ten thousand dollars. Clearly, there was something awfully unusual occurring. Samuel was perplexed as to why the coin dealer thought that the silver dollar was worth $1,230 and that the man thought he could sell one of Samuel's twenty-dollar gold coins for $1,500! Most amazing of all was the agitation the coin dealer showed over one three-dollar gold coin. The coin dealer was doing his very best not to handle or stare at that one coin. Samuel realized that this three-dollar gold coin was the one coin the dealer wanted most of all. Samuel realized the coin dealer thought this coin was worth thousands of dollars. Samuel understood the dealer did not know the value of the three-dollar coin, yet the dealer did realize the coin was very rare and valuable. Samuel saw that the coin dealer planned to resell one of his ten-dollar gold pieces for $750! How can that be he thought? Why would anyone want his buried money that much? Samuel saw the coin dealer return from the bank and hand Sarah the nine thousand dollars.

Sarah carefully counted the pile of money twice. Then she handed over the gold and silver coins. Part of Samuel wanted to grab his coins back, but this he realized he could not do that. His coins were gone now.

Samuel's mind was also in complete confusion as to why the man had just paid Sarah nine thousand dollars! Why had that coin dealer given Sarah nine thousand dollars for his coins? Samuel was in complete astonishment as nine thousand dollars was enough money for eight families to retire for the rest of their lives and live well in their old age!

Samuel's partner simply said, *"Well, let's follow her."*

Samuel and his partner followed Sarah out to her old car. They followed her as she drove to the Black Angus Steak House. There, Sarah ordered a rib-eye steak dinner with an iced tea. Samuel watched her eat the meal. When the waiter brought the bill for the dinner to her, Samuel was looking down on Sarah from above and he was simply astonished that a steak dinner could cost twenty dollars with a tip! Why, the last time he purchased a steak dinner in Creede, Colorado he paid fifteen cents. Why a bottle of wine cost a dime, and they charged her two dollars and nineteen cents for an iced tea!

"Hell," Samuel thought, "for twenty dollars I would sell anyone two 1,200 pound steers!"

Slowly, Samuel realized that something must have happened to the money supply of the United States. The paper money had become worthless! Then Samuel recalled how Confederate currency became worthless after the fall of the Confederacy in 1864. Slowly realization occurred to Samuel, that only the old money, like his gold and silver coins were worth anything now days! United States paper money had become worthless!

★★★★

When Sarah got back to Durango, she returned to work at Wal-Mart. Everything had returned to normal except for Sarah's racing mind. Her thoughts were on getting a passport, getting time off from work, and taking a trip to England. Her dream of vacationing in England was coming true! Sarah decided that with the nine thousand dollars she now had that she would set aside half the money towards a dependable vehicle and the remaining half would go for a dream of a vacation in England. First, she would get her passport photos and fill out an application to get a passport. While waiting for her passport she would check on the internet to find all the places she wanted to visit in England and Scotland.

Slowly it dawned on Sarah's family something was different about their daughter. Her brothers felt she must have recovered *their* treasure, and they wanted it. Clearly, Sarah was being greedy and keeping all the money to herself. They would not be so angry with her if she would have been fair with them. Sarah had always been the greedy one, they thought. If their sister would just give them each, one or two hundred thousand dollars--they could understand her wanting to keep *some* of the money for herself.

They told her it was only fair she give them their rightful share, if she would just give them two hundred thousand dollars each they would still be friends. Why did she have to be so greedy, even with her own family, they asked her?

Sarah was mad that they had repeatedly refused to help her when she had asked. They had never offered to help pay for the metal detector, instead they had constantly ridiculed her idea of searching the old adobe ruins. Now that she had worked hard and she could make her dreams come true, her greedy and lazy brothers wanted their "fair share" of her treasure. Sarah intended to give them their "fair share" of her treasure in proportion to the effort they had made in helping her. Since they had refused to help her in any manner, Sarah felt their "fair share" was nothing!

Sarah knew that if she should ever tell her brothers what she really found, all they would want was everything! Then they would still believe that there was more and in time they would use violence against her, when verbal threats and harassment did not work.

Within a month of Sarah returning from Dallas, Texas her brothers and their wives were all threatening to kill Sarah unless she gave them their entire fair share. As the story grew in her brothers' and their wives' minds, with each retelling of the event, they were sure she had dug up several Wells Fargo strong boxes of gold. The calls and threats came on her phone both day and night.

Shortly thereafter, Sarah took to carrying a Glock handgun for self defense. She told a police officer she had been getting many threats on her life. The police officer volunteered to spend the weekend teaching her how to shoot the Glock, should the need arise. Sarah accepted the police officer's offer for handgun training and spent sixteen hours with him learning to effectively use her new Glock. She took the police officer out for lunch and dinner both days, as her way of thanking him.

A month later, Sarah Williams moved to Seattle, where she got a new apartment and a new job. She was no longer speaking to any members of her family. Sarah's family knew she was rich, and she was just holding out on them. Her parents had opened Sarah's mail and seen her new U.S. Passport, and they had also opened the travel brochures that had arrived from the travel agencies. Sarah's parents told her brothers and their wives about Sara's unusual behavior after she searched the old adobe ruins. First she had taken off from work for a week to take a vacation in Dallas, Texas. Now she got a passport in the mail and she was getting travel brochures to travel overseas. Wal-Mart must be paying their employees pretty good money for them to be able to take several vacations and fly overseas. It was her greedy nature, they told each other. They had always seen that part of her nature. They said that was why they had not helped her dig up all those Wells Fargo treasure chests, she would not have shared it with them. They told themselves they still would be speaking to their sister if she had just been fair to them and given each of them *one or two hundred thousand dollars each!* She was always the unreasonable one. They would not have broken into her apartment so many times looking for their share of the money, nor busted her car windshield, nor slit her car tires if she had just given each of them their share. They knew she was just a selfish female in heat, by not sharing her money with them.

Everyone knows that housing in Seattle costs a half a million dollars! When she moved to Seattle that simply confirmed to them that they were right. She had dug up several Wells Fargo treasure chests, each with millions of dollars of gold and simply would not give her family members their fair share.

★★★★

Once Sarah got settled in her new apartment, she began looking for a new job. It took her three weeks and twenty-two job applications before she started work again. In the evenings Sarah went to the library to use the internet. The next time she went to sell a coin she felt she would get a more honest price for her coin if she knew its true value. She began with an 1880 ten dollar gold piece, minted in Denver. The coin was in perfect condition. The value she found on the internet was $810; so her goal was to get 80% of its fair value. So Sarah figured she needed to hold out for $648 in cash. She had nineteen more gold coins to appraise at their honest value. Her oldest gold coin was minted in 1853 and no coin was newer than 1880.

★★★★

Sarah was still dreaming of a vacation to England. She planned to take a nice vacation as soon as she had accumulated enough time at her new job to take two weeks off. She planned to see it all, and slowly she was building up her checking account with money from the sale of her gold coins. In six months she could write a check to a travel agency for her trip. Sarah was allowing two thousand dollars for the travel agency to pay for her trip. For any shopping and all other expenses she would take another two thousand dollars, and she would go to another bank and get a thousand dollars in traveler's checks for emergencies. To realize her dream of a lifetime since she was a little girl would cost her four thousand dollars, and she smiled to herself there was still a lot of money still left over in her safety deposit box.

Sarah picked up the book she had picked up at the library and began reading the book on her couch that night. She thought it was time to start doing her homework. She had a book on Western Outlaws, and another book on the history of Montana, from a government program called "The Federal Writers Project." Sarah began reading about a dishonest Sheriff called Henry Plumber, in the book on Western Outlaws. Beside her laid a notebook and ink pen. If she was going to make another recovery, she figured research was the key which would lead to more recoveries.

★★★★

On the weekends Sarah often took walks along the water front. Though she knew nothing about the different boats she saw, she liked looking at them. Maybe someday she would go fishing for fresh salmon. That would be exciting, she thought. One Saturday she went to see a boat dealer who rented out small fishing boats called Cape Dories. In the back of her mind she wanted to go for a ride in one. As she looked at the boats at the dock, she saw a Cape Dory coming into the dock from out in the Pacific Ocean. It came right up to the dock she was walking on. To her surprise there were two teenage girls about her age running the boat.

Sarah started talking with the two teenagers and learned the names of the two women were Dancing Wind and Molly O'Brian. She wanted to know all she could about boats and where the girls had gone. Molly told Sarah that they had just gotten back from Wrangle, Alaska. Dancing Wind suddenly offered to take Sarah out to dinner this evening after they got cleaned up. Sarah said she would love to hear all about their trip over dinner. They agreed to meet at a restaurant near Fisherman's Wharf for dinner.

For the three teenagers, this dinner was the beginning of a lifelong friendship. In time their friendship would grow so that they would go prospecting, treasure hunting, boating, canoeing and even tracking. In time, their friendship would grow to where Sarah would put her life in the hands of her friends Molly and Dancing Wind and she would stand by them protecting them to the limit of her existence. Such friends that can be counted on in times of need are truly priceless, but I am getting ahead of myself here, as these adventures are yet to come.

Sometimes in life there are those coincidences, which turn out to be major turning points in our lives. Often we refer to them as simply coincidences, while in fact our Guardian Angels are working hard to make the events occur. Such was the case for the "chance" meeting between Sarah, Molly and Dancing Wind. Throughout our lives, we all have these events occurring. So, when your Guardian Angel has been working for weeks to arrange a meeting with a person who might become a very good friend to you, are you open to the opportunity? Or do you ignore the stranger or hurry up and walk on by, leaving your Guardian Angel in the dust wondering why they just went to all that effort to try and help you. You might consider the possibility that you should ask the individual you encounter or seem drawn to, the question or thought which first pops into your mind no matter how crazy it may sound. It may be the beginning of a lifetime friendship both of your Guardian Angels have been working hard to arrange.

★★★★

That night, after the initial bond had been forged, Sarah felt she could share many of her secrets and plans with Molly and Dancing Wind. She was afraid her car with 321,000 miles on it would give out shortly, so she told them that she was planning on buying a new pickup truck with the cash she had from the sale of her gold coins set aside in the bank safety deposit box. She told them that she had eighteen gold coins and eight thousand dollars in her safety deposit box. She proudly said how she had opened her bank account with seven hundred and fifty dollars, which she still had not touched. She explained to them she had used one gold coin to buy her Glock handgun and a second gold coin had been sold to pay for her apartment rent and security deposits.

She told them she planned to pay cash for the truck by selling some of her gold coins so she would not have to worry about making payments.

Immediately, Molly and Dancing Wind told her "No, you must not do that. If you go to buy the new pickup truck and you pay cash, the IRS, the Treasury Dept., and Home Land Security will be notified of your actions and they will probably begin several investigations of you! *You must be discrete with your cash!*"

They told her she would have to make payments like most people do, or she would be explaining to Uncle Sam why she suddenly came into thousands of dollars.

Realizing the trouble she almost got into, Sarah realized the necessity of being more discrete with her cash. They also told her that while the banks reported cash deposits of three thousand dollars or more to the Treasury Dept., smaller sums of money could be reported if the bank thought they were unusual. They told Sarah she needed to keep her transactions down below five hundred dollars to be reasonably safe from government investigation.

Sarah told Molly and Dancing Wind about her plans for a trip to England and they suggested that on payday she begin slowly building up her bank account as she deposited her pay check. They told her to bank about half of her check, that way when she went to take a vacation she could just write a check to the travel agency. Sarah told them she would follow their advice on building up her checking account balance so that in six months she could write a check to a travel agency for her trip.

Sarah told Molly and Dancing Wind about how she had picked up some books at the library and began reading the book on her couch that night. She thought it was time to start doing some homework on the past if she expected to find any more treasures. She had a book on Western Outlaws, and another book on the history of Montana, from a government program called "The Federal Writers Project." Sarah had begun reading about a dishonest Sheriff called Henry Plumber in the book on Western Outlaws. Molly and Dancing Wind told her research was indeed the key to making recoveries occur again and again.

That evening Sarah began the story about her recovery of the cigar box of treasure which had given her new opportunities in life. She described the site of the old adobe thirty miles south of Durango where she discovered her treasure after three days of hard work. She spoke of the stories she heard as a child about it being haunted by an old outlaw and how glowing lights were sometimes seen around the old outlaw adobe cabin. Molly and Dancing Wind looked at each other and began laughing. Sarah was wondering why they were laughing until Molly began describing Sarah's brothers. Sarah was astonished at first, but then she came to realize that Molly and Sarah had been asked by her brothers to find any treasure she had failed to locate in the ruins of the old adobe home. So Molly said to Sarah, "Let me tell you the rest of the story."

★★Six months earlier★★

The two brothers, Jake and Silas got to thinking: if Sarah had gotten one or two strong box of gold out of the cattle rustler's hide out, then there must be many more treasure chests of gold there. So the brothers each looked over the site but did not see any gold lying around. Next they invited their friends to help them dig and recover their treasure. After digging two randomly-dug holes, they quickly tired of the effort required to make a shovel move dirt. Their next step was to use the internet to look for someone to find their treasures for them. They left some postings on the internet and offered a ten-percent reward of the recovery.

They really did not intend to share anything, but by offering a ten-percent reward, they planned to recover their treasure. When the two treasure hunters talked to them, the brothers claimed there were three or four chests full of gold and silver which needed to be located and dug up. The brothers insisted the treasure was near the old outlaw hide out, or possibly located in the mountains nearby. Actually, they intended to pay the treasure finder nothing, as it was really their gold. They were sure whoever came and found their treasure for them would be happy to give the brothers all the treasure if they were kind enough to spare their lives.

★★★★

Molly saw the posting on the internet for someone to come and recover a treasure. The claim was that there was a lot of gold and silver buried on the property. She was told there were also one or two ghosts or spirits watching over the treasure. Molly talked to the older brother, Jake, and he invited her to come up and meet him. Molly told him that she worked for equal shares for everyone, with Dancing Wind and her and the two brothers it would come out a four way split of twenty-five percent for each of them.

Jake told her, "Go to Hell! You will take the ten percent I am offering you or nothing! I can always find people to work for that cut of all the gold there. It is ten percent or nothing. That is all you will get."

Because she had not gotten paid for tracking a trail in three months, Molly Reluctantly agreed to the ten percent in order to be able to make her Jeep payment, which was coming due at the end of the month. Dancing Wind accompanied her partner Molly, but Dancing Wind knew that the two brothers, Jake and Silas, never intended to share the treasure. Dancing Wind decided to chalk this one up as a learning experience for Molly.

At the last minute Dan told both teenagers he was going to accompany them while they tracked this trail. Dan is a wise old Indian medicine man with a traditional appearance: long silver hair worn in braids, brown leathery skin and a slow raspy voice he uses, almost as a medal of honor, to pass the oral history of his tribe to younger generations. Dan had taken the two teenagers under his wing and he taught them to track the trails of animals and man. Dan was always encouraging them to develop their tracking skills. When he accompanied the girls, his wisdom brought a deeper understanding upon the ancient trails he continued teaching them to track. Molly knew that with Dan along they were sure to know the location of the treasure. Yes, Molly thought, this trip is looking up. In reality her old teacher and Dancing Wind had only accompanied Molly to ensure her safety, as they felt the two brothers lacked dignity, honor and honesty.

The two brothers Jake and Silas asked the two trackers to sign an agreement that they were only to get ten percent before they would take them to the site of the treasure. The trackers were going to have to split the ten percent between all three of them; the two brothers planned on keeping the rest. Dan noticed that Silas had pocketed both copies of the agreement promising the trackers their share as soon as the teenagers had signed the agreement, so the trackers had nothing in writing. Dan was aware that the two brothers intended to pay them nothing after Molly and Dancing Wind found the gold that they had ultimately been unable to find.

The old Indian seemed to relax in Molly's Jeep and fall asleep. In reality, Dan was extremely aware of what was occurring as well as what would occur. Dan sensed the two hand guns as well as the knives the brothers concealed under their clothing.

With the "contract" signed, the brothers led the search party to the old adobe where

Dancing Wind and Molly began walking around the property. They observed Samuel's spirit watching them from beside an old piñon (pine) tree he was leaning against, as he watched the two trackers walking over his property. Clearly, in the back of Samuels mind was the last time a woman had come on his property. As a ghost, Samuel was apprehensive about what would happen next. For the first time in over a century, he realized someone not of the spirit world could actually see him. Often a spirit will know what is going to occur before a person on the physical level does. He talked it over with his partner two weeks earlier when his partner told him these three trackers were coming to look for his two treasures; Samuel knew exactly what he had to do. His riding partner told him all about the three trackers that would be coming. He was even told that these trackers would be able to see him and talk with him. If his partner had not reassured him it would work out alright, Samuel would have really been worried. Samuel's gut feeling was that these trackers were really skilled at following a trail.

The first woman had stolen one of his three wooden boxes of treasure and she had been unable to see him. These three new individuals who could see him and speak to him represented a greater danger than he had ever faced before.

Samuel would have lost his composure and tried to stop the two teenagers from searching for his treasure if not for the fact that now he had the support of a friend to help him. Samuel had complete faith in his friend; and a friend like that is a treasure beyond price.

Samuel watched the two teenagers and smiled, for this time Samuel had an ace up his sleeve. He knew he could take the two women in a game of cards. Samuel knew he would win a poker game, as his partner had told Samuel that he would win. All Samuel had to do was what his partner told him: get the two teenagers' "words of honor," on a bet over a game of poker, and then win the game of cards. Samuel knew these trackers would find his treasure, so a game of poker was the only way to stop them.

Samuel was not any good at poker, but his partner told him that if he engaged the girls in a poker game and won, the two women would keep their word and leave his treasure alone.

Samuel would never forget he had been unable to stop Sarah from walking off with one of his boxes of treasure, yet he was extremely confident he would win this round of cards. Samuel's riding partner had warned him of the women who would come, and he explained that they were women of dignity, honor and integrity, so after Samuel honestly beat them in a game of poker they would keep their word and leave. Samuel's partner was further back in the piñon watching everything that was occurring. Samuel knew his partner was pretty smart so Samuel decided he would do it his partners' way. Certainly he had no chance of stopping Sarah from walking off with the first chest of his treasure. Samuel planned to give one of his cigar boxes of gold and silver to the crippled young girl and the old woman that he and his partner checked in on when they made their night rides.

When Molly and Dancing Wind walked up to him, he held out his hand to shake their hands. Dancing Wind looked at Samuel long and hard, but she made no effort to reach out and shake the offered hand. Dancing Wind could sense the men Samuel had shot and killed as well as the men Samuel had robbed as he rustled cattle. Dancing Wind looked closely at Samuel, with his out-stretched hand offering friendship. But Dancing Wind also realized that no one has the right to judge another. Only GOD can judge another person. . As Dancing Wind and Molly looked at the out stretched hand offered to them, Samuel surprised them by saying

"To the highest good of all".

Both Molly and Dancing Wind immediately shook Samuels's hand.

Samuel said, "I have been expecting you. My partner told me that three trackers would be coming to find my treasures."

This further surprised both teenagers, but they let Samuel talk. Dancing Wind wanted to sit down so Molly and Samuel followed her example. Under the piñon tree in the shade, they talked as they enjoyed the afternoon breeze.

★★★★

The two brothers watched the two teenage girls walk around the property. Then they saw the two teenagers sit down together under the tree. As they walked around the property Jake said they must be lesbians, since the women clearly showed no interest in the two brothers. Then the two teenagers started talking to themselves, as anyone could see that there was no one else under the tree with them.

Silas said "Obviously it's been a mistake to hire these two teenagers; they certainly did not know anything about finding treasure! I guess they probably are not all there, upstairs in their mind." The two brothers nodded to each other.

Jake thought that they had not sound that crazy when he had talked to them on the phone and said, "I guess you just never can tell."

★★★★

"My partner told me that I am supposed to play a game of poker with you. Then the winner of the one hand gets to keep the treasure,"

Samuel told them, "Once you gave me *your Word, it was a promise I could bet my life on.*"

Samuel talked to the two teenagers as he began shuffling a deck of cards. Neither teenager had accepted the proposal that they play cards, nor had they rejected the proposal. As Samuel shuffled the cards, he talked about his partner with whom he went riding at night. He told the teenagers about his idea of giving forty percent of his gold and silver to the crippled young girl and the old woman who had no one to care for them. Samuel told the teenagers that if they gave him their word that forty percent of the gold and silver would go to the two women he spoke of and regularly checked up on them that he could easily give them the winning poker hand.

"I will just fold my cards and put them in the deck so you will win," he said.

Molly told Samuel that if the two brothers had been fair and honorable with them they could do as Samuel asked and give the crippled girl and the old woman forty percent of the treasure but since the two brothers would only give them ten percent, they had no negotiating room to enable them to keep such a promise.

Samuel replied, "The two brothers Jake and Silas are very greedy. They never will give you the ten percent they promised both of you."

Molly told Samuel that the two brothers' greed would prevent them from going home today with half the treasure—one cigar box with about $ 350 in gold and silver coins. By being greedy, instead of one box of treasure which the three trackers could locate today for them, the brothers' insistence on ninety percent would actually result in recovering nothing today, or in the future.

Samuel said he would be helping the brothers find his treasures himself if they would be willing to help the two women that Samuel intended about half his money to go to, but they are too selfish and only think of themselves.

"Do you realize that both brothers have concealed weapons under their belt? You know the brothers will never let you leave here alive with any gold are silver. The guns and knives they are carrying is how they intend to pay you off when you recover the treasure," Samuel asked Molly and Dancing Wind.

Dancing Wind asked the spirit if he would be alright when they left, or if he would like them to take Samuel *home*. Samuel told them he would be alright, and his partner said,

"In another five or ten years some more trackers like you will come, and they will help me keep my promise to the two women, then the two of us will ride out of here together."

Molly asked Samuel: "By the way; what is your partner's name?"

Samuel replied, *"He has some strange Hebrew name, it is: Je-zus Yaw-Kheed Yo-safe, is the way I think it is said*

Samuel asked the two teenagers: "Are you ready for me to deal the cards now?"

Samuel began dealing them each a hand of cards in the poker game. Tears were streaming down Dancing Wind's face as she took her hand of cards and picked them up. Then she reached over and took Molly's hand of cards from her and without looking at either hand of cards she pushed them into the deck of cards laying down on the ground.

She looked at Samuel and told him: "It looks like you won this game of poker. Molly and I fold."

Dancing Wind told Samuel, "We have to make a search for your treasure. We will use a Fisher Gold Bug metal detector with an eight-inch detection depth. I know your treasures are hidden about twelve inches and thirty-one inches deep so we will not find them."

Then Dancing Wind hugged Samuel and told him: *"Via Con Dios"* (Go with God) as tears streamed down her face.

★★★★

For three hours Jake and Silas watched the two teenagers search the old ruins and the property around it. Both brothers knew it had been a mistake to have the two teenage girls find their treasures. Obviously women cannot do a thorough search like a man does. If they had the time they would search the ruins themselves. Silas knew that men like themselves could recover the treasure in an hour, but the football game would be coming on soon at the bar. After a hard day of work, watching the two teenagers search the old adobe ruins, both men needed a cold Coors beer. Just like they figured, they noticed the two teenagers could not find anything!

"Well I guess we can go to the bar now and get a couple of beers," the brothers said to each other as they watched the two teenagers put their metal detector in the Jeep and get ready to leave.

★★★★

Just as the teenagers were putting the metal detector in the Jeep, Dan told them to wait and give him a minute, as he had to stretch his legs. Dan slowly walked over to where Samuel stood under the piñon tree and hugged Samuel and whispered a few words into his ear. Then the old Indian walked over towards Samuel's partner who was standing kind of hidden in a group of piñon trees, so you could not make him out clearly. Dan said a few words to the man dressed in the white wool robe of a shepherd and gave him a hug. Then Dan walked back and jumped into the back of the Jeep.

Dan told Molly, "Well let's go."

Molly took off on the dirt roads. Shortly thereafter she hit the main road and headed

southeast towards Abiquiu.....

As they drove, Molly turned to Dancing Wind and asked her, "How do you suppose Samuel's friend knew that we were coming here before we even knew ourselves?'

"Wasn't it kind of unusual that Samuel said that after the two women get forty percent of his gold, that he and his partner would be riding out of here together? Could he have meant that his partner would be taking him *home* to heaven? Well Dancing Wind, did you recognize that funny name Samuel told us, his partner is called? I think he said he calls him: *Je-Zus Yaw-Keed Yo-Safe* I clearly saw it had an impact on you; I saw the tears running down your face."

Dancing Wind replied, "The name is in Hebrew and translates as: *Jesus, son of Joseph*"

Molly pulled the Jeep over to the side of the highway as tears streamed down her face, too. Their Native American teacher, Dan was left to drive home.

★★★★

When Dancing Wind finished telling the story she was quiet for a few moments.

Sarah then told her, "You are full of shit! I would admit that you had me going there for a few minutes as your description of my two worthless brothers was very accurate, but then I recalled I told you about my brothers first. So what is your angle here? How was your swindle of me supposed to go down?"

Dancing Wind frowned as she never expected her story to be thought of as anything other than truthful.

Then she simply told Sarah, "What I told you is true."

"Do you really think that I am that stupid? I never saw a ghost at the ruins. So what is your swindle? Let me guess, the ghost sent you here to get his gold back. So then you tell me you have to take the cash and the rest of my gold coins back to Colorado and return it to your imaginary ghost. Am I right so far?"

Molly O'Brian was very angry, and was getting up to leave. Dancing

Wind reached out and pulled her back down into her chair as she shook her head 'no'.

Molly said, "We are not trying to steal any of your treasure."

Dancing Wind looked at Sarah and said, "You taking the coins from Samuel, the cattle rustler, was actually a wonderful gift to Samuel, though he did not realize it."

Sarah said, "Say what you said again. Why are you saying it was a wonderful gift to Samuel?"

Dancing Wind replied "For over a century Samuel stayed, watching his gold and had you not come along, five centuries from now his spirit would still be at the site watching his gold. As a result of your actions four series of events were set into motion.'

"The first series of events was your recovery of the treasure and the new life path it sent you on: it resulted in your moving to the Pacific Northwest. This will result in your visiting England, which has always been a dream of yours. It has also given you some financial freedom.

"The second series of events you set into motion was by searching the ruins and the ensuing recovery you were in a position to realize your brothers' true natures. Sometimes money brings out the best in human nature, but unfortunately sometimes it brings out the worst in human nature too.

"You were fortunate enough to protect your assets from your greedy brothers. Had you given them anything …no matter how much, they would have wanted more. Even if you had given them every cent you recovered, their greed would have eventually led them to taking you out and torturing and killing you as they would never have been satisfied with taking everything! Your brothers would have always felt you were holding out on them keeping most of the treasure for yourself. Frankly speaking, deceit and greed was their character so they would assume that you were as greedy as they are.

"The third series of events you set into motion was the involvement of Dan, Molly and myself going to the site, meeting your brothers, and the eventual meeting here along the waterfront of the three of us. In all likelyhood, it was your Guardian Angel working with ours that set up this chance encounter along the waterfront.

"Tonight we can leave here as friends and meet again and again, or we can go our separate ways; the two paths are open to you. Each path in life will have a different outcome. The path you take in life is for you to choose. Throughout your life there will be many different paths and many choices you will make. You will chose the education you desire, the jobs you want, the man or men you marry, the cars you drive, where you will live and who you chose for friends.

"The fourth series of events you set into motion was purely accidental. By taking Samuel's treasure you scared him. You scared him so much the possibility occurred to him that he could lose everything he had worked his life to save. It would all disappear so he called out to GOD for help.'

"His urgent appeals to GOD in his time of desperation resulted in Jesus coming to help him. Over time Jesus was able to help Samuel see the needs of two needy individuals and their difficulties in life. I imagine that over time, as the two of them went on their night rides, Jesus was slowly raising Samuel's vibration until he is ready to go *home*."

Sarah asked, "If that was really Jesus, he could have instantly taken the man *home* and just as easily given the two treasures to the woman in the wheel chair and the old woman living all alone, couldn't he?"

Molly told Dancing Wind, "I have got this one.'

"Jesus will not force Samuel to go *home,* as he will respect and honor Samuel's free will that GOD has given everyone. Clearly, Jesus will want to take Samuel *home,* yet he will have the patience to wait with his friend until he is ready to go. And it is likely he will set into motion the chain of events that will lead to another group of treasure hunters to the ruins where Samuel stays."

"Well if Samuel is a cattle rustler, are you sure Jesus will take Samuel *home*? I figure Jesus will take him to hell to pay for his sins."

Molly replied, "Everyone makes mistakes in their life; that is why our spirits come here and are born--to live, to learn life experiences. Earth is simply a school where everyone is learning lessons. Some people learn their lessons and go on. Some spirits do not make much progress in their lifetime.

"Yet when they die, their Guardian Angel is always ready to take them home. It does not matter what religion you practice or if you practice no religion at all, when your time comes to go *home*, The Angels will be there to take you.

"As for giving the treasures to the two individuals Samuel chose, sure, you are right Jesus could have instantly given them to the two individuals in need. Yet in practice that is not the way it works. Most often individuals who are full of GOD's love and grace like Babaji, Jesus, Buda, Mohammad and Krishna let the Angels of GOD arrange lessons for our spirits on earth as part of the life lessons they chose to experience or learn.

"Just suppose in your life, had you not worked and struggled to save the money you earned at Wal-Mart for the metal detector. Would you have valued the treasure as much and protected it from your brothers, who wanted to steal it? The dream that you could recover a treasure, the struggle to save the money, the actions of your brothers helping you dig out the root cellar, or more correctly, refusing to help you at all, were all part of the lessons you chose to experience and learn from. Just as your trip to Texas was a learning experience, your trip to England will also be a learning experience. They are events you chose to experience in life."

Over dinner then throughout the night as the three teenagers walked along Seattle's waterfront they talked. Misunderstandings were resolved and the beginning of trust established. As they parted company, Dancing Wind and Molly O'Brian wished Sarah the best on her trip to England. They told her when she returned she was welcome to join them on a prospecting trip to Arizona. They were going to explore a place called Cañada del Oro, just north of Tucson.

Ask Angels for Guidance
For they surely know
The Path that is right
For you to go

"It's Our Inheritance"

Molly and Dancing Wind were getting their hair done in a beauty shop in Santa Fe. As they were getting perms done, the beautician working on their hair told them about a family in Taos who struck it rich after finding their family treasure. It seems that everyone in Taos knows the story about the family who found their treasure. Yes, the rumor going around Taos was that the family struck it rich, finding their family's inheritance of gold bars. They had always talked about the treasure on their land, when suddenly the entire family just disappeared. Everyone just knew they found their treasure since they walked off taking nothing--why, they even left their old clothes and cars at the house when they up and left. Everyone said they would buy new clothes, cars, and houses when their plane landed in California. They had struck it rich! Some people just seem to have all the luck. The lucky ones are always finding treasures or striking it rich by winning the lottery. As Molly was getting her hair perm, she closed her eyes and let her mind drift back to a trail she had tracked a year earlier.

★★★★

During the hot days of summer in New Mexico, Dancing Wind and Molly were told about a Spanish family up in Taos upon whose land there were a large number of Spanish stone markers. The old Hispanic family believed that a rich treasure of gold bars existed on their land, mined by their ancestors who settled upon this land in 1667.

Dancing Wind and Molly arranged a visit to see the land owner, Juan Blanco, through a man in Española who was often a guest at the Señor Blanco hacienda. Señor Juan Blanco was more than happy to show the two teenage girls around his property and the numerous Spanish markers erected by his ancestors more than three centuries earlier. He showed them the large stone face which overlooked the stream flowing through his property. In addition to the stone face, there were dozens of other stones one could clearly recognize as stones shaped by the hand of man.

Stone Eagle

Upon the estate of Señor Juan Blanco were dozens of stone images representing thousands of man hours of work. There were stone faces of man, faces of animals like fish, dolphins, alligators, foxes, bears, coyotes, ducks, gila monsters, snakes, buffalo, owls and eagles.

There were also two-ton flat stones set on smaller boulders like a table a giant might sit on or use as a table. These were called compass stones, which the Spanish used to give directions to travel or to enter the underground stone structures they often built to conceal their gold and silver. There were even a dozen stone eagles, some on nests with young fledglings, flying eagles and several standing eagles.

Juan showed the teenagers the Spanish Markers upon his lands in the hope that they could show him where his inheritance was buried. Juan Blanco was running out of time to save his land, as he had mortgaged his land to the bank to support his lifestyle of shop and spend. Now the bankers wanted to steal his land simply because he had not made payments on his two hundred thousand dollar mortgage! The bankers did not understand that he and his sons could not work, as they had to keep an eye on their land so no one came and stole their treasure. When they found the treasure he would pay the bank; he just did not know where the treasure was hidden.

Juan Blanco's father had told his son about how hundreds of years ago his family worked a mine, half way up on the East side of Taos Mountain. There the gold poured out of the rich mine and provided his family with anything they desired. They had two dozen Indian slaves working the mine and smelting the rich gold ore into gold bars. They had Indian servants waiting on their every need in the hacienda, cooking their meals, and tending their crops. Juan Blanco longed for the good old days.

Because of the 1680 Indian revolt, his family had been forced to flee to Mexico to escape the savage Indian attacks. When the family returned from Mexico they could no longer enslave the Indians, nor could they find the rich gold mine. Juan Blanco suspected that the Indians on the Taos Pueblo had filled in and concealed his mine so that they would no longer be enslaved and forced to work it. All that remained of his family's wealth was the bars of gold his ancestors had hidden on his land. Unfortunately, his great grandfather had taken the secret of the gold's location to his grave when he had a sudden heart attack and died. Since then his family had been looking for their inheritance.

After Dancing Wind and Molly had toured the property and viewed all the Spanish markers, they told Juan Blanco that they would be happy to track the trail and try to locate the inheritance he had spoken of, but they never worked without a written contract and they charged five hundred dollars a day up front, plus they wanted an equal share of the recovery for each person involved in the search and recovery of the gold. Dancing Wind explained that he should expect approximately four days to locate and enter the cache site in order to have a reasonable chance of finding the gold.

To stall the trackers so they would not leave, Juan Blanco insisted that the two trackers must accept his hospitality and stay for dinner. Juan told the two teenagers, "Mi casa es su casa" (my house is your house). Over dinner Juan asked the trackers numerous questions about tracking old trails. Dancing Wind and Molly answered all his questions in a general manner so as to show they understood how to track the ancient Spanish trails, but they did not talk or give specific answers about the site they had just viewed. They knew that if they told Juan their hunch of the general location of his treasure he would not hire them to track the trail. The trackers made their income tracking old trails; as trackers they needed jobs which paid their bills. After an hour of conversation Juan Blanco agreed to hire the trackers and wrote a check for two thousand dollars if they would start tomorrow morning.

The teenagers immediately declined as they told Juan that they did not bring their Ground Penetrating Radar and the Pulse Induction Electronics' that they normally employed. To get their equipment they would need two weeks. With the check they told him they would pay some bills and bring the equipment needed for the job in two weeks. That would give Juan plenty of time to look over the contract, sign it and mail it to them before they returned. With the two thousand dollar check in hand, the teenagers left with the understanding that they would be back in two weeks once the signed tracking contract would be mailed to them. They thanked Juan Blanco for his tour of Spanish Markers and left.

Juan Blanco was furious with the two trackers. If he had had a gun he would have made them lead him to his gold now! He thought to himself that is not a mistake he will make again. The next time they returned his two sons Amador, Poncho and he would all have a handgun.

Imagine how dishonest those two girls were, they actually wanted to be paid to track a trail!

No girl is worth five hundred dollars a day to Juan Blanco! Did they think he was a stupid gringo (white person)? They should be grateful that Juan Blanco was willing to allow them on to his land. What infuriated him the most was they wanted to steal his inheritance—they actually thought they should be given a share of his treasure for finding his lost gold! Juan had given them a worthless check for two thousand dollars; had the women stayed and tracked the trail in the morning, they would not have had time to go to the bank and find there simply was no money in the checking account. Now because the check would hit the bank tomorrow but the trackers would not be coming for two weeks, he would have to get two thousand dollars tonight to deposit in the account so the check would clear the bank. Otherwise, the trackers would not return to find his treasure.

Juan Blanco sat around the dinner table with his wife, Consuelo, his two sons, Amador and Poncho, and his two daughters, Maria and Gwen. No one was happy about the turn of events; the treasure was practically in their hands with the arrival of the two trackers. Yet it was clear the trackers were obviously very greedy, as they had refused to tell them the location of their own treasure. Imagine the nerve of those two putas (woman who sell themselves to married men), they thought, wanting part of their treasure!

Although the family was opposed to paying the trackers anything, they foresaw three problems: First was the fact that if they did not deposit the money in the bank to cover the check, they would not get the trackers to return. The second problem with not paying the trackers was they had been unable to locate the treasure in sixty years of looking, so they would have to give the trackers two thousand dollars of they wanted to locate their treasure.

The third problem that arose was that if they did not sign the contract promising the trackers an equal share of their money, the thieving trackers would not come back. Without the help from the two trackers following the ancient markings they would never locate their treasure. The entire family discussed this difficult problem.

Amador and Poncho said, "We cannot give them an equal share. We need all the treasure for ourselves. There just is not enough treasure to share as the greedy bankers will want to be repaid for the two hundred thousand dollar mortgage."

Consuelo spoke up and said, "Why, if there is only eight hundred thousand dollars in gold, their certainly is not any money to pay those thieving trackers. If we are forced to pay the bank two hundred thousand dollars for the mortgage, there will only be six hundred thousand dollars left to split among us . That only leaves us with one hundred thousand dollars each. There is hardly enough for us, we certainly cannot pay the trackers too!"

At last, the family reached an agreement that satisfied them all. They would pay the trackers for four days of tracking so they would find the treasure. The foolish trackers had said that each person who helps gets an equal share. So instead of just Juan Blanco signing the agreement and there being a three-way split of their treasure, they would all sign the agreement so that the treasure would be split eight ways. Those gringos can be so dumb, they thought. They would let the trackers find their treasure, and then they would pull out their handguns so that the trackers could not steal any of their treasure. They would tell them they were trespassing on private property and they would force them to leave without a penny of their gold! Yes, they agreed, this plan just might work out just fine; soon they would have their inheritance.

Juan Blanco told his two sons, "Take one of your 4-wheelers to Pablo the thief and stolen-weapons dealer. Tell him you need $ 2,000 and three handguns."

"How do we get him to give us the cash and guns?" they asked their dad.

He replied, "Give him one of your 4-wheelers".

"But we paid $ 10,000 each for those 4-wheelers," Amador and Poncho protested.

"Do it!" Juan Blanco told his sons. "Soon we will have all the wealth you desire."

When Amador and Poncho arrived at Pablo's house and told him they needed two thousand dollars and three hand guns, Pablo immediately smelled that there was money to be made here. So Pablo asked why his two good customers of stolen goods needed the cash.

Amador told him, "It's to pay two trackers to take them to our family's treasure."

"We need the hand guns to prevent the trackers from stealing our gold."

Pablo told the two brothers that, while he would like to help them out, he was short on cash. While he had often offered five thousand dollars for the 4-wheelers which cost ten thousand dollrs when new, he could sense the desperation in Amador and Poncho so he immediately dropped his cash price to a thousand dollars. Then he told the brothers that three of his handguns would cost an additional thousand dollars. Amador and Poncho were furious with Pablo. Literally, Pablo-the-thief was stealing their 4-wheelers!

Pablo went into his bedroom and removed two thousand dollars for Juan Blanco's sons from a shoe box up high in the closet, leaving eight thousand. Pablo had the money to pay a fair price for the four wheelers, but since he was dishonest he decided to take advantage of his good customers of stolen merchandise. Then Pablo went into the basement and looked over his stolen gun collection. Carefully he picked out the three most unreliable hand guns to give to his friends. He was selecting his most worthless junk to give them. If he had to kill them before the month was out, he did not want them shooting at him! He selected a .32, a .25 and a .22 caliber to sell to Amador and Poncho. After a lot of haggling, Juan Blanco's sons left walking on foot, taking with them two thousand dollars and three handguns.

As soon as Amador and Poncho left, Pablo called up two of his business associates who specialized in burglarizing houses and told them they needed to cancel all their plans as he had a job for them. They needed to watch Juan Blanco's hacienda and report to him everything that they saw. Pablo thought it was time he retired and any way he looked at it, he planned to come out a winner. If the Juan Blanco family found their gold he would just have to kill them for it. In the event that Juan Blanco killed the two teenage trackers, he could always blackmail Juan Blanco. Let's see, he thought; didn't he own 80 acres? If Juan Blanco or his sons killed the two trackers, he could get Juan Blanco to deed him 20 acres for his silence. Of course, a couple of months later it would be another 20 acres until eventually he had all the land! Yup, any way he looked at it he was going to come out a winner. As he looked at the 9mm Ingram's sub-machine guns in his basement he was happy he kept his best firepower for the Juan Blanco's family.

Soon he would have their hacienda.

What was that saying? " Su casa es mi casa."

★★★★

Two weeks passed since the teenagers had received the two thousand dollars from Juan Blanco and the signed written contract before they returned to track the trail that Juan Blanco had paid them to track. As they drove up, they saw the two men hiding on the side of the driveway, watching them. They had a hunch that the men were up to no good.

Juan Blanco and his family greeted the trackers and were anxiously waiting for them to find their gold. The two teenagers observed the red and jagged black auras's around all of the Juan Blanco family. From the color of their aurora they knew that the family had no intention of treating them with dignity, honor, or fair play. Simply stated, from observing their aurora, they had a bad feeling that the Juan Blanco family planned to cheat them out of their share. Molly observed that the Juan Blanco's family had the shovels, picks, digging bars and ladders that they had told them they would need to recover their treasure. Yet, the trail to the treasure must first be tracked, Dancing Wind told Señor Blanco. Next, Molly ordered measurements of every rock while Dancing Wind wrote down the measurements in her notebook. So the day began with the sons and daughters of Juan Blanco measuring the distance between each rock throughout five acres of Juan Blanco's property. As the day wore on the teenage girls had all the measurements of the direction and distance between each rock.

Hiding behind some Piñon trees the burglars, Pablo and his two accomplices, watched everything. After measuring between every rock, the two trackers soon had Blanco's sons and daughters holding the tape measure and measuring the distance between each tree and even the tree stumps. Often, as the two sons walked by the trackers, they took the time to make insulting comments. Never did the teenagers reply to the insults. Yet Pablo noticed that the more Juan Blanco's sons insulted the two females or made sexual suggestions, the more it seemed to him they were wading across the stream measuring rocks or trees that Molly seemed to need exact measurements of. After two hours, Pablo-the-thief could barely contain his laughter, because he realized that the two female trackers were simply play-acting while wasting away the hours of the day.

The teenagers had Maria, Gwin, Amador and Poncho measuring between every tree and rock they could think of as the afternoon wore on. Often times the angle between the stones was carefully measured. Amador and Pancho were becoming exhausted from crossing the stream so frequently as they carried a hundred foot tape measure and then measured the angles of each stone on the property. They had not worked so hard in months. Watching everyone, Juan Blanco was proud of how hard his family and the trackers were working. Last night he had a premonition in a dream that today he would find his treasure. He was so excited, he was ready to dig now.

Spanish Compass Stone—These stones weigh 1,000-8,000 pounds. They give directions to travel or the location of the Spanish treasure sites. They are always placed on a stone base and have stones holding up the upper flat portion with a clearly seen air gap between the base and the top stone.

At approximately forty-five minutes before sunset, Dancing Wind and Molly O'Brian had the two brothers stand up on top of the large compass stones. They carefully made sure Amador was standing in the center of one compass stone, while Poncho stood in the center of another. Dancing Wind wrote down the total distance as the brothers measured the circumference around three of the compass stones, which formed a triangle. These compass stones are flat, one- to two-thousand-pound stones which were set up off the ground on small, round boulders so that light can be clearly seen beneath the stones. From the southern-most compass stone, Molly had Maria and Gwin measure true south one hundred yards which was the circumference through the stone's center going around the three compass stones. The trackers directed the family of Juan Blanco to dig here for their treasure.

As the sun sank in the western sky, the shovels threw dirt out of the hole, as all of Señor Blanco's family took turns digging for their treasure. Darkness had descended when the outline of a stone door came clearly into view. Using shovels and digging bars, the ancient stone door was forced open. Behind the stone door was the tunnel leading to the treasure! Juan Blanco and his sons and daughters knew it was now time to pay the trackers.

All three men pulled hand guns out from under their clothing; pointing the guns directly at Dancing Wind and Molly. Juan Blanco screamed at the two teenagers, "You are not stealing my gold....it's my inheritance...now get off my land! If you do not go now I will call the sheriff and have you arrested for trespassing."

The two trackers quickly got into their vehicle and drove off in the night. As they drove away, the silence was broken by Molly, as she studied Dancing Wind:

"You knew they would not share the gold with us! I can tell you knew! You knew!"

Dancing Wind just smiled as she looked at Molly and said, "Had you asked your Guardian Angel if they would treat us with dignity, honor and fair play, you, too, would have known how this was going to turn out."

"Then why did we do it if you knew they planned to cheat us the whole time?'

As she drove the Jeep south, Dancing Wind just smiled in the darkness and told Molly, "Think of all the wishes that GOD granted today.'

"You and I both got out safely, we both earned one thousand dollars to pay our bills; Señor Juan Blanco and his family also got their wish too, they found their inheritance."

"I noticed the more insults you heard from the brothers it seemed to me that you sure had his sons getting wet crossing the stream an awful lot of times measuring from tree to tree and rock to rock. Now tell me, didn't you have trouble controlling your face at times to keep from laughing or smiling as you had them measuring the distance between each rock and tree? I bet you most of these trees you had them measuring from did not even exist 320 years ago!"

Molly replied, "It was the attitude of his sons to us that really pissed me off. They were simply not very nice to us, there is never a good reason to degrade or insult another person."

★★★★

Juan Blanco and his family pushed the large flat stone sealing the entrance to their treasure site up upon a pile of dirt that had been concealing the entrance. Then they got ladders from the shed and flashlights from their house and descended into the tunnel far below. All six family members rushed down the ladder so as to be the first to find their treasure.

"Well," Pablo told his two accomplishes, "This is better than I could have planned.

We know where the treasure is and we do not need to even dig their graves. Let's go kill them and get our treasure."

Nine greedy individuals entered the tunnels leading to the treasure room.

Juan Blanco and his wife, Consuelo, took the first branch of the tunnel going to the right.

Before them on a mantle they saw two gold candlestick holders and two bags of coins.

As they grabbed the treasures from the mantle, they heard a loud roar. The roof of the room collapsed, just as their ancestors had designed it to do. The trap was designed to kill anyone trying to steal any of the family's treasures.

Poncho and Amador raced down the second corridor to the right. Suddenly they saw the treasure chest in front of them. They yelled, "It's here. It's here!" There, on top of a treasure chest, they saw two beautiful, shining, brilliant bars of gold. As they raced down the floor, neither brother noticed the solid stone floor had suddenly changed to sand. As they raced across the sand the floor collapsed, sending them falling into a thirty-foot deep pit. After they crashed to the bottom they were never to speak again, for they had gone into spirit like their parents who had unfortunately preceded them.

Pablo and his two associates descended into the tunnel and caught up with Juan Blanco's two daughters, Maria and Gwin. In front of them was the treasure room. Over the portal entrance to the room, carved into the stone, was a heart with the bottom center of the heart divided by a jagged lightning bolt. A foot to the left and the right of the broken stone heart were two more jagged lightning bolts, but in their haste to get all the gold, they failed to consider what the barely-observed symbols foretold. As they all walked into treasure room, they saw a stack of gold bars before them. In walking towards the treasure, suddenly the floor descended a foot and a half and there was a grating sound of stone upon stone. Suddenly a giant boulder slammed the entrance into the treasure room closed. There was no way out of the treasure room!

There was more gold in front of them than they would ever spend in their lifetime. Unfortunately, there was no way out of the treasure room. They pounded on the solid, stone boulder that sealed the way out, but they simply could not budge the immense stone.

Pablo, in frustration, aimed his 9mm Ingram submachine gun at the stone boulder and opened fire. Suddenly, the air was filled with stone chips and ricocheting bullets as they bounced off the stone walls and careened around the room. In moments, everyone was bleeding from the bullets' metal fragments or stone chips which had hit them. Maria and Gwen started screaming in frustration; they were trapped!

★★★★

A storm front moved east from California. Soon, as the storm clouds built up on the Sangre de Cristo Mountains, the lightning and thunder spirits started playing with each other. The Wind Spirits and the Rain Spirits started playing around with each other. The winds and rain were much needed in New Mexico. As the hard-driving rain fell on the loose soil, the freshly-dug, loose dirt became saturated with rain water and turned to mud. Suddenly the heavy stone that had sealed the entrance to the underground tunnel slid down the mud and again sealed the entrance where it had rested for centuries. It would again rest there for centuries to come.

★★★★

In Taos, the police chief noticed that home burglaries had finally decreased. Maybe the increased police patrols are finally paying off, he thought. Well, at least with fewer burglaries he stood a better chance of being reelected as sheriff.

★★★★

The banker was working late in his office, he hated to have to reposes another piece of land where the land owner had failed to make the mortgage payments. Well the bank would take a small loss but when they auctioned off the property they would recover most of the two hundred thousand dollar mortgage. There was a heavy demand in Taos for land for building new homes.

★★★★

There was a rumor going around Taos that one family struck it rich. They had always talked about the treasure on their land and suddenly the entire family had disappeared. You just knew they found their treasure, as they walked off taking nothing; why, they even left their old clothes and cars at the house when they up and left. Yes, people said they would buy new clothes, cars and houses when their plane landed in California. They had struck it rich! Some people just seem to have all the luck. The lucky ones are always finding a treasure or striking it rich by winning the lottery. Suddenly Molly was startled awake from her thoughts as the beautician told her, "That will be ninety-five dollars, please. You look great with your new perm."

Angels believe in Karma,
Which is justice from above;
Angels believe in Grace,
Which is like Divine Love;
Angels believe in reincarnations,
Where you come back again and again;
Angels believe in You!
For one stands at your side!

Fisherman's Karma

Dancing Wind and Molly had driven up to Seattle, Washington to take a vacation. On impulse they had decided to rent a small boat and go cruising along the coast line. At a boat rental dealer they saw the perfect boat for them to rent. A small Cape Dory looked like it was the perfect boat to explore the coastline and small islands along the rugged coastline. So both teenagers looked in the Yellow Pages for a boat dealer who would rent them a Cape Dory.

The boat rental dealer threw up his hands in exasperation. Women were impossible, he decided. The Cape Dory the two teenagers wanted to rent had a perfectly good engine on the boat; it was the engine the factory recommended. He promised the teenagers they would not have any problems starting the 75 horse power Johnson outboard engine.

There was an electric starter and it would start the outboard engine just like the car engine is started by a battery.

That red-haired girl, Molly O'Brian, looked him in the eye and said "And what happens if the battery dies or the charger on the engine quits working? How are we supposed to start the engine then she asked?"

He told her, "If the battery dies or the charger quiets, well, it just is not possible to start the engine."

"Exactly," Molly replied. "That is why you are going to install two new Mercury 9.9 horse power engines on the back of the Cape Dory."

"Do you realize what those cost?" he asked her.

Molly replied, "A lot less than my life is worth."

"They would cost three thousand dollars to buy and install," He replied.

"Well a simple solution," Molly replied, "is for you to install them, and I am sure our rental fee will leave you with two new emergency spare engines."

Some times in life compromises are necessary. In the end, both parties made compromises. The dealer agreed to install one new spare outboard engine with its own fuel filter and spare fuel tank. He also provided some basic tools and spare parts for the Mercury outboard engine.

The Cape Dory was loaded up with food, fuel, crabbing and fishing supplies, camping gear and clothing for both women. Then the teenagers got out the "Charlie Chart" of the area they planned to go cruising and exploring. Before leaving they left a written copy of their plans with the United States Coast Guard as well as with the Marina where they rented the Cape Dory.

The Cape Dory traveled north along the inside passage. They tried to keep the distance they traveled north broken up into short jaunts that would not leave them exhausted at the end of the day. Sometimes they climbed up and explored waterfalls or the surrounding forest at the sites they camped. Ancient Douglas fir and cedar trees hundreds of years old and five to ten feet in circumference filled the forest. The teenagers often encountered the cabins of fishermen or trappers along the coastline. Crabs were plentiful and catching a half dozen at low tide was easy. Fishing was an angler's dream and each teenager was able to easily catch plenty of fresh fish for dinner which they fried in a skillet.

The custom when you spend the night in the cabin of a fisherman or trapper is to leave the log cabin as good as- or better than you found it. So if you build a fire to keep warm, then you should cut the wood to replace what you used, plus a little extra. If you use the matches then in a jar replace the matches with a new box of wooden matches. If the food shelves are almost bare; leave a few extra cans of food. It just might be your life or your neighbor's life you save should an emergency force you to take shelter in the log cabin.

★★★★

Jim Thomas and his sons, Dave and Paul, lived along the coast making a living by whatever dishonest method their imagination and cunning could contrive. When salmon fishermen cast gill nets to catch the salmon they depended upon to making a living, the Thomas boys were not averse to helping the owner of the net, by emptying the net of fish so the net owner did not have so many fish to sell.

When homeowners were out working, the Thomas brothers would visit the owner's home. There, they would steal whatever they could easily resell for a quick cash sale. The Thomas brothers hurt dozens of families as they robbed their houses over the years. When the police put more effort into catching the home burglars the brothers just switched who they robbed to something unexpected, always staying one jump ahead of the police.

When crabbing season came, the Thomas brothers would work catching crabs to sell to the packing houses. Jim Thomas and his sons ran about a hundred and fifty crab pots. The crab pots would be baited every two- to four days and left in the deep water for the crabs to enter the crab pot and take the bait. Once inside the crab pots, the crabs would become trapped. About every two- to four days the pots would be hauled aboard the boat, the crabs removed, and the pots rebaited and replaced into the water. The crabs would be sold at the packing house.

To increase their catch the Thomas brothers would carefully watch where the other crab boats were working and at what interval they checked their crab pots. Then the Thomas brothers would steal the crabs from the other fishermen who were making a living crabbing. Often times the other fishermen or crabbers never knew that the Thomas brothers had emptied their crab pots stealing their crabs. Often times the other fisherman just thought they were having a poor day at that location; so they would move their crab pots to a new location. Sure enough, at the new location the crabbing would often be better, as they had moved away from where the Thomas Brothers were stealing the other fisherman's catch.

When fur-trapping season came along in the winter months, the Thomas brothers would hit the trapper's cabins taking any pelts the trapper had accumulated. As the brothers liked to really piss off whomever they robbed, it was not unusual that they would take the trappers' furs, food, kerosene fuel, lanterns, and even the sleeping bags off the bed. The Thomas brothers thought it was always much more profitable to rob the trapper of his furs than go to the work of trapping the animals themselves.

After a long day at work it was not unusual for the trapper to return to his cabin and find he had been cleaned out of everything. Lock, stock and barrel; everything was stolen by the Thomas brothers. Remote fish camps and vacation homes were also targets of the Thomas clan. Many homes over the years were vandalized and their contents emptied.

20 years later

As Dancing Wind and Molly cruised north they sometimes stopped at the fisherman camps as well as the trapper cabins. Frequently they were located in the only sheltered location one could safely get a boat in or out of in rough weather. Sudden storms could come rolling south across the Bering Sea, making the sea conditions along the Alaska coast some of the worst in the world.

One night along this remote coast line, Dancing Wind began hearing an owl hooting. Suddenly she felt the urge to find the owl she heard hooting from somewhere close by. As she moved closer to the hooting owl, a small stream leading into a quiet cove of water appeared before her. Molly, too, wanted to explore the small stream coming out of the coastline. As they entered the sheltered cove, they noticed that on the bluff overlooking the cove there was a lonely log cabin which seemed very old and abandoned. Tall pine trees sheltered the cabin and the cove from the winter storms, making this an ideal spot to seek shelter from a winter storm. As they tied up the Cape Dory and examined the site, it seemed the perfect hideaway. Strangely, the old log cabin seemed empty as though no one had lived there for years.

Inside the log cabin was the typical Alaskan wood stove. It was a 55-gallon steel drum converted into a wood stove for cooking and heating the log cabin.

Molly was looking at the wood stove when she suddenly exclaimed "I cannot believe what I am reading on the wood stove."

Embossed into the steel 55-gallon drum were the words: "Property of the U. S. Army Air Corp."

"That is before the United States had its Air Force! That is a very old steel barrel."

Dancing Wind and Molly decided to spend the night in the log cabin—they cut fire wood for the night plus an extra three days. In a jar they added a full box of wood burning matches. The jar would protect the matches from any mice wanting to chew on the sulfur match heads, and possibly causing a fire. They also placed some canned soup and corned beef on the empty shelves. Clearly whoever had been there before the girls had not shown the proper manners.

After dinner the teenagers turned in for the night. They were tired and wanted to get a good night's sleep. In the morning they planned to take off early, just after breakfast. There was a little left over food which they left near the wood stove and the fire was still burning in the cabin, keeping it warm as they turned in to sleep.

★★Twenty five years earlier★★

Jim Edwards came into the cabin after a fourteen hour day running his trap line. Jim was looking forward to a hot meal, a warm bed, and a nice fire. When he reached his cabin he would build a nice fire in his 55-gallon barrel wood stove. He always got a kick out of the US Army Air Corp stamped into the metal. It brought back memories of when he and his dad used to work the trap line before his dad had passed away. Right now he could use a nice, hot meal.

As Jim Edwards arrived at the cabin, he immediately sensed that something was wrong. His canoe out front was gone! He opened the cabin door and his temper exploded; they had robbed him again! Everything was gone! His food, his matches, his kerosene and kerosene lanterns, even his pots and pans and knives! They had stolen his extra traps and all his furs! All the work he had done for the last four months was gone; he had no furs left to show for a winter's work of trapping. It was like Jim Edwards was kicked in the gut by a mule! He just felt like he was at the end of his rope; it was the last straw.

Jim Edwards said, *"GOD, that is just not right. That is just not right what those thieves have done to me."*

Jim Edwards had no family to turn to for help. He had no money in the bank. He simply had no way of replacing his traps or all his belongings! Thirty days later, Jim Edwards went into an old folk's home. Everything he owned was gone! He had no one else. He had no place else.

★★20 years ago★★

Jim Thomas lent his sons Dave and Paul his fishing boat. Jim told them before they took off he wanted them to change the oil on the marine diesel engine as well as the fuel filter. Cleaning out the rich tourists houses along the coast had become an annual trip for Dave and Paul. Dave and Paul expected they would score a number of hunting rifles, laptop computers, and high-priced cameras from the vacation homes they robbed. Yes, this was easy money. Dave and Paul looked forward to this trip twice a year, once in the spring and once in the fall. They were impatient to see what they could steal on this trip up and down the coast. Dave and Paul were in too big of a hurry to waste their time changing their dad's boats diesel engine oil and the fuel filter. They would let Jim (their dad) change his own oil and fuel filters.

★★★★

The sky had turned gray as Dave and Paul cruised along the coast line. Paul had a bad feeling about this trip. He had been uneasy, even as they loaded up their fishing boat with the plunder from the houses they robbed. As the wind and the waves rapidly increased, Dave and Paul knew they had to find shelter from the storm coming at them from out of the Bearing Sea. The diesel engine had not been running right, as the engine RPM had constantly climbed or fell with the rolling of the boat in the heavy seas.

The trouble was that neither man could remember the last time they had changed the fuel filter on their engine. As the boat was tossed in the heavy seas, the sediment in the bottom of their fuel tank was sloshed throughout the fuel tank, clogging it, and soon found its way to the engine. Both brothers had been too lazy to change the fuel filter before they started on the trip. Nor had the brothers made the effort to buy and carry a spare fuel filter. The engine RPM constantly climbed and fell, as the engine was starved for fuel. The trouble was that Dave and Paul needed all the power they could get to control the boat in the heavy seas. Already the diesel engine's RPM had fallen from 3,000 RPM to 1,100-1,700 RPM. Unless they could fix the problem, they might not live through the day.

As the day wore on, the storm increased in intensity. Finding shelter was critical before the waves over came and swamped their fishing boat. Paul remembered an old trapper's cabin from years past. As they headed for the site it looked touch-and-go, as the twenty foot seas threatened to sink the fishing boat. Suddenly the engine gave one final gasp and died. Thirty seconds later, the first of a series of large waves crashed over top their fishing vessel. Where once their feet were firmly planted on the deck, they were both now swimming for their lives!

In the process of swimming through the surf, their clothes were torn off their bodies. They helped each other escape the crashing surf and made it up out of the water, reaching the shore by some fluke of luck. They were naked, exhausted, and cold. They started walking to the trappers' cabin they remembered three miles up the coast.

The wind howled as they traveled up the coast line; they were shivering and shaking as the cold winds turned their skin red and then blue. Their teeth began an uncontrollable chatter. Their arms were shaking. They had to reach the cabin if they were to survive. A fire, a meal and a warm bed meant that they would survive this day.

Upon reaching the cabin on the small cove they had to wade across the small creek to reach the shelter of the cabin. Once the two brothers reached the cabin and entered inside they wanted to scream in horror! But they were simply too cold to scream as their teeth rapidly chattered due to their extreme cold. For inside the trappers' cabin it appeared just as they had left it the last time they were here. There were no sleeping bags on the beds! There was no food on the shelves! There was no firewood cut for emergencies or someone arriving late at night! There were no kerosene lanterns! There was no kerosene! THERE WERE NO MATCHES TO LIGHT A FIRE! The house looked exactly like they had left if when they robbed it years earlier!

★★Twenty years later★★

Dancing Wind and Molly fell asleep in the warmth of the cabin. Late that night, the front door suddenly opened. In staggered two men, their teeth chattering. Their skin was blue and they were shaking from cold. As the teenagers awoke from their sleep, there before the wood stove, were the spirits of two naked men. With their backs to the girls; the spirits of Paul and Dave were trying to warm themselves by the wood stove. Every month on the day they had died, the spirits relived their last minutes on earth before their death due to exposure. They relived the sinking of their vessel, the struggle to get ashore. They experienced the dangerous surf with its waves pounding against their bodies. They felt the icy water pounding their bodies and their freezing walk up the beach to the cabin. When they arrived at the trappers' cabin they experienced their horror at realizing that the cabin was totally empty just as they had left the cabin after they had stolen everything belonging to the old trapper,, Jim Edwards. Their last moments on earth were shivering and shaking from cold in front of the old two-barrel wood stove before going into spirit. But they were trapped here now as ghosts, reliving their last hours.

Dancing Wind and Molly got dressed, and then asked the Spirits to get some clothes on. When they replied their clothes were torn off as they swam ashore in the surf Molly told them if they think of warm clothes now, that they were sure GOD would instantly provide them. Moments later the two ghosts were dressed in warm clothes. When they said they were hungry, Dancing Wind said you are welcome to share our food with us. As Dancing Wind talked, Molly fixed four plates of food.

Dancing Wind spoke with her Guardian Angel for a few minutes so as to understand what was occurring and what had occurred here. Dancing Wind was pissed, as she herself had been robbed several times. When the two ghosts and the two teenagers sat down to talk, Dancing Wind was not in the best of moods, she was angry! Dancing Wind's words cut like a knife as she asked the two spirits or ghosts, who had stolen the bedding, food and matches and fuel from this log cabin. The ghosts looked at the floor as they knew the answer; for it was one of a number of houses they had robbed. Dancing Wind asked them if they realized the harm they had caused the old trapper who used to live here. They both knew exactly the harm they had caused, as their Guardian Angels showed them the damage they had wrought upon the old trapper as the completely discouraged and totally broken man checked himself into an old folks home. Dancing Wind told them in their next life time they will have to undo the damage they caused by setting things right. If not by helping the man they hurt, then by helping another individual in need. She asked them if they understood that they had damaged and hurt dozens of families living up and down the coast.

She asked the men, "Don't you know that what comes around goes around? What you did to the other families will all happen to both of you unless you can set it right!"

She told them that karma may be explained as a simple cause and effect so that divine justice is achieved. "

"A thief who steals from a number of houses may in turn have his house robbed so that all his efforts were in vain, "she explained, "Or when he goes to sell his stolen goods he may sell them to a police officer and hence be arrested for the crimes he committed. What you did was WRONG! The most I can do is help you go *home*, if that is what you want to do.

"Otherwise, you can keep coming back to this empty log cabin, freezing cold and shivering, as you relive your last hour before you went into Spirit. You will do it time after time until you finally realize that you need to ask GOD for his forgiveness and ask him to send you some Angels to take you *home.*"

"Would you help us go *home* now?" they asked the teenage girls.

Dancing Wind and Molly assured Paul and Dave that they would help them to go home now. They asked both men to say a prayer to GOD. At the same time the two teenagers prayed to GOD for his help. When they ran out of words to say they simply said "The Lord's Prayer". When Dancing Wind and Molly reached the part where they were saying "Forgive us for our sins ..." two Angels of the Lord appeared. Between the Angels was a door of light, into which walked Paul and Dave. As GOD's Love filled the room, the Angels smiled at the two teenagers, just as suddenly both Angels were gone. Molly and Dancing Wind could feel the love flowing all around the room, so there was no more sleep that night. They stayed up and talked around the warm fire burning inside the old wood stove with "U. S. Army Air Corp" embossed into the steel.

Pray to the Father
Pray to the Son
Pray to Mary
And We (Angels) will Come

Arturio; A Man of Honor and Integrity

In centuries past, as now, men of dignity, honor, honesty, loyalty and integrity were extremely scarce. This is a story of just such a man. Arturio had come over from Barcelona, Spain as a lay brother to help the Catholic Church with its work in the new world. In Mexico City he was told there was a pressing need to have priests attend the spiritual needs of miners as well as the savage Indians, and to run a church mine so as to keep money flowing into the Catholic Church and give it funds for its ministry work.

Before being ordained as a priest, Arturio was given a three month crash course on running a gold and silver mining operation, assaying and smelting, codifying church maps and documents, Indian customs and traditions, agriculture, church prayers, and his duties as a priest at his future parish.

Arturio was told it was important to get the mines on *Sierra de los Minas* into production, as the church was desperately short of money and needed a dependable flow of revenue to support its works of charity in Mexico and New Mexico. The Archbishop told Arturio that they were counting on him to meet the needs of the Franciscan Ministry. In return they would get Arturio the help and supplies he needed for his work.

They would see that fruit tree seedling, garden seeds, sheep, food like dried fruit, flour, mining supplies, like gunpowder and drill steel, and labor would arrive to help him in his work; these items would be shipped north along the El Camino Real (Royal Road).

Three months later, having walked 1,300 miles north from Mexico City to Abiquiu along the El Camino Real, Arturio arrived in a remote village in northern New Mexico to begin his work as the local Franciscan priest. His only possessions were a Bible, his personal journals and a pocket full of apricot seeds. He planted these seeds in Abiquiu by the church as well as at the three Indian pueblos. His was the first church mass held in years, since the murders of the last priests. He had sick to attend to, children to baptize, mass to hold every Sunday, as well as get the church mines back into production to help the church in its work.

Father Arturio worked tirelessly to get the mines producing the gold and silver required by the Archbishop. Immediately he noticed everything he required: axes to cut the timbers for shoring, rifles for hunting and self-defense, gunpowder for blasting, iron digging bars for the miners work crews and food supplies were lacking in this northern outpost. Arturio found he also needed honest miners to work the mine and these were in very short supply. Doing his best to overcome numerous obstacles, Arturio worked long sixteen hour days.

After six months of hard work, Arturio had a shipment of gold and silver from the church mine ready to move south so the priest requested that the Royal Soldiers put the tax stamp on the bars of gold and silver, providing proof that the Royal Fifth of all the mined gold and silver went to the King of Spain. With the shipment of gold going out, the Father asked the commanding officer of the detachment of soldiers out of the Santa Fe Presidio (fort) to ship some of the churches gold along with the king's gold down to the Archbishop in Mexico City. The officer was happy to help the priest out, and he was proud that the priest had entrusted him with the church's gold. He would protect it with his life.

Arturio also asked the commander to deliver a letter, asking for the supplies needed to operate the mine including honest miners. Four months later the letter, along with a small gold and silver shipment, were delivered to the Franciscan's Mission in Mexico City.

The Archbishop at the Franciscan headquarters in Mexico City was an astute man, and was able to place the priest and the brothers in jobs that fit them well. He appointed the priest to controlling receipt of gold and silver, converting that to cash, buying the necessary supplies and then sending those supplies to the missions. He was an excellent quartermaster, but did not have the qualities necessary to interact with people the way a parish priest should. This man got the highest price available for the gold and silver while paying the lowest price available for supplies. He received all supply requests from the outlying missions and did his best to provide the necessities for the missions; that is, except for Arturio's request. The quartermaster was a jealous man and was quite upset that he had been passed over for his own mission by a lay brother. Every four months Arturio sent a shipment of gold and silver and his request for supplies and honest men to work the mine. Every four months the quartermaster converted the metal to cash, brought the supplies requested by the outlying missions, and hid Arturio's request in his files.

Never did Arturio receive the supplies or help he requested. Arturio felt that he was in an extremely precarious position, but since he knew the Church desperately needed the funds, he shipped to Mexico City and he had given his word to the Archbishop, he would not quit or leave his work. Arturio's word to the Archbishop was that he would do all he could to further the work of the Franciscan mission; as an honorable man he felt bound by that promise and would not halt his work because of the hardships he was experiencing. The Archbishop had impressed upon him that the mines in *Sierra de las Minas* provided twenty percent of the funding for the Missions in Mexico, and were thus necessary for the success of the order throughout the whole of the new world.

As the mining operations were now under the direct supervision of Arturio, it really angered a number of men from Abiquiu who had chosen to help out the Church as they had thought the padre would not notice their stealing most of the mine production. On the contrary, the first three men would never forget the lecture from the Bible about the Ten Commandments they got when Arturio caught them. When Arturio explained each of the Ten Commandments to anyone caught stealing the gold from the Church and the King of Spain, Arturio would violently impress upon them his displeasure, as his powerful fists slammed into their bodies as he thoroughly explained all Ten Commandments. It was not unusual for the offender to recover from unconsciousness to find they had several broken bones. Never had Abiquiu seen or experienced a priest like him.

Slave traders were allowed to capture and enslave the "wild Indians" like the Utes, Lakota, Cheyenne, Comanche, Arapahoe and Apaches. This was encouraged by the Spanish authorities, as it weakened enemies of the Spanish Crown. The civilized tribes like the Pueblo Indians had agreed to provide both food and man power to the Spanish upon demand, so they were not supposed to be captured and dragged off as slaves.

The first time the slave traders stopped in Abiquiu and started to grab some of the local Pueblo Indians instead of the wild uncivilized Indians, which they were allowed to kidnap and enslave, the priest explained the difference to the slave traders in a manner that they would never forget. The big burley slave trader who knocked Arturio aside when the priest told him he could not take his (the priest's) Pueblo Indians found himself suddenly grabbed from the rear of his pants and the scuff of his neck. His head was then pounded repeatedly into the wooden sides of the two wheel ox-pulled carreta he had been loading the kidnapped Indians into. Then Arturio removed the kidnapped Pueblo Indians from the carreta and he threw the unconscious slave trader into the wagon. When the slave trader awoke two hours later and six miles east of Abiquiu, he found his head all bruised and bloody and he had no desire to ever see that priest again!

One cold winter morning, Arturio had some of the Abiquiu Pueblo Indians cook up a big pot of beans and deer meat. When the priest returned in the evening and found the pot of food stolen by several lazy men in Abiquiu, he asked the Indians who had taken it. The Indians just pointed toward an adobe house. Five Spanish men were looking forward to their hot meal when an angry Arturio walked in the door. One foolish man told Arturio he was not touching their stew pot. Arturio did not argue with him; he just lashed out with his powerful fist and slammed it into the side of the man's head right behind his ear, and he fell unconscious, partly falling across the fire the men were heating the pot of food on. Arturio grabbed up the pot of food, and as he walked out the door he said,

"Thou shall not steal."

As Arturio left, one man got up and rolled their companion off the burning fire and dumped a pitcher of water onto the burning clothes of the unconscious thief. The remaining four men had nothing but bare cupboards, as they had been too lazy to plant crops and tend them. The remaining four men looked at each other and said, "Now what are we going to eat?"

When the king's soldiers came through Abiquiu they would accompany a carreta loaded with the Royal Fifth, one fifth of the gold and silver that had been mined from the rich gold and silver mine on Sierra de las Minas. Sixteen men in Abiquiu got to talking and they decided that if that carreta was loaded with a ton of gold for the king of Spain, there must be much more gold up at the mine Arturio was working at. Far better that they should have the gold and silver, than the church waste all that money building churches, feeding the poor, or wasting it on widows and orphan children.

They would put the money to good use in the cantinas and the houses of women who entertained men. So it was agreed that they should go to church and attend the next mass the priest gave. Then they would repent and tell the priest they wanted to help out the church and turn their lives around by working for the Church. Then, as soon as they saw where Arturio stored the church's gold on *Sierra de las Minas*, they would arrange an accident and murder the priest! All sixteen men reached an agreement: assassins they would be—and their first victim would be the Catholic priest.

The sixteen assassins went to work up on *Sierra de las Minas*. While the mine was rich in gold and silver, none of the assassins wanted to work for the honest wages that the priest paid them. Instead, after they'd had a hot meal, the sixteen men went to a small clearing in the woods and discussed the best method of murdering the priest. They decided to arrange an "accident" down inside the mine, where they would roll a large boulder onto the priest, crushing him to death.

They set their plans into motion and prepared a large boulder to roll on top of the priest. One man ran to the priest, calling him to come quick, saying the mine timbers had slipped and a miner was trapped. Arturio ran into the mine to try to save the life of the trapped miner. Unfortunately, what he found was not a trapped miner, but a trap set to kill him. As the boulder was pushed toward him, Arturio jumped aside, but the boulder tore a jagged gash in his leg.

The priest clinched his teeth together to keep from screaming as the intense pain shot through his left leg. Blood streamed out of his wound. The priest escaped the mine and told two companions what had occurred. They tore a strip of cloth off the bottom of the priest's robe to make a bandage to wrap up the wound, and tried to stop the bleeding.

The Pueblo Indians working in the mine quickly disappeared, as they did not want to get involved in a fight between the Catholic priest and the group of assassins. The word of any Spaniard was always believed over that of a Pueblo Indian. In a trial, the Spaniards were allowed to tell their side of the story; whether it was the truth or a complete fabrication. Then the Indian was sentenced to his fate, whatever the judge determined was appropriate, like being tortured to death, executed, or sentenced to work in the mines as a slave until he died. Indians were often considered property of the king, and as property they were usually not allowed to say anything in their defense before the judge sentenced them to their fate. So the usual punishment for an Indian attacking a Spaniard was death. Even though the Abiquiu Pueblo Indians supported Arturio, they chose not to engage in a battle with the sixteen Spanish assassins because they felt that regardless of the outcome of the fight, they would die; at the hands of the group or at the hands of the king's men.

The sixteen men came out of the mine and again returned to the small clearing in the woods. They must murder the priest along with anyone who stood loyal to him tonight, for if word of their action reached the Spanish garrison, the soldiers would come and hang them all. The assassins circled Arturio and the two men loyal to him so that they could not escape. When darkness came, they planned to finish the dark deed that they had begun in the mine. Using bows and arrows, knives and swords they planned finish this afternoon's work.

That night on *Sierra de las Minas*, Arturio lay against an immense stone boulder to protect his back. Sitting beside him were two friends of the priest. They believed in the priest and all the good he was accomplishing, so they chose to stand by and support their friend in his time of need. All Arturio had was a wooden walking stick to defend himself because the gun powder and weapons he had repeatedly requested had never been sent north from Mexico City. His two loyal companions had one sword and one steel digging bar as their weapons. As darkness fell they heard the movement of men in the woods around them. Arturio requested the two men to help him up, as he was unable to stand without assistance. Arturio did his best, fighting to the end. With his back leaning against the huge boulder and his two friends standing beside him, they fought for what they felt was right.

The sixteen assassins came out of the woods in a rush, and in a ruthless attack they murdered the Franciscan priest and his companions.

At the end of the battle, the bodies of the murdered priest and his companions lay upon the ground. The spirits of the three men came out of their bodies ready to continue the fight, but their spiritual bodies were not even seen by the assassins, nor could they continue the fight as their physical bodies lay lifeless on the ground. The spiritual bodies of the two men who had died fighting protecting their friend took on the spirit form or a translucent outline of the physical form of they had when alive. The priest was a more enlightened spirit and did not hold on to his physical body's previous form, but took the form of a single beam of light about twenty feet tall. As the seasons came and went, all three spirits remained at Arturio's camp site where they had been murdered on *Sierra de las Minas.* If the average person saw them in the early morning hours, at dusk, or on the anniversary of their murder, they would probably say they saw three ghosts at the camp upon the mountain.

The assassins were victorious! They celebrated the victory and got drunk. They were all excited and happy; they were all rich beyond their wildest dreams! In the morning they shot arrows into the knife and sword wounds to conceal how the priest and his companions had died. They would say they came up to assist the priest, at his request, and when they got to his camp, they found that he and his companions had been murdered by raiding Comanche Indians.

The assassins agreed that in two or three months they would return and steal all the gold and silver from the treasure room in the mine. For now, they would cover up the mine entrance so no one would even know that there was a mine on the mountain. For the next two days they worked to remove all trace of the mine. Now their gold would be safe, as they did not think that anyone could possibly find the mine. Then the assassins returned to Abiquiu to let everything cool off before they disposed of their stolen gold and silver.

★★★★

A week later a detachment of Spanish Soldiers rode into Abiquiu. They rode straight up to the sixteen assassins who were loafing around the Abiquiu plaza. The commander of the soldiers looked over the lot of scoundrels. They were a sorry looking lot, not worth the powder to blow them away. As the Commander looked over the men, they grew quiet and nervous under his stern gaze.

Then the officer said, "I have been told you murdered the priest and have stolen the King's gold. If I had proof of that now, we would not be talking, but I would be showing you Spanish justice. If I ever learn that you are selling gold or silver you have stolen from the king I will personally take great pleasure in carrying out swift justice. I will tie your arms to two different horses and your legs to another two horses. Then I will whip the horses, so the four horses pulled you in four different directions, and as painfully as possible quarter each one of you thieves into four pieces! I will take great pleasure in administering justice by killing anyone stealing gold from King Charles of Spain!

"No one but the lowest of assassins would murder a priest. You all know the penalty for murder. If I had proof I would administer the king's justice now. One of you is going to slip up and get caught spending the King's gold and when you do, I will have all the evidence I need to provide swift justice to all sixteen of you. Then may GOD have mercy on your souls as I will show you murderers none!"

The sixteen assassins were never able to spend the gold they murdered to obtain. To this day it lies in the Santa Fe National Forest, stored up upon *Sierra de las Minas* southwest of Abiquiu. When the Spanish Treasure Armadas sailed to Spain every fall, they were bringing back to the Old World the wealth from the New World. It was hundreds of rich gold and silver mines, like the mines upon *Sierra de las Minas* worked by honest, hard-working men like Arturio that filled the ships with priceless treasures.

★★★★

Over a hundred and fifty years has passed since Arturio last worked the gold mine on *Sierra de las Minas*. If one were to look inside the mine, just as Arturio left it, the stacked bars of gold and silver bars are ready to be shipped to the Franciscan Mission in Mexico City as well as to the King of Spain, just as they were on the day of the attack. On the metal bars of gold and silver is the tax stamp of the Royal Fifth, showing the tax to the King of Spain has been paid. Beside the treasure room, spirits of the twelve assassins stand guard to block entry to anyone. Four of the assassins felt the best way to get their hands on the treasure was to go *home*. These four spirits then reincarnated into individuals now living in Abiquiu today.

The assassins continue to watch over the treasure to ensure no one touches the gold and silver that they murdered to obtain. If you were to walk down the ancient tunnels, I am sure that you would see the assassins--they are the color of dark muddy water, and in shape they are like an upright broom stick or a spear. While their appearance may be a little frightening at first, if one asks GOD to put a white light of protection around you and you *actively work to hold the protective light all about oneself, they cannot hurt you.* They cannot buy a drink with the gold, nor can they buy an enjoyable evening with a beautiful woman; as they had planned to do many times. The ghost cannot use the treasure to buy fine clothes, fine horses or large estates as they had thought of doing when they planned their evil deeds. Everything they dreamed of buying with the gold is impossible for them, for they are ghosts now. Yet they cannot let go of what they murdered to obtain for their greed holds them there, like chains of the toughest carbon steel, to a room of treasure which they cannot spend! These spirits have literally created, through their actions, a prison of their own making.

Gold and silver did not have any lasting effect upon Arturio's spirit, as he was not affected by greed. Arturio was a man of dignity and honor; there was simply no place for gold to corrupt his character. Arturio realized that the gold and silver was simply a tool—which could be utilized by the church in helping the less fortunate. *Arturio's path in life—literally his life's mission--was to help humanity.* Arturio believed *we need to put humanity back in the human race and his actions throughout his life were to help the needy and less fortunate.* Yet Arturio tells me: *"Make no mistake about my principals. Never do I believe in giving someone a fish to eat!"*

Arturio believed that you teach someone to fish. Arturio would always be willing to give a person a helping hand—even to feed them—but he expects that person to work and do his part too! The reason that there are now apricot trees in Abiquiu, is because Arturio brought seeds up from Mexico and planted them. Arturio felt that it was your responsibility to care for the trees if you wanted to enjoy the fruit of the apricot tree. Arturio felt that if you wanted to enjoy a pot of beans and elk meat for dinner it was your responsibility to help plant the beans and care for them or you should participate in the hunting of the elk and butchering the meat.

There are men today who have both transported and handled millions of dollars in gold bullion whose duty, integrity and honor would not allow them to touch one bar of gold except to deliver it as they were entrusted to do. Such men, like Arturio, have honor and integrity beyond price. Then there are men who pay lip service to honesty, integrity and honor and are the first to point out another's lack thereof (lack of honesty, honor and integrity) , when they have none of their own. These individuals are no different from the assassins who murdered Arturio. So where do your priorities lie? Can you look the two Angels in the eye as you walk between them when you return *home* and enter the tunnel of light? Or when you die will you be like the sixteen assassins who murdered Arturio and be bound in chains of greed of your own making? For truly the path you walk, is the path of your own making, as GOD has given you free choice.

★★★★150 years after the death of Arturio★★★★

It started with the drought. The land was dry and food for the bears was very scarce.

Dancing Wind and Molly drove their Jeep up into the mountains. Dancing Wind felt the hunger of the two bears that lived upon *Sierra de las Minas*. Taking Molly along to give her a hand, Dancing Wind had come to do what the New Mexico Fish and Game department was unwilling to do: She had come to feed the bears to help them get through the winter.

Dancing Wind knew that to feed the bears she must not draw them in towards houses, nor should the bears associate the food with people or cars or she would be endangering the bears and the people who would come into the mountains for a drive. So the path that Dancing Wind chose was to ask her Guardian Angel how to feed the bears and where the best spot to do so was.

Dancing Wind's Guardian Angel thought this would be the perfect opportunity to resolve two problems at one time, so she suggested that Dancing Wind go into the Santa Fe National Forest with two twenty-pound bags of dog food and two big jars of honey. Guiding Molly and Dancing Wind to the north side of *Sierra de las Minas*, the Angel showed them a small rise, or hill, that would be an ideal spot in which to feed the bears. Dancing Wind and Molly parked the Jeep nearby and each strapped on a backpack loaded with twenty pounds of dog food and a jar of honey and hiked to the top of a small hill about ten minutes walk away. Here the green grass grew tall and they saw bear sign on the ground. The Angel told Molly and Dancing Wind that they were feeding two black bears so they needed to make two piles of food about six feet apart. They each opened their backpacks and poured the dog food in a pile on top of the ground and topped each pile off with the honey. Then they placed the sticky honey jars into the dog food bags and placed the trash into a trash bag they had brought along in their backpacks.

Next, Molly and Dancing Wind went to call the bears to the piles of food they had given them as a gift. Had not Jesus said "When GOD's children are in need you be the one to help them out. And get into the habit of inviting guest home for dinner or, if they need lodging, for the night." Romans 12:13. Molly asked her Guardian Angels to tell the bears' Guardian Angels that there was a meal here on this mountain for them. Next, Molly just pictured the hill in her mind. Then she pictured the pile of food for the bear on top of the hill. Then she pictured the two bears eating the food. Molly pictured the hill again and how the hill looked. For five minutes Molly repeated these thoughts about the hill, the food, and the bears eating the food. Molly was doing her best to communicate with the bears, telling the bears through the pictures where they could find a nice meal.

Dancing Wind had the same intent as Molly, but she went about it slightly differently.

Dancing Wind asked her Guardian Angel to show her where the bears were located.

Dancing Wind's Spirit then flew with the Angel to the bears. Addressing the bears and the bears' Guardian Angels she told them, using pictures of where they were, where the piles of food were and the shortest path that the bears should take to reach the food. Immediately the two bears took off, traveling rapidly towards the small hill where the food was awaiting them.

On the hill the two teenagers suddenly jumped up off the ground.

Dancing Wind told Molly, "We have got to get off this hill fast; the bears are on their way."

To the south of them on *Sierra de las Minas* they heard the bear growls in the distance. They rapidly moved off the hill to the northwest to their awaiting Jeep. When they were safely inside their Jeep, Molly turned to Dancing Wind.

She said, "Did you hear the bears growl like I did?"

"I certainly did," Dancing Wind replied. "Yes," she said excitedly, "I think we did this one right!"

Molly turned to Dancing Wind and said, "Do you think we could go up on top of that mountain and watch the bears through our 30X spotting scope?"

Dancing Wind told her, "I don't see why not, as long as we stay 200 yards away from them."

★★★★

Driving to the south, Molly and Dancing Wind came to an arroyo (dry wash) traveling to the East. They drove their Jeep up the wash to where the wash narrowed down. Here they both removed the trash from their backpacks and put it into trash bags. Then they repacked their backpacks with a compass, knife, magnesium fire starter, wooden matches in a Ziplock bag, two water bottles, first aid kit, satellite global positioning system (GPS), a 9mm Glock, and a spare ten round magazine. Molly carried the spotting scope. From there they walked a while further east up the dry arroyo. Then they climbed up the mountain to the north. On the mountaintop they set up the spotting scope on a large boulder and watched the two black bears feed.

About an hour later, they decided to head back to the Jeep. Since they were in no hurry, and to make the descent easier, they were taking a roundabout path, which put them in a saddle of the mountain. Dancing Wind was in front leading the way and suddenly she stopped so fast that Molly crashed into her. Molly started to apologize for bumping into her friend, but abruptly stopped when she saw her friends face and manner.

Dancing Wind and Molly suddenly reinforced their White Light of Protection they had asked GOD to surround them with. They visualized a White Light of Protection all around them. Then Dancing Wind asked GOD to surround her friend Molly with the White Light of Protection for good measure. Molly had already surrounded herself with the White Light of Protection, and then for good measure she asked GOD to also surround Dancing Wind with the White Light of Protection, as well. Slowly they scanned the area about them. Watching them from a huge boulder was a Franciscan priest and two companions. The priest and his two companions were ghosts. Both groups of individuals looked each other over for several moments, appraising each other.

The priest and his companions were as surprised by the sudden appearance of the two teenage girls as the teenagers were surprised at running into a priest and his two companions dressed in ancient clothing. Then Dancing Wind greeted the priest and his two companions; saying hello and telling them her name. Then she introduced her friend Molly to the Franciscan priest.

For the next hour, Dancing Wind, Molly, and the Franciscan priest, Arturio, talked. Arturio talked about his missionary work in Abiquiu and his mining here upon *Sierra de las Minas*. Dancing Wind asked Arturio if she could help him *"go home"* and Arturio sadly told her:

"Dancing Wind, I have been here so long that I simply do not know my way home anymore. I certainly do not know how to find my way home."

Dancing Wind told him, "There is a woman with red hair who misses you a lot and she is waiting for you now." Dancing Wind was constantly talking with Arturio, yet at the same time she spoke with Arturio, she was also listening to her own Guardian Angel, Lily. It was Dancing Wind's Angel, Lily who told Dancing Wind to tell Arturio about the woman with the red hair.

"Let me help you "Go Home," she said.

As they talked, Dancing Wind told Arturio she would return

to this spot the following weekend and help Arturio and his two companions *"return home"*. At this point in her life, Dancing Wind lacked a lot of the needed experience she would later obtain in helping spirits return home and calling in the needed Angels. Dancing Wind wanted the help of the Lakota medicine man, Dan, to ensure she performed the necessary spirit work properly. So it was agreed among everyone that she would get Dan's help, and a meeting was set for next weekend.

★★★★

True to her word and her honor, Dancing Wind returned to the site of their meeting with Arturio the week before. Along with her came Molly, as well as her dear friend and spiritual teacher, the Lakota medicine man, Dan. Together they all climbed the hill and met the three spirits who had asked for their help in going *home*. They sat down together and talked about their worries and concerns for a while. Arturio told Dancing Wind, Molly, and Dan that they could have his gold mine. The Franciscan told them that he was familiar with approximately a dozen mines in this area and that this was the richest gold mine of them all. Arturio told Dancing Wind that if she chose to utilize the wealth that she expected, she would respect and honor his wish that none of his assassins profit by her actions. Arturio also expected that 20% of everything would be used as follows: *12% was to go the church and to help the poor and 8 % was to go to his daughter Angaline Maderia in Barcelona, Spain.*

"Just remember," he told her, "Be patient and be persistent. As you open the door it is one foot down for each letter in my name Arturio= 7 feet deep." Then he gave Dancing Wind instructions about how to enter the mine and what she must be careful of or avoid inside the mine.

Arturio told Dancing Wind, "Stay away from the mantel with the gold *candlesticks and the leather bags of gold and silver coins; I do not want you to go near them nor to take them,"* He also told her, *"Do not open the rocked up stone wall at the end of the tunnel. What lies behind the stone wall is not for you."*

Arturio's last advice was: *"Take The Path Of The White Buffalo"* (the Spiritual Path).

Then Dan began slowly drumming, as Dancing Wind and Molly lit incense in a small circle in the clearing. Dancing Wind began walking in a circle. Molly, the priest, and his two companions followed in behind. Dancing Wind and the Franciscan priest could be heard saying the Lord's Prayer. As they walked around the circle for the third time, suddenly two Angels of the Lord appeared. Between them was a golden door of light that the priest and his two companions walked through. As Dan looked on, the priest, Arturio, turned and waved to Dan, Molly and Dancing Wind.

Arturio said *"Remember: Arturio de la Ascheron (Ascheion) is your friend!"* Then the priest turned and flew down the tunnel of light into the arms of a lifelong friend, a woman with red hair and a beautiful smile on her face.

The two Angels standing guard on each side of the door turned and stepped into the door of light. In a flash the door and the Angels were gone.

Molly turned to Dan and asked, "Who was that woman with the red hair, waiting in heaven for Arturio?"

Dan just smiled and grinned as he shrugged his shoulders; if Dan knew he wasn't telling. Molly turned to Dancing Wind for the answer, but she opened her arms wide, holding the palms up, indicating she did not know or was not telling. Molly wondered if the woman with the red hair was from Barcelona, Spain; where Arturio was born and had grown up.

Epilogue:

"It has been many years since Arturio went home to heaven where he belongs, and although many years have passed, my thoughts often return to Arturio, for I seldom encounter men of his honor and integrity. When one walks through Abiquiu in March and early April and sees the pink and white blossoms of the apricot trees in bloom, I realize that they have been there for centuries because Arturio made the effort to hand carry the seeds from Mexico, up the Camino Real for 1,200 miles, to plant the apricots in Abiquiu.

When a memory of Arturio comes to me, I know that he wanted everyone to know about the early Spanish mining and not to forget the history or the hardships of the early settlers and miners in New Mexico. Foremost though, I know how much importance he placed upon putting humanity back into human actions.

A simple act I saw recently, that of a woman seeing a homeless man hitchhiking on the side of the highway, then seeing the woman drive to a restaurant and buy the man a Coke and a hamburger, simply reminded me of Arturio and the actions he spoke of. Over a century and a half has passed since Arturio, my friend, has died; yet, as I walk through the mountains and I encounter his campsites, his memory is as fresh on my mind as yesterday and the tears flow down my cheeks."

- - Dancing Wind

When everything is hopeless
Do not Despair,
For Angel Love
Can be found Everywhere!

The Woman Who Loved Na Che Hee

In the 1750's along the Chama River there were a cluster of Indian pueblos near Abiquiu. These pueblos were the home of hundreds of Pueblo Indians. There were two pueblos, just to the East of the dry arroyo where Bob Trujillo's store is now located. Another of the Indian pueblos was located where the town of Abiquiu is now located. It was here that the woman who loved Na Che Hee was born.

Her parents were of Pueblo Indian decent. She was born on a night as the Rain Spirits were fast approaching Abiquiu to water the crops, supported by the coming and going of the gust of the Wind Spirits. Therefore, when the newborn baby arrived into the night she was called Dancing Wind.

Dancing Wind was born at a sad time—a time in which the freedom the Pueblo Indians knew was replaced by servitude and enslavement by the Spanish Conquistadors. The Pueblo Indians still raised their beans, squash, pumpkins and corn but the Spaniards would take the food away from her people at their choosing. So all the Pueblo Indians growing crops had to raise extra food for themselves and the Spaniards. If food became short in the winter it was the Pueblo Indians who went without eating--certainly not the Spaniards whom would steal their food as needed.

Should any Pueblo Indian object to the treatment accorded them by the Spaniards, either a finger pointed at them or a word or two to was exchanged with the frequent slave traders who visited the Pueblos, and the Indian would be hauled off by the slave traders and seldom heard from again. The Conquistadors always needed extra slave labor to work in the fields and gold mines, which was simply a death sentence. Slaves working in the mines had a very short life due to harsh working conditions, underground cave-ins, mistreatment, and malnutrition.

As Dancing Wind grew into her teenage years, she grew to be both wiser and more beautiful with each passing year. By the time she was twelve she was always traveling alone into the mountains to gather healing herbs or dropping in to visit the two Pueblos two and four miles east of her pueblo in Abiquiu. Dancing Wind was always welcome, as she had the kind of bubbly personality which lit up a room with her sweet smile and friendly personality. When she saw a sick or injured Indian she would not say anything, but she would take off into the hills to gather the herbs or plants which would alleviate the suffering or help to heal the individual. When Dancing Wind did not know what combination of plants would be most effective in healing she would simply ask the little Katchinas (Nature) Spirits that she encountered in the forest, mountains or along the streams. Sometimes the plants would speak to her, showing her the most effective manner to use them in treating sickness or injuries.

Dancing Wind put pictures in her head of what she needed to heal or a problem she had in order to talk to the plants. The plant, if it chose to speak with her, put a picture in her head of what it wanted to show her. That is how Dancing Wind and the plants communicated.

By the time Dancing Wind was thirteen years of age, her reputation as a healer was well established throughout the Rio Grande valley. While she certainly was not rich enough to own a horse, she found that one would be made available to her where ever she chose to travel. When the Pueblo Indians on the flat top mountain with the spring up near its top (this is approximately 3 miles southeast of the present location of Abiquiu Dam) and northwest of Cerro Perdenal required her services in healing, they sent word to Abiquiu for her assistance. This request was accompanied by an escort of three warriors to ensure her safety.

Where ever Dancing Wind traveled she was always greeted in a manner of honor and respect. The first time she made these journeys her parents were worried about her safety, but in time they were able to control their concerns for their daughter's safety. As a healer she was very skilled; not only because of her healing skills but also due to the fact she would carefully consult the Katchinas as well as the plants spirits to get their advice.

Na Che Hee was eighteen years of age when he took notice of the quiet healer known as Dancing Wind. She seemed the type of woman he wanted for a wife: she was wise, an excellent healer, she had the respect of the important tribal elders, not only in Abiquiu, but in the surrounding pueblos…and she was tall and beautiful, too.

Na Che Hee began his courtship of Dancing Wind by bring her family the hind deer quarter of a deer he killed on a hunting trip. Whenever he had extra wild game from his hunting trips it usually ended up on her family's dinner table. Soon Na Che Hee would be accompanying Dancing Wind as she gathered wild herbs or plants like water crest, cattails and rush root bulbs for the dinner table.

The Spanish had drafted Na Che Hee without pay, as well as half the men in the Abiquiu Pueblo, to make a series of stone traps to protect their treasure room and construct a secret treasure room. The men of the Pueblo had been constructing these stone faces and markers for five months when the slave traders arrived in Abiquiu.

★★★★

Before long Dancing Wind looked forward to the arrival of Na Che Hee, the walks they would take together and the time spent in each other's company. As the years passed, Dancing Wind looked forward to the day Na Che Hee would ask her to marry him. She felt that day would come on her sixteenth birthday. The month before her birthday, Na Che Hee gave Dancing Wind the leather hide of a deer he had killed on a hunting trip. This Dancing Wind lovingly made into a pair of moccasins. When finished, she put on her new moccasins and walked outside into the Abiquiu Pueblo. She planned to walk up to the place of the warm and cold springs, about ten miles south of Abiquiu and take Na Che Hee some bread she had made in the horno, an outdoor oven for baking food, and show him the moccasins she had made.

★★★★

The slave traders arrived in Abiquiu, having come down the Rio Chama bringing back Indians they had captured and enslaved. Coming into the pueblo, the leader of the slave traders noticed the lovely Pueblo Indian girl. When he saw her, he instantly realized she was worth more than all the slaves he had captured while raiding up north. So the slave trader simply took what he wanted. He nodded to his men and pointed to the Pueblo Indian girl. He and his men simply grabbed her hands and started to bind them. Dancing Wind screamed and struggled to get away, but she was no match for the strength of the three slave traders. A sharp blow to the side of the head and she simply collapsed. When she came to an hour later, she was in an ox-driven carreta (two wheel cart) traveling up towards the mountains south of Abiquiu. Dancing Wind was bound hand and foot with strips of leather hide. Dancing Wind felt she must escape or all was lost. As the carreta carried her further away from Abiquiu, she leaned over the rear of the cart and snatched up a sharp jagged rock with which she would try and cut the leather strips of hide binding her. Slowly, she worked the sharp rock back and forth across the leather as she cut the leather bonds that bound her.

After cutting the bonds, she indicated to the other Indians that she would free them too. This she began to do, and she had secretly freed two more captives when the carreta arrived and was passing by the other Abiquiu Pueblo Indians who were working making stone figures for the Spanish ten miles south of Abiquiu.

Dancing Wind jumped out of the carreta and ran straight for the man she loved, Na Che Hee. She held him in her arms and with tears running down her face, she gave him the moccasins that she wore on her feet. Then she took off running to the southeast, past the stone chess piece of the knight (a stone horse head).

Na Che Hee screamed out "NO!"

Then he chased after Dancing Wind. Many Pueblo Indians who loved the healer with the bubbly personality and her healing manner also ran after her to stop her. The other Indian captives took this distraction to try and make their escape. The entire workforce of Pueblo Indians had suddenly taken to disobeying the Spaniards who enslaved them. The Spaniards were fearful of another Indian rebellion!

Dancing Wind had actually chosen to die rather than be sold as a slave and raped by her new owner, so her last acts had been to give the man whom she loved her moccasins, then she ran past the stone knight chess piece, a twenty-five foot high horse head, and into the mountain she ran. With tears streaming down her face, Dancing Wind ran to the only place she knew where she could escape the slave traders and the dishonor they would bring upon her.

As Dancing Wind ran into the mountain she traveled down a horizontal mine shaft in which the Spanish had cached their treasures. She knew that to run down the corridor would bring about her death, as a Spanish death trap would be tripped. Behind Dancing Wind ran a number of her fellow Pueblo Indians who were trying to prevent her suicide, for the other Pueblo Indians clearly understood her reasoning. They knew that Dancing Wind intended to live free or die before she would submit to being a slave and raped by her new owner.

The Spaniards, on the other hand, saw her action as leading another Indian Revolt against them, and clearly she was taking all the Indians into the mine tunnel where they had placed their treasure of gold and silver. There was nothing the Spanish were more protective of, or guarded more jealously than their treasure, so to protect their stored treasure of gold and silver, the Spaniards drew their weapons and began slaying all the Native Americans. Men, women, and children all died under the slaughter wrought by the Spanish Conquistadors; for they mistakenly believed the Indians were revolting.

The Pueblo Indians had no interest in the yellow devil metal the Spaniards lusted after and which caused them to go crazy. Yet as the Spaniards began slaying them, they fought back trying to prevent their slaughter. Three Spaniards were killed in the same massacre that resulted in the deaths of thirty-eight Pueblo Indians. Dancing Wind and Na Che Hee died in the underground tunnel, but due to the emotional and violent physical response of the Spaniards and the violent deaths of all the Indians, only Dancing Wind was able to choose the path of the Angels and travel *home*. The remaining Spaniards and Pueblo Indians were caught up in the violence and unable to find their way *home*.

★★★★★

In 2002Dancing Wind learned from her spiritual teacher, a Lakota medicine man Dan, how to take Spirits *home*. These spirits who did not know how to find their way *home* were encountered by Dancing Wind when she explored a huge rock formation like a horse head or chest piece called a Knight. As she walked through the area of the knight (chess piece) she encountered many spirits or ghost who died in a battle. As Dancing Wind spoke with several of the Indian spirits she realized she knew them from her previous past life living in Abiquiu.

For literally Dancing Wind was the reincarnation of Dancing Wind born two centuries later.

There was a Spaniard in spirit whom was always cracking jokes. He would tell Dancing Wind that he was happy she brought her shovel so that she could dig lots of holes looking for treasure; but he did not think that she would find any today.

When Dancing Wind would politely offer the joking spirit food and water, he would laughingly tell her "No, thank you. Thanks to your dad hiding caches of food in the mountains and planting fruit trees I always have plenty to eat."

Dancing Wind doubled over with laughter at this spirit's joke, as she saw the humor the joking spirit had shown. You see, the spirit did know who her dad was, even though she had never told the spirit. The Spirit also knew that it was her dad who planted fruit trees as well as the caches in the mountains. Dancing Wind knew that often people think, when one goes into the mountains or the remote desert that no one is watching or seeing what you are doing; but in fact most of your actions there are always known or watched by other spirits.

While it was true that her dad placed small caches of food, the spirit was jokingly saying that is why he had plenty of food. When a spirit goes and eats an MRE (Meal Ready to Eat) after eating his fill—to you or I; the MRE will appear untouched and everything is still in the brown package. So the full meal is still there, except the spirit will have eaten!

As a general rule to go by: *It is always polite to offer any spirit you encounter food and water.*

As the teenage girl walked through the killing ground, she noticed where the Spanish had buried two Spaniards whom had died in the fighting. They were buried side by side in their graves. Their bodies had long since returned to the earth whence man comes; but the spirits of the two men were still lying in their graves. They did not know what they were supposed to do or how to return *home,* so they just lay there where they were buried.

"What are you doing there?" Dancing Wind asked them.

The two Spaniards replied that: *"This is where we were placed after we died."*

So Dancing Wind asked them if they would like to come out of the ground?

"Yes," they both replied, *"but we don't know how."*

The Indian girl told them it's easy; "Just reach up and grab my hand," she said. Dancing Wind got down on her knees and reached her hands towards the two spirits. Both spirits reached up their hands for Dancing Wind, and as soon as they clasped each other's hands Dancing Wind stood up. Beside her stood the two Spaniard spirits, who were so happy that they went off singing and dancing. They had not had so much fun in hundreds of years! Dancing Wind was going to ask them their names, but the two Spaniards were gone in the blink of an eye.

Next Dancing Wind talked to some Pueblo Indians from Abiquiu. She comforted these spirits and told them it was time to go *home* , but they were anxious to do so.

Dancing Wind told them that next weekend she would return to help them go *home,* but she would like them to also do her a favor and pass the word around to all the spirits that she would be happy to help all the spirits whom chose to go home to do so, here in the small circular meadow a week from now.

Down in a small arroyo (gully) to the north of the meadow, Dancing Wind caught movement out of the corner of her eye. So she went over to the arroyo to investigate.

There she saw a little five year old Indian girl take off running to hide behind her mother.

The mother and daughter had died in 1750 when the Spaniards had slaughtered every Indian they encountered in the imaginary Indian revolt where Dancing Wind had also died. The mother, NaKa, had come here to feed her husband his lunch when the Spaniards had slaughtered everyone. The mother and daughter had been killed by the Conquistadors, just as her husband had been. Dancing Wind sat down to talk to NaKa and her daughter. NaKa's daughter was hiding behind her mother, peeking out from behind her toglance towards Dancing Wind. First Dancing Wind wanted to calm NaKa daughter's fear of her.

NaKa's daughter told her mother that *"There is something strange about that girl; her hair is blue."*

So Dancing Wind explained she was wearing a blue cap. Then she took the cap off her head and shook her hair so the little girl could see it. Then she held out the cap so the little girl could examine it. Before long the little girl was sitting beside Dancing Wind as all three of them talked about going *home*. Dancing Wind promised to return next weekend and help them return *home* and she asked them to pass the word on.

Another Indian spirit Dancing Wind spoke with was alongside the old dirt road.

This spirit appeared as a swirling cloud of dust. This was the first time that Dancing Wind had observed a Spirit that had a swirling energy pattern which made a five foot high swirling cloud of dust. It was possible that this spirit had a good relationship with the Wind Spirits.

This spirit had also been slain by the Spanish and had remained with the other spirits who had died that day. Dancing Wind showered him with all her love, compassion and understanding as she encouraged him to let go of the pain and anger and return *home* to the Spirit; Who Moves Thought All Things.

Next Dancing Wind talked to Na Che Hee. This was very emotional conversation for Dancing Wind, as they talked of the old days, as well as their love for each other. It had been intended for Dancing Wind and Na Che Hee to be married in 1750, before Dancing Wind had been captured in the Abiquiu Pueblo by slave traders. Both had died together here on that fateful day in 1750 when the Spanish had misunderstood the Pueblo Indians' actions in trying to prevent Dancing Wind from killing herself as a revolt to steal all the Spanish gold. The Spaniards' paranoia about anyone trying to steal the gold they accumulated resulted in their massacring of the peaceful Indians.

Na Che Hee told Dancing Wind he still loved her, he always had and he always would. As he held her in his arms he told his love he knew she would return. Tears streamed down Dancing Winds face as Na Che Hee told his love that she must not forget him. If he was to go *home* next weekend she must not forget to bring her moccasins for him. Clearly, both lovers remembered this was the last thing Dancing Wind did, giving the man she loved her moccasins before she died about two hundred and fifty years ago!

On the east side of the circular clearing where Dancing Wind had found the two Spaniards, she believed there was an underground door opening into a treasure room.

So after she helped the Spirits go home, Dancing Wind intended to hire a backhoe to dig a hole and see if she could gain access inside this treasure room. She believed that there would be gold and silver bars of metal inside this treasure room. She felt a couple of bars of gold would help her pay her college bills and pay for a car to drive at college.

While she was walking around the surface of the ground trying to figure out the possible location for this treasure room, she was examining the ground from different angles when a pickup truck suddenly rounded the curve at this remote location. The driver saw the beautiful Indian teenager with the long black hair and decided he wanted her! No one would notice him kidnapping a girl in this remote location. Quickly he slammed on his brakes and jumped out of his old red pickup truck.

Carefully he looked all around to ensure there were no witnesses to what he intended to do! Then he started after Dancing Wind, but the driver had taken no more than five steps when out of the woods Dan appeared, looking like a Lakota warrior on the warpath, for Dan had been accompanying Dancing Wind on this day as he instructed her in matters of the spirit. Immediately the driver fled back to his truck. Jumping in, he spun his wheels in a cloud of dust and gravel as he sped away!

Sometimes when one is in the mountains, desert or other remote locations; the greatest dangers are from the two-legged wolves.

A week later, Dancing Wind and Dan returned to the small clearing where they had told the spirits to meet them. There were thirty eight spirits who had come to the small clearing to return *home*. Dan removed incense from his back pack and directed Dancing Wind to make a big circle and place the lit incense in the ground in a circular pattern. Then Dan played a soft slow mellow tune on a flute. Dancing Wind began drumming as she walked in a circle immediately outside the circle of the incense.

As she walked and drummed, she would invite the spirits she passed to come along with her as she walked in a circle and drummed. She continued around the circle, very slowly picking up the pace and speeding up the beat of her drumming. Shortly she was walking and drumming very rapidly as Dan, too, had increased the speed of the flute melody. Suddenly a door of light appeared on the outer perimeter of their circle. As they walked by the door of light, the spirits looked inside and, seeing their loved ones, they left this dimension as they traveled into the tunnel of light; accompanied by the Angels, they returned *home* to GOD.

The next week Dancing Wind returned to the South end of the meadow. Accompanying her was a backhoe operator she had hired to dig a hole where she thought the treasure room was located, but the only thing the operator found there was dirt. . Where she though the Spanish treasure room was located, the only thing the back hoe operator found was dirt. Clearly she made an error, for nothing but dirt was in the hole. This was Dancing Wind's first hole she dug looking for treasure. After refilling the hole with dirt, the back hoe operator and Dancing Wind spread the native dry land grass seed that she had brought along to replant the area. When the seed sprouted after the next rain the land would be covered in a new carpet of grass. It would not be the last dry hole she dug, either, for when one looks for buried treasure one should expect to dig a number of holes before one makes a nice recovery. In the future she did in fact often dig holes uncovering rusty cans, bits of metal, and even the shoes of a horse that must now be running around barefoot, as the horse had lost his shoes! Without persistence, correcting one's mistakes and effort, one cannot learn to track a trail, accomplish one's goals, or achieve your dreams. I hope you persist in your goals so you achieve your dreams. Dancing Wind had not yet learned to follow the shadow arrows, nor read the Indian hieroglyphs. Future lessons she had yet to learn would include pulling the data and true directions off the Spanish Death Traps which protected a treasure site. As this was her first hole she dug, she did not understand about the sight hole, the stone maps, the shadow animals, and stone eagles giving directions to the stone door she desired to enter. These lessons were all in the future, as they were a part of the learning process she was going through as everyone does who is to become a professional in their field of work.

That Dancing Wind failed to find her treasure of gold and silver at this site is a fact. That Dancing Wind helped the Angels take *"home"* thirty-eight Spirits home to GOD's house is also a fact. Now, some inexperienced trackers might say she failed, though more experienced trackers realize that there is a learning curve all persistent trackers pass through if you hope to set the standard of excellence that a tracker can achieve. Certainly, every Angel there who witnessed the events going down was more than happy with what occurred. Never think a good tracker does not make mistakes. Good trackers correct their mistakes and persist in learning to be better trackers. *Maybe in time they will even accompany you; teaching you, helping you, in tracking the trails your Guardian Angel is teaching you to track!*

Beauty is in the Water
Beauty is in the Snow
Beauty is in LOVE
Just beginning to Grow

The Treasure of Miguel Schreiber

Miguel Schreiber was a Jew in Seville, Spain. It was becoming apparent that he needed to take his family and flee his country. The other neighbors he knew were being taken away from their house and thrown into dungeons, interrogated and tortured. After they confessed under the torture to secretly practicing Judaism and exercising their religious freedom to be Jews, their house and land was confiscated. Then, whether he was guilty or not, as anyone under enough torture often will confess to anything just to get them to stop the torture, the offender was killed or burned at the stake. Their family then was thrown out penniless on the street to starve as all their assets were also seized. It was only a matter of time before the authorities came and hauled he and his family away.

Miguel Schreiber talked with four of his neighbors who he was friends with and they decided the safest course of action to ensure the safety of their families and themselves was to sell their houses and land at a very low price to get a quick cash sale. Then they planned to take a ship with their families to the New World. In the distant lands of

New Mexico, they thought that they were unlikely to be victims of the Spanish Inquisition.

Preparations were made and they sold everything they owned to buy passage on a ship coming to Mexico. Miguel Schreiber boarded a ship for the new world at Seville, Spain. Accompanying him were his five neighboring families. To his surprise, aboard the ship he met another five families of Jews from France who had the same idea that he had of traveling to a remote location in the new world where they could have their own homes and lands to raise their families. Over the three months it took to sail from Seville, Spain to Veracruz, Mexico; the ten families became good friends and decided they would all stick together and work together for mutual safety.

★★★★

While crossing the Atlantic Ocean, the stories of storms and shipwrecks is sure to come up as a topic of conversation between the passengers and the seaman. It was while crossing to the New World that they learned of the loss of the 1715 Plate Fleet. These ships were wrecked off the wretched and barren coast line of this horrible place called Florida. Here in this worthless land with barren sandy beaches and numerous miles of swamps, the poor seamen were shipwrecked. While there was the beautiful blue ocean water everywhere, none was drinkable as it was all salt water! The few desperate survivors, whose extreme thirst drove them to drinking the salt water that was all around them, immediately went into convulsions. The seamen suffered horribly from thirst. Then those who survived the hurricane and the lack of water were each greeted by hundreds of hungry blood-sucking mosquitoes.

Most of the officers were given their position by their family's political connections; seldom was it for their intelligence or for their ability to handle emergency situations. This resulted in officers who valued the treasures of gold more than the lives of the seamen who had faithfully served them. The officers had one large boat about eighteen feet long. Instead of filling the vessel with hurt or injured men and then sailing north to the Spanish Fort at Saint Augustine for help, the officers instead loaded the boat with gold.

So much gold was placed aboard this small vessel that they loaded it down so it had only a few inches of freeboard (the height of the side of the vessel above the ocean). Shortly after the wooden boat was launched into the ocean and began to leave the survivors behind a wave just rolled right over the tiny boat. One minute the boat was sailing away and the next minute the boat and the greedy and selfish officers slipped beneath the waves. The next minute the Devil was welcoming his good friends home! There are times when payback occurs promptly, and you immediately reap the results of the good or the bad actions you have set into motion.

So the survivors sent another rescue party north and after three days of traveling, they reached the Spanish Garrison at Fort Augustine. The rescue party promptly headed to the location of the wreck. But the commander of the Spanish forces was so focused on rescuing the gold that he had little regard for the shipwreck survivors' lives.

To ensure that no one stole any of the gold, Governor Martinez from the Spanish fort at Saint Augustine lined the survivors up and ordered them to be searched. Governor Martinez knew how to ensure every thief was punished. Any shipwreck survivor with any gold was promptly executed on the spot. Of course, if you were innocent of any wrongdoings it was your misfortune to be executed too. A single gold coin was often the reason you were executed. Even though you may have saved the coin from your pay as a seaman or won it gambling in a game of chance, no excuse was accepted; you were executed as a thief.

Many a seaman who thought the rescue party was there to save them found themselves murdered by their own compatriots. One seaman summed up his feelings about Florida saying :

"If there is a hell on earth it is Florida, and the devil himself put Governor Martinez in charge of that swampy mosquito and malaria infested hell hole."

Many Angels cried that day, at the senseless slaughter of the men who they watched over since birth. Who would have guessed that centuries later that many individuals would still be fighting and arguing over the Plate Fleet Treasure. Once Mel Fisher began diving and recovering the treasures of the Plate Fleet, then many individuals, the state of Florida, as well as the U. S. Government all did their best to steal the treasure. Greed has a way of bringing out the worst in human nature.

★★★★

Veracruz is a beautiful seaport on the east coast of Mexico. Beautiful green forested mountains surrounded the harbor where their ship docked. It is from this port where the fabulously wealthy treasure ships of the Spanish Plate Fleet are loaded with their treasures of gold, silver and precious gem stones then they sail for Spain with their treasures. Protecting this port is the Spanish Fort San Juan de Ulua. Overlooking the harbor of Veracruz and the Gulf of Mexico, this fort, with her thirty five foot high gray stone walls and cannons, was built to protect the port of Veracruz.

It was here at Castillo de San Juan de Ulua that Miguel Schreiber first saw the treasures which provided Spain with her wealth. Ox-driven carreta which are large two wheeled carts pulled by oxen arrived, loaded down with silver bars. Pack mules loaded with gold were also unloaded inside the Spanish Fort. Tons of precious metals were there for all to see—but not touch!

It was here that Miguel first thought "GOD, I wish I could find a gold mine so we could be wealthy too." Miguel talked to the men bringing in the gold and silver and tried to learn all he could about how to find a rich gold or silver mine. All day and late into the night Miguel talked to the miners and mine owners about finding and mining gold.

In the new lands they could raise their families, and if they were careful about it, also practice Judaism, their religious beliefs. From Mexico City the ten families traveled north, staying together along the El Camino Real (Royal Road) to a remote area in New Mexico called Ojo Caliente and north through Vallecitos. Here the ten families settled down and built homes, where they raised sheep and crops to provide for their families.

Because the official and safe religion to practice was the Catholicism, they practiced this religion in public, but in the privacy of their homes they also practiced many of their Jewish customs. They would celebrate the Catholic holidays as well as the Jewish holidays like Hanukkah and Passover, and for Christmas they would place a Star of David on their Christmas tree.

Miguel Schreiber must have been born under a wandering star, for after he built his adobe hacienda, a house built of mud and straw bricks, built irrigation ditches to water his crops, and had sheep in his pastures, Miguel would explore the mountains. These trips took Miguel further and further afield as he was always exploring the new lands and rugged mountains. Sometimes Miguel would leave his family for months at a time, riding his horse as he explored the remote regions.

To explain his wandering and explorations to his wife and family, he would always say he was just off hunting elk. It was on one of these trips about seventy-five miles to the northwest that Miguel discovered another nice hot spring. These hot springs were even nicer than the ones at Ojo Caliente. These hot springs are now called the Pagosa Hot Springs. These hot springs had been a favorite stopping place of the Ute Indians for centuries.

On another trip into the San Juan Mountains north of the Pagosa Hot Springs, Miguel encountered some Ute Indians. He was about to ride down a trail in the mountains when fifty yards away he saw a black bird suddenly take flight. Then he saw a small war party appear where the bird had been. He quickly but quietly moved his horse up a side canyon to stay out of sight of the Ute war party. To prevent the Ute Indians from lifting his scalp and stealing his horse after killing him, Miguel rode up a remote canyon off the Piedra River to hide from the Indians. Here, while hiding from the Ute Indians, Miguel discovered the deposit of gold and silver ore that he was literally sitting upon.

After the Ute Indians had left, Miguel loaded up his saddle bag with the rich gold ore. Using a rock, he would break the barren pink quartz rock away from the small chunks of gold. Over a period of five days Miguel accumulated enough gold mixed with a little silver to fill up his saddle bags behind his saddle. Miguel used his tomahawk to cut blazes on trees, marking his trail as he started riding back to Vallecitos. The blazes were to ensure he could return exactly to his gold deposit in the San Juan Mountains. Because the black bird had saved his life, some of the blazes he made were of a bird's head.

On his return to Vallecitos, Miguel shared the news of his discovery with the other Jewish families. . Miguel's friends had looked out for his family when he was away as well as on the long difficult trip over crossing the Atlantic Ocean and the difficult trip up the Camino Real from Mexico, so he was willing to share his newly discovered wealth with his friends, to him, though he had a difficult time expressing his love for his friends. To Miguel, his friends and neighbors were treasures beyond price.

Taking a trip to Santa Fe, Miguel bartered his gold for a new rifle, a ram's horn full of gun powder, lead balls for his muzzle-loading black powder rifle, salt, and his biggest accomplishment, a sturdy mule. On Miguel's next trip to the mountains he would have a sturdy mule to haul back his treasure of gold. After showing his friends and neighbors what he had purchased with one saddle bag of mostly gold, but that also contained some silver, they too, were excited about accompanying Miguel Schreiber back to the San Juan Mountains so they could enjoy the luxuries that gold would allow them to afford.

That summer Miguel went with nine of the fathers or sons of the Jewish families that had accompanied him to the New World. These friends of his accompanied him into what is now Colorado. Three days easy ride north of the Pagosa Hot Springs, up along the Piedra River they mined their gold and silver. From other miners they talked with, they learned how to remove the waste rock and cast their raw gold and silver into bars of bullion, which were easier to transport. These were then taken to Santa Fe to trade for anything they desired. The first fall season they literally went on a spending spree, buying mules, pigs, sheep, looms for their wives to make cloth and blankets, new rifles, gun powder, lead bullets, soap, salt, dried fruit, yet even after buying whatever they chose, they found they still had gold left over.

The following year they returned to the San Juan Mountains and mined the gold and silver for three and a half months, but as they returned south they recalled how they had to flee Spain. While they dreamed of returning to Spain as rich men, their fear of the Spanish Inquisition tempered their desire to return to their home land. Since they recalled how they were forced to flee Spain's Inquisition, they decided it would be prudent to cache the gold and silver bars well away from their homes. As they were mining in a remote area, by locating there treasure room closer to their homes they could still gain easier access to it if needed. Yet their treasure store house was not near their homes in case they ever had to take their families and flee because of their Jewish ancestry.

The men discussed it around the campfire at night and they decided to make a bank or depository for the gold and silver. This depository was to entail forty days of work. Their depository was built at a much lower elevation, so it would be accessible ten months of the year. They located it three days' ride from Vallecitos. The ten men built a concealed bank vault to hide their treasures of gold and silver. Here, on the east side of the Chama River, on the top of the hill they placed the concealed entrance to their treasure room. Throughout the area of the depository there are still the black bird's head; just as it is on the original trail markings going up to the rich gold and silver mine in the San Juan Mountains as well as the main cache site west of Vallecitos, New Mexico.

On this hill where the treasure is hidden there are stone figures of human faces, as well as life size human figures; one example would be a fifty foot-tall Indian smoking a pipe. Animals of every kind are here too. There are elk, foxes, bison, snakes, alligators, birds, tools, fish, dolphins, burros, and mules, all carefully made out of stone.

But since they were Jewish, they also had the Star of David near the door of the treasure room. Over time they also added many Death Traps to prevent unauthorized access to the treasure room. This treasure room was not above ground, but buried beneath the surface of the ground where it would not easily be found. For fifteen years treasure was added every year to the underground store room when they were forced to stop their mining in Colorado.

The Ute Indians, who had been somewhat friendly and peaceful, had become very war-like and hostile due to the Spanish slave traders attacking their villages and hauling away their loved ones in chains.

As the Ute's were trying to protect themselves from the slave traders, their anger at having their wives or children kidnapped turned upon any Spanish intruders in their territory. While the French and Spanish Jews were not responsible for enslaving the Indians, the angry Indians struck out at anyone, as often the slave traders were no longer there as they immediately left the area to avoid reprisal Indian attacks.

★★★★

Today if you were to visit the village of Abiquiu, slightly northeast of the Abiquiu Church, is the O' Keeffe house. One of the original rooms in this house is a guest room. The guest room is painted solid black and has two foot thick walls. The guests who stayed in this room were the poor kidnapped Indians who had been hauled away from their villages with their hands bound tight in rawhide or their legs secured in chains. The Indians were kept in this guest room, which has no windows and is equipped with a heavy solid door that bolts from the outside until the Indians could be either trained as slaves or sold in the slave markets.

★★★★

When Miguel Schreiber and his friends first mined the gold in Colorado and transported the treasure closer to their houses in the region of Ojo Caliente through Vallecitos, the men originally dreamed of returning to their homeland in Spain as rich patrons and buying vast estates. But as time passed and they raised their families and their children had children of their own, they came to realize that the true treasure was their friends and family. There was nothing that they needed, as they owned cattle and sheep and had their own irrigated land where they grew their crops and they had also planted fruit trees. Over time the trips to the treasure vaults became less and less frequent.

When Miguel Schreiber and his wife Maria attended first his son's wedding and later his daughter's, he came to realize that he was really at home. Vallecitos had become his home and never would he move away and leave his children. His neighbors and friends were some of those rare men whom Juan could trust with his life; and if needed he would protect them to the limit of his existence. In time, as the fall of his years came upon Miguel and his wife Maria, their love for each other and their children was what he considered his greatest treasure.

★★★★

In time, the existence of the treasures on the mountain became just a distant memory for the French and Spanish Jews who lived in the area between Ojo Caliente and Vallecitos, New Mexico. Like the hardships of their ancestors and their Jewish ancestry, their history has been mostly forgotten by their children.

★★★★

Molly O'Brian asked Dancing Wind if she had ever ridden on an old-fashioned coal-burning steam train? When Dancing Wind replied that she hadn't, but thought it sounded like a great idea, Molly called the Cumbres Toltec Railroad about getting tickets for both of them to ride the train from the Chama station up to Osier Station where they would have lunch. From Osier Station they could continue on to Antonio, Colorado or take the return train back to Chama. They decided on the shorter trip from Chama, NM to Osier station. The trip would take all day. They would have to get up early if they were to make the morning departure of the train from Chama.

Molly picked Dancing Wind up at her trailer in Abiquiu and they were off to Chama. As Molly drove her Jeep north towards Chama, Dancing Wind leaned her seat back, kicked off her tennis shoes, and placed her feet up on the dash. Dancing Wind thought she would take a short nap on the drive to Chama.

The curve threw her against door and the glass window. Wouldn't you know it, when she had just closed her eyes for a moment, Molly's driving would wake her up. Dancing Wind thought Molly did the sharp turn on purpose, to prevent her from catching a nap. Dancing Wind opened her sleep-heavy eyes to see what was going on around her. On her right, through the window, she saw the landscape flying by at 50 to 55 miles per hour. Then she saw the Death Trap on the mountain slope, and another and another. In the span of ten seconds it took for Molly to drive by the ancient site, Dancing Wind counted four Death Traps and a set of entrance markers!

★★★★

Some people will tell you it is impossible to track an ancient trail made centuries ago while traveling at 55 miles per hour. Some people will say it is impossible to look at a mountain slope and pick out four Death Traps in ten seconds. And you know what? For them, they are right! If you believe it is impossible to do something you will not even try. So if you believe something is impossible, and are unwilling to even give it an honest try—then literally the task at hand is impossible for you!

Now, on the other hand, there will be individuals reading this story who will say "I can find the actual site that Dancing Wind saw: the four Death Traps and the Entrance Marker ." They, too, are right—they can! They will say the description is so detailed they can locate the site where the ten families hide their gold and silver; and they can! For what you believe possible, and you do your best to learn, correcting your mistakes as you persist in achieving your goals, you have a good chance of achieving!

It was often Dancing Wind's attitude, her willingness to be open and learn, coupled with her persistence that determined what she could achieve and accomplish in life.

The fact that Dancing Wind can track a century or two century old trail did not happen overnight; it took a lot of hard work and effort upon her part! If the trail you chose to track leads to a new car or a new job, the path you follow will require effort and persistence upon your part. If you say it is impossible for you, it is! And if the path you chose to follow in life explores the frontiers of possibility, you will be in for a lot of adventures. The choice to say it is impossible is yours, as well as to choose to do what most consider impossible. Because when you feel it is impossible, you do not give it an honest try or effort on your part. And if the trail you choose to track in life is taken with optimism—if you say I can do it; I am going to persist until I achieve my goal—I may have to make changes, learn all I can, and continually adapt and persist to achieve my goal, then you are already halfway there, as you are willing to try and do your best until you achieve your dream.

★★★★

Molly noticed the attention her sleepy partner was suddenly focusing upon the mountain. She looked inquiringly at Dancing Wind and Dancing Wind told her that she had just counted four Death Traps upon the mountain slope and she saw a pair of entrance markers too! Every two seconds Dancing Wind was identifying a death trap so carefully concealed that thousands of people drive by this site every year and fail to recognize the treasure door markers or the explosive danger that the numerous death traps could unleash upon an unsuspecting individual. Each trap had been build to have the maximum killing radius possible so as to safeguard the treasure room the stone traps were built to protect. The distinctive entrance markers were there to give guidance on how to enter the treasure rooms. Dancing Wind told Molly that she was reasonably sure that there was a treasure room up on that mountain!

Molly said "Ok," and simply kept driving north to Chama. Molly did not even slow down as she drove away from a treasure room which could easily contain a million dollars in gold and silver artifacts. Molly filed the information away in the back or her mind, but she had already learned from Dan, that when they were tracking one trail, they would not get side tracked by every trail they come upon. If one is following a trail, or a path in life, the rewards come to the ones who follow it to the end. Today, the path Molly and Dancing Wind were following was one of exploration and fun aboard the Cumbres Toltec train.

The treasure room, with its protective death traps and false entrances designed to kill intruders, had been there for centuries. It would still be their tomorrow, and it would be there a year from now. Maybe the stone storeroom was full of treasure; maybe the stone storeroom was empty, but it would only be by tracking the trail to the end that would she learn the whole story.

★★★★

At Chama they parked the Jeep in front of the train station. Walking into the train station, (www.cumbrestoltec.com) they purchased two tickets to Osier station, round trip, for sixty-two dollars each. Both tickets were for inside the coach, in case it turned colder or rained. Preplanning for contingencies never hurts and it may on occasion be what it takes to make a trip more enjoyable or occasionally even save your life. By riding inside the coach, they would not turn as black from the soot of the coal-burning steam engine. Since they were allowing all day for the train ride, they also planned to eat on the outdoor picnic tables at Osier, Colorado station. Molly planned on having the meatloaf dinner with mashed potatoes, peas, carrots and corn. On the other hand, Dancing Wind preferred the turkey with mashed potatoes and gravy, green beans and cranberry sauce.

With several blasts of the steam whistle, the train slowly pulled out of the train station at a walk and began building up speed as it headed for the mountains. As the train rolled down the tracks it seemed to have two motions. It rocked both side to side and backwards and forwards, making it difficult to walk a straight down the center aisles. The combination of motion, however, makes it easy to fall asleep in the unceasing rhythm.

Dancing Wind fought off the sleep and was able to watch as breathtaking meadows, forest of green timber and golden yellow aspen. Possibly you will see families out riding horses as you pass through the Carson National Forest. Often the train riders see large elk the size of a horse. Sometimes one might see an elk herd of a dozen elk and occasionally you might see a large group of fifty elk.

As the train climbed up into the mountains, Molly turned to Dancing Wind and said "You will not believe, this but look at that Spanish Marker of a fifty foot-high profile of a man's face. To the right is a shadow bird."

To the right of the shadow bird was another man's face with a beard. Obviously the Spanish had a gold or silver mine up in these mountains too, but today the teenagers just wanted to enjoy the train ride. By the time Osier Station was reached, Molly and Dancing Wind were ready, really ready, to eat. As they ate lunch they discussed how it seemed that when tracking an old trail like this steam train ride which they had just taken for enjoyment they always seemed to get one or two more leads on trails or treasure hunting they might want to follow up on in the future. In a single day while planning to go enjoy themselves with a train ride, the teenagers had located two different Spanish treasure trails from centuries ago.

Along the return trip, Molly and Dancing Wind watched the train ride take them through spectacular scenery, but the day had been a long one and soon they fell asleep to the rocking motion of the old steam train.

★★★★

It is the time around dusk that the veil or wall separating us from the spirit world is thinnest or most easily pierced by thought. That evening at dusk, as Molly drove by the same site where Dancing Wind had observed the four death traps and entrance markers to a treasure room, Molly too had an unusual, to her, physic experience. Suddenly the stones began talking to Molly! It was all Molly could do to keep the Jeep on the road and negotiate the turns!

"Dancing Wind", Molly whispered under her breath with some urgency.

Dancing Wind, who had been dozing in the passenger seat, suddenly opened her eyes and noticed the alarmed expression on Molly's face. Not knowing the reason for Molly's distress or alarm she quickly put a white light of protection around both of them, as well as around the Jeep. She was prepared to grab the steering wheel if needed, but she actually had not detected any hostile threat or danger about. It was dusk and there were no other cars on the road within sight.

Molly turned a quick glance towards Dancing Wind and said, "The stones are talking to me!"

"Don't you mean the stones are communicating with you?" Dancing Wind light-heartedly replied.

"What is the difference?" Molly asked her.

Dancing Wind replied that usually "talking" means there is a voice or sound that all can hear.

"While if the stones are talking to you, I would hear the sound of them speaking too, if the stones are *communicating* with you, the stones are hearing or understanding your thoughts, interests or intentions, while you, in turn, understand the rocks' thoughts or concepts the rocks are conveying to you.

"That is communication, which is slightly different than the rocks actually verbally talking with you. The rocks are communicating directly between your mind or consciousness and theirs."

Molly said, "Well, it came as a shock to me that the rocks talk!"

Dancing Wind replied: "You mean the rocks were communicating with you."

"Well, communicating or talking, they were talking with me. As each rock talked with me, I knew which individual rock was talking with me; Seven rocks spoke with me."

Then, as Molly began to calm down a little, "Now that eighth rock just talked to me!" She said, as she pointed to a boulder across the river.

"Well what did the rocks say to you?" Dancing Wind asked Molly.

"It was different with each rock," Molly replied. "It was just different. The first rocks just said 'feet,' and the next rock said it was giving me 'distance and direction (compass direction to travel),' and the third rock said 'Position.' Then, the fourth rock said: 'Bird's Head' or 'Travel in the direction of the birds head,' and the fifth rock said 'Compass Bearing.' The sixth rock just said the word 'Position,' while the seventh said 'Trail Marker' and the last talking stone, which was miles to the south of the other stones said it was 'Compass Bearing.'"

"Well it seems that the stones are willing to teach you and help you should you choose to work with them," Dancing Wind told Molly, "I guess your understanding is growing and extending beyond yourself to also encompass another aspect of GOD's creation!"

Two weeks later, the teenage girls began tracking the trail of the French and Spanish Jews who had built a treasure cache where they stored their gold and silver. As they tracked the trail into the cache, they often stopped to talk to a rock or group of rocks. Sometimes they encountered boulders which had been split length-wise, and then they were laid together. Sometimes a six- to twelve inch gap of air space was left between the boulders, which created a black shadow line which could be seen at a hundred yards away. The line drawn by the meeting of the two boulders or the black shadow line gave Molly and Dancing Wind a compass direction to travel. Often, if you were traveling the wrong way, there would be one or two stones placed within a couple feet of the boulders and these stones would be at a right angle to the direction you were sighting. Symbolically, these right angel stones in your path were blocking your path and telling you that you were traveling in the wrong direction. Dancing Wind called these stones "Stop Stones," as they told you to stop as you were going the wrong way.

As the days passed tracking the centuries-old trail they frequently encountered the black bird's head. The way the bird beak faced often told Molly and Dancing Wind the way they should travel, but sometimes the black bird's head pointed in the wrong direction. That was the early miners being extra careful: if the bird faced in an incorrect location, then there would be a big black shadow line showing the correct direction for properly following the trail into the cache site (treasure site). Then there would be a shadow line or wedge showing the correct direction to travel. Once there was a black line formed by boulders behind the black bird's head. The black line then pointed to the correct direction of travel.

On the fifth day, they got an early start. Today the trackers thought that, GOD willing, they might find the entrance to the treasure room. If their luck held they would be recovering bars of gold this week! They climbed the mountain slopes, pushing hard to be in the correct location. As the sun approached noon, the two teenagers lay on their stomachs on the ground. Opposite them a hundred and fifty yards away lay their treasure hill. Their breathing was fast and heavy as they had to very rapidly climb this last hill to be in the proper position to observe the sun signs. Beside Dancing Wind, her Chesapeake Bay retriever found some shade from the hot desert sunlight. Removing their backpacks they both pulled out their binoculars.

As they scanned the treasure hill opposite them, Molly suddenly exclaimed "Son of a B_ _ _ _!"

Dancing Wind was saying What the F_ _ _."

On the opposite hill as the morning sun peaked over the hill tops it created four shadow black birds' heads forming a perfect "X" by the way the rocks were positioned on the rocky slopes. For literally "X" marked the spot to dig!

In the center of the "X" was a freshly-dug hole. Beside it was a giant pile of freshly-dug dirt and the deep tracks of a backhoe. Beside the pile of dirt was the stone entrance door which the Backhoe (tractor) had removed. Wrapped around the stone door was a heavy, new 3/8 inch thick chain. The backhoe operator had used the chain to help open the heavy stone door. Leading away from the hole were the wide lug tire tracks of a backhoe on the freshly disturbed brown dirt. Someone else had beat the two teenage trackers and their reddish-brown Chesapeake Bay Retriever to the treasure and left them an empty hole!

And Behold, there arose a great tempest in the sea,
Insomuch that the ship was covered with waves.....
And he said (Jesus)... "Why are ye fearful, O ye of
Little faith?" Then he arose and rebuked the winds
And the sea; and there was a great calm.

Matthew 8:24-26

The Ghost and the Guardian Angels

When the first winter storm of year moved across the Mediterranean Sea from the west, Captain Economidies was not worried, for he had been through many storms over the years. At most, it might slow the ship down and delay their arrival at the refinery by one day-- possibly two. He had 400,000 barrels of crude oil to get to the refinery. As the storm engulfed the S. S. Acropolis, the seas built up from five to twenty feet and occasionally a larger wave slammed into the tanker, sending sheets of freezing water over the ship and coating the decks and superstructure with sheets of ice. Throughout the day, the winds and the seas continued to build in fury. As darkness came the storm only seemed to intensify.

Below decks, in the galley where the meals were prepared, Little John the cook prepared cold sandwiches, as it was not possible to cook the normal meals due to the rolling of the ship in the heavy seas. Little John had a member of the stewards department take the ham and cheese sandwiches up to the bridge where Captain Economidies navigated the ship through the storm.

It was 1:57 pm when everyone felt a shudder as the Acropolis slammed into something. Whether it was another ship the S. S. Acropolis hit and sent to the bottom of the ocean or a steel container off another cargo ship lying submerged just below the water's surface, no one aboard the ship knew. Neither the lookout nor the helmsman could see anything except the stormy Mediterranean Sea. Nevertheless, over the next twenty minutes the bow of the ship sunk lower and lower. No longer did the bow rise up out seas instead most waves broke on the bow sending up sheets of spray like waves hitting the shallow water of a coral reef.

Captain Economidies knew the S. S. Acropolis had five water tight bulkheads to prevent the sinking of his ship. Three watertight bulkheads were forward of the superstructure on the ship. One watertight bulkhead was on each end of the engine room. The last watertight bulkhead gave the ship one compartment behind the ships superstructure. Whatever he hit had ruptured the watertight integrity of his ship and flooded the forward hundred feet of his ship.

Captain Economidies ordered the radio operator to begin putting out a distress call. The radio operator began transmitting: SOS,SOS,SOS and then he gave his ships position. All the crew began putting on life jackets. Forty minutes later, the second watertight bulkhead ruptured. The stormy seas now were slamming into the main superstructure. Waves of white frothing water twenty- and thirty feet tall rolled across the decks from the bow, which was now underwater to the stern of the ship. Captain Economidies ordered the crew to abandon ship. If another bulkhead ruptured no one would have time to even launch a life boat. When the third bulkhead gave way the Acropolis would just be another ship lost at sea.

Twenty three men worked as fast as humanly possible to launch the number one life boat over the side. Captain Economidies asked if everyone was there as the men climbed down knotted ropes into the lifeboat. A seaman told the captain that the cook was missing. The Captain ordered two seamen to find the cook, Little John, and to get him to the life boat. They returned and reported that Little John refused to come, and had taken a butcher knife in each hand and told them he was not leaving the ship, and if they tried to force him into the life boat he would just have to kill them both as he was not going anywhere!

The Captain told his men it was not worth dying to try and save one man. The two seamen climbed down the lines into the life boat and the captain followed. Moments later they released the lines securing them to the davits and the men in the life boat lost sight of the stricken tanker S. S. Acropolis.

★★★★

Little John was nine years old when his dad was lost at sea. His dad had gone fishing for the afternoon and he never returned home. Ever since that day Little John was terrified of the sea. Though he was terrified of the sea, he concealed his fear from everyone, as he did not want the other children his age to tease him about his fear. Even Little John's mom, Helen, did not realize her son was so afraid of the sea after that awful day her husband went fishing for the afternoon and never returned. Helen always wondered how her husband died, as the weather was nice the day her husband, Sebastian, went fishing. Neither Sebastian nor the boat was ever seen again.

Oh, how Helen missed her husband. Sometimes he got her so mad she wanted to hit him with a frying pan. Sometimes he did little things that made her so happy she had chosen him for a husband. GOD, she missed Sebastian. Sometimes she thought she heard him come in the house or she would remember the way they made love or she thought he was watching over her and his son, Little John. When she was alone in the house, sometimes she talked to Sebastian as if he were still with her. But then she thought she must be an old woman imagining things. Sebastian was gone.

The the nick name Little John was in humor. For Little John always seemed big for his age and in humor his friends always refered to him as as being small. He got a job cleaning up at nights in a restaurant, as he was bigger and stronger than most kids his age. In his free time Little John learned all he could about cooking and baking, as he knew that they earned more money for a day's work than the workers cleaning the tables and mopping the floors. John always helped his mother with the bills and since times were hard there was little money for himself. They got by the best they were able until one day the kitchen had a grease fire and the restaurant burned down.

A friend of the family told Little John that there was a ship in the harbor called the S. S. Acropolis and the baker had just gotten sick, so the captain would probably hire a new cook. Even though Little John was deathly afraid of the sea, he desperately needed work and so Little John reluctantly went down to the harbor to look at the ship, S. S. Acropolis. After talking to the captain about the cook's job, the captain told Little John he would give him a try for three days and if he could perform the job then he would hire him. The captain told him he wanted to see fresh bread, rice, goat meat and curry on the dinner table if he wanted to hold his job through dinner.

So Little John rationalized with himself: he was just cooking in the kitchen, but in the back of his mind Little Joe always knew that his kitchen or galley, as the seaman called it, was on a ship at sea. For years he cooked and sent home fifty dollars a month to help his mother and the other fifty dollars of his pay each month he saved for a rainy day. Little John was always able to control his fear of the sea, so that no one realized he was horrified. Little John was especially terrified of the storms, which he imagined must have swallowed up his dad and his fishing boat.

★★★★

Sebastian had gone fishing on a beautiful day. Sebastian primarily went fishing to catch fish to put food on the table, but he also simply liked being out on the water. He enjoyed the peace and serenity he experienced when he was out on the water. Sebastian was thinking of his son when the chest pains hit him. Sharp pains ran down his left side and across his chest. Suddenly the man could not breath as his heart attack ended his life. He fell against the side of his ten foot fishing boat and it leaned over in the water, for his little fishing boat only had eight inches above the water. As he fell against the side of his boat in his dying moments, the boat tipped so that only five inches of freeboard kept his wooden boat afloat.

Sebastian's Guardian Angel thought, "Now it is time to take Sebastian *home* and I have completed my duty and promise to watch over him. Sebastian started down the tunnel of light, but Sebastian was not concerned about himself, all his thought and energy were focused on his nine year old son, Little John. It was in that instant as he entered the tunnel of light that he realized that his son was going to drown when he grew up and worked on a merchant ship that Sebastian abruptly turned around and raced out of the tunnel of light that would have taken him to heaven. Sebastian's Guardian Angel raced after him as he realized that where ever Sebastian's Spirit or Ghost would go, he must follow.

Sebastian's ghost rushed towards the little fishing boat and with all the force and energy he could manage to employ, he pushed the low side of the boat lower in the water. Sebastian's ghost was trying with all his might and energy to sink his boat. There were five inches of freeboard above the water on the low side of the boat and Sebastian repeatedly slammed all his energy into the gunnel on the edge of the boat trying to capsize and sink his boat.

Sebastian's Spirit cried out: "GOD help me! as he attempted to sink his boat.

Two Angels of the Lord appeared and watched Sebastian repeatedly try to sink his boat. They realized his intention was that his boat and his body would be lost at sea and that his son would grow up afraid of the water so he would not drown at sea like his father had foreseen inside the tunnel of light.

The Angels of the Lord did not approve of what he was doing, but it was not even the Angels' place to judge anyone, for only GOD can judge anyone. The two Angels nodded to Sebastian's Guardian Angel then all three Angels assisted Sebastian in sinking his boat. Sebastian's boat slid beneath the Mediterranean Sea off the coast of Greece and was never seen again.

★★★★

The S. S. Acropolis was a thirty year old oil tanker owned by a Panamanian Shell Corporation. The Shell corporation was in turned by another Bahamian Shell Corporation which in turn was owned by another Panamanian Shell Corporation which in turn was owned by a another seven Shell Corporation's intended to hide the identity and eliminate the liability of the ship's owners should an oil spill occur doing millions of dollars in environmental damages. The owners usually made a profit of a hundred thousand dollars on every shipment of Saudi Arabian crude oil hauled from Ras Tanura offshore oil loading facility to the Lago Oil Refinery at Aruba, an island in the Caribbean Sea.

Years ago the S. S. Acropolis was owned by an American oil company but when she could no longer pass the United States Coast Guard safety inspections she was sold to a Panamanian Shell Corporation as Panama was known as a country that had very few and only superficial safety inspections. With the sale of the vessel, the American seaman and officers also lost their jobs as the new owners replaced the crew with a Greek captain and seamen. The Greek captain and his crew were happy to get the jobs and they worked for one quarter of the wages paid to American crews, for it was money that determined where the ship was registered and the crew that manned the ageing oil tanker. The owners were concerned with maximum profit and so when maintenance was required, seldom were the repairs made unless it was essential to keep the ship turning a nice profit.

Captain Economedies did his best to maintain his tanker, but his requests for repairs were almost aways turned down. Then his men who were repairing the life boats his bosun (like a foreman on a ship) informed him that in some places he metal had so deteriorated and rusted away that only the paint prevented one from seeing thought rusted out sections of the life boats. The lifeboats were so unsafe that only the floatation under the seats would stay afloat for very long. .

To solve the problem honestly without money to replace the life boat was impossible, so Captain Ecomonidies ordered the bosun to remove all identification from the number one life boat. Then one night they stole another ship in the harbor's life boat and left their life boat in the place of the one they had stolen. Now the ship had at least one life boat that would float! In the morning their new life boat had Acropolis lettered on it in wet paint.

Most people do not realize it, but a ship usually rusts away from the inside out-- such was the case with the S. S. Acropolis. While working below decks, seamen had pointed out to the bosun that the water tight bulkheads had simply rusted through in sections. The bosun told the captain about the weak watertight bulkheads, but like most repairs on the ship, they were never made. The owners were more concerned about profits and that is why the tanker had Panamanian registry.

★★★★

Even though he was told the ship was sinking, there was no way Little John was getting into the tiny life boat! He would kill anyone trying to remove him from his kitchen (galley)! There was no way anyone was going to force him into the life boat. After the life boat was launched, Little John went and used a pipe to hammer all the steel dogs which held the steel water-tight doors closed to seal out the breaking waves. Then Little John went through each compartment of the ship and sealed the metal dogs on the portholes to prevent water entry into the ship. He could think of nothing more he could do, so he went up to the radio room and broadcast on the radio: SOS , SOS, (... --- ... , ... --- ...) This was the only Morse code Little John knew.

★★★★

Dancing Wind and Molly O'Brian were taking a vacation to Greece. They had come to see the tourist attractions that most tourists come to see, like the ancient Acropolis, the Temple of Olympian Zeus, Ancient Agora and the Parthenon at Acropolis. It was here, while visiting Acropolis, that they heard of the oil tanker sinking in a storm. So among the ruins of the ancient Parthenon they sat down and prayed to GOD for his help for the ship and the seamen aboard the ship. You must always realize that GOD hears your prayers; and prayers always help. But when one says a prayer they do not always result in things turning out the way we want or with a happy ending.

★★★★

The sun dawned on a new day as the storm moved off to the east. The winds and the waves calmed down on the sunny winter day. The storms, like most storms in life, had passed on. The Greek Coast Guard helicopter hovered up above the stricken oil tanker S. S. Acropolis. A basket was lowered down and a cook was hauled up aboard the helicopter. Little John had never ridden in a helicopter.

★★★★

Four hours later, a life boat was located by the Greek Coast Guard. Twenty four men were in the life boat and all were covered in ice. Everyone aboard the life boat had died of exposure.

★★★★

As the Coast Guard helicopter lifted off the S. S. Acropolis and headed back to Athens, Little John thought he saw a momentary flash of light. Sebastian nodded to his Guardian Angel and smiled. He had been able to save his son's life, even though he had died twenty-seven years earlier. Together, Sebastian and his Guardian Angel disappeared in a flash of light as they entered the tunnel of light as they shot *home* to heaven.

A calmness or serenity came over Little John as he flew in the helicopter over the blue Mediterranean Sea. Little John thought if he could survive a storm like the one he had just he gone through, a ship which did not sink in a fierce storm, a ride in a tiny basket, and a ride in a helicopter, there was really no reason for him to feel scared of the sea. As Little John got out of the helicopter when it landed at the Greek

Coast Guard station, he thought he would love to go for another ride in the helicopter, as surely that is where the Angels must play.

Dancing Wind and Molly heard the news that one man aboard the oil tanker had survived. Upon hearing the news they thanked GOD for the miracles that had prevented a massive oil spill and allowed one man to live. Don't forget to thank GOD for answering your prayers, even though they did not come out exactly the way you wanted. You can always ask GOD for the highest good to occur.

Angels are crying
Angels are praying
Angels are working
To set things Right
And that is why
You may see Angels
In flight; tonight!

La Cañada Del Oro

There is a high, rugged mountain along Cañada del Oro (Canyon of Gold). 8,000 years ago, pre-historic man and woman took shelter among its rugged and protective heights. Here they had small gardens growing squash, corn and beans catching the runoff from the occasional rains to water their crops. Along Cañada del Oro these ancient people hunted and camped and, when pressed or attacked by enemies, they took shelter here on top of the tall gray granite and black shale oblong mountain.

It took four warriors to ensure the safety of their clan against all intruders; for there were four entrances by which man could enter this mountain. One entrance is on the south-east side of the mountain. There is another entrance on the northwest side, which is visible in the setting sun. As the sun sets in the western sky, it cast long shadows. It is due to the long shadows of the setting sun, that the stone steps cut into the sheer cliff face become visible. The most easily accessible entrance is on the northeast corner of the round mountain where access is easiest as there is a fault or crevice enabling a person to enter the mountain by only having to climb a low thirty foot high cliff. There is a twenty foot high stone face that looks directly towards the northeast entrance into the mountain. The location of the fourth entrance is unknown to Dancing Wind; she had never seen it, nor did she know where it lay. Yet Dancing Wind knew that the fourth entrance existed, as it was from her Guardian Angel that she learned of the existence of the four entrances. Her Guardian Angel only pointed out three of the entrances, and since her guide did not discuss the fourth entrance, Dancing Wind did not press the matter with her. Dancing Wind assumed her Guardian Angel did not want Dancing Wind near the fourth entrance. The access point that her Guardian Angel advised her to use was the entrance on the northeast corner of the mountain, and this was what was most important to her as she moved about exploring the oblong mountain. If she chose to explore the secrets of the mountain, she would heed this advice. .

Dancing Wind, Molly O'Brian, and Sarah had originally gone by the mountain as they followed an Old Spanish Trail up Cañada del Oro. As this is an area which has many dry stretches where water is absent, as they were traveling past the mountain they noticed a giant shadow of a "7" engraved into the rocks. Immediately they changed their path of travel to enter a small box canyon with high gray and black cliffs where the "7" was located on the canyon walls. The seventy-foot high shadow "7" was only visible from noon to one, as it was the sun's angle to the cliff face which allowed the seven to be visible for this one hour during the day.

Molly knew that the "7" commonly had eight meanings to the Spanish explorers: The seven meant:

1. That this is a camp site.

2. This site is capable of being protected or defended in a fight.

3. There is water here for people and horses.

4. The "7" often led one to a stone map containing directions to what is important to the Spanish.

5. On some occasions, the seven is used by the Spanish to represent gold or the trail to gold or the treasure.

6. In the Bible, it was on the seventh day that GOD rested; the "7" was used by the Spanish to represent a place to rest that had water where they could camp.

7. The seven was sometimes used to represent GOD. So this leads to the eighth meaning of the "7:" the seven was referring to GOD as the treasure or gold that you seek. An example of this is that a "7" is often at a treasure and or cache site guiding one to the treasure.

It was Molly's curiosity about the water source in this dry canyon that led her to look for where the spring was located. As she neared the end of the box canyon there, there was a stone. Engraved upon its face were symbols showing half of a sun face with a small arrow pointing to the spring. There before her she found a pool of water about two feet wide and eight feet long. She understood that knowing the location of hidden pools of water when traveling through desert country can be the difference between life and death. This spring is not on any topographical map, so Molly was proud of herself for having seen the "7" and having realized its importance.

As one learns to track, there are milestones of progress one never forgets. One such milestone is acquiring the ability to communicate with one's Guardian Angel. Gaining he ability to follow the trail of one's choosing for mile after mile is another, as well as the honing of one's ability to find water, especially when one is tracking in the desert. Another important skill is that one needs to be able to recognize danger or when danger is approaching. If one is to interact on the spirit realm, you need the ability to communicate with spirits--in a safe manner. And most important of all is when one begins to bring all these spiritual gifts together to achieve positive results for the highest good of all.

If one looked at the spiritual path Dancing Wind, Molly and Sarah were traveling with the Angels, they would see that each lesson built upon the prior lessons and each lesson progressed in difficulty as their skill in dealing with physical and spiritual difficulties grew. They were free to walk away or stop the lesson, just as they were free to accept another lesson and another challenge. And so the Angels tell me this is true for you too!

Never think that you failed when you failed to achieve your objective. Certainly as Dancing Wind, Molly O'Brian and Sarah track the trails of the spirit they do not always achieve what they set out to obtain or achieve. Only if you quit and never try again have you failed.

Should you look back at Dancing Wind's first lessons, like *Tracking Through Time*, her Guardian Angels knew the lessons that they wanted to teach Dancing Wind. Certainly, they did not take her to a location with a treacherous spirit like the one found in *Path of the Angels* until she had some experience under her belt and the Guardian Angels who were watching over her had confidence in her ability to handle the challenges she would encounter.

Just as Dancing Wind's ability and Molly O'Brian's spiritual gifts are different, so, too are your gifts and abilities different. You should use the ability you have to do the best you can, showing love, dignity, honor and integrity. That is all the Angels expect or want! There are some individuals whose idea of a great weekend is to pop a top, and drink a few cold ones as they watch TV on their big screen. There are some individuals who will plant fruit trees and berry bushes. There will be some who help a person in distress and there will be some, like Dancing Wind and Molly, who track the old trails and try to leave their path a better place after having traveled there. Your path is yours to choose! So choose wisely!

Dancing Wind and Molly O'Brian have chosen the path of tracking with Angels. If you were to track a trail through the Sonoran desert, and in so doing you saw stone turtles or a "7" guiding you to water ,you have a right to smile and pat yourself on the back or thank your Guardian Angel for helping you learn and expand your understanding of Mother Earth. For it is within this framework of expanding your understanding, that you have the opportunity to grow and expand your spiritual understanding, too. For you it may start with simply getting out into the wildernesses of the world, taking simple hikes in the woods or canoeing along a stream; that you are allowing your Guardian Angel the opportunity to open the beginning of an unfolding dialogue with you. As your understanding develops you may chose to interact with your Guardian Angel or possibly even dozens of Angels. After all it is your choice, whether you chose to interact with one Angel or dozens of Angels or none at all.

And so it was that as Molly slowly moved away from the spring and marveled at her discovery, her mind was open to allowing her Guardian Angel to show her the stone turtles placed centuries ago along the trail she walked guiding one to water.

Dancing Wind then removed some garlic bulbs and asparagus seeds, which she planted in the small holes that Sarah dug near the waterhole. The teenagers were trying to help any hungry individuals or animals whom could use the plants to provide them with a meal. Then, moving away from the water hole, they selected a place to camp for the night. They wanted to leave the desert animals that would come to drink from this water hole, plenty of freedom to come and go, and to drink the life-giving water as well.

Molly, Sarah and Dancing Wind quickly erected their tent, as they knew that, often, teamwork makes the job at hand go quickly and easily. Outside their tent they watched the sun set in the western sky then they talked awhile as the stars began to appear; the arrival of nightfall ended Dancing Wind's, Sarah's, and Molly's first day at the round mountain.

The second day began after breakfast, as the teenagers explored the mountain beside Cañada del Oro. As they were walking down a narrow trail on the western slope, their Guardian Angels pointed toward a small, twenty foot high hill. As they walked down the trail, they noticed that their Guardian Angels walked in front of them. The Angels then hiked up to the top of a small hill. Following their Angels' suggestion, they followed them to the top of the hill where there was a thousand pound boulder with a crack or split going half way down the boulder. Watching their Guardian Angels' actions, they saw their Angels walk up to a large boulder on the top of the hill. Then their Guardian Angels each took a turn looking through the crack or split down the top of the boulder. Their Angels showed them that the crack was intended to be looked through and on the horizon, at the top of the cliff in the distance, was a U-notch on the skyline. The ancient sight stones were guiding one into the mountain. This marker had been in place to guide people to a place of safety inside the mountain for eight thousand years. These stone markers had stood the test of time.

Molly stood in awe of one giant sixty foot stone eagle. Sarah had no idea how such a giant stone bird could be constructed. Dancing Wind talked with the Guardian Angel standing beside her, and the Angel told her that the Eagle was here to tell them about two important sites they might chose to see. For centuries, the stone bird had stood as a silent sentinel watching over the oblong mountain.

As they walked back to their Jeep they retraced a portion of the trail they had taken, walking in on the western side of the mountain--it was then they made an alarming discovery. On top of their footprints were the paw impressions of a mountain lion who had been tracking them! Maybe the mountain lion was only following them out of curiosity. Perhaps the mountain lion was planning to invite the teenagers to join him at his dinner table. In time, the lion's decisions would become very clear to the teenagers.

Dancing Wind said "Well, we will need to remove our Glocks from our Jeep and start putting them in our backpacks from now on."

They had blown off the advice and counsel of the old Lakota Indian, Dan, to always carry a weapon for self-defense when out in the back country. As they saw the four foot stride of the tracks of the mountain lion, they realized they had made a serious mistake which they needed to correct before it cost one or all of them their lives.

"When we see the lion we will have to remove the semiautomatics from our backpacks should the mountain lion approach us. I do not want us to kill the lion but I do not want the lion having us for supper either. From now on we need to be a lot more careful and avoid locations where the lion can easily ambush us," said Dancing Wind.

The next day they never saw the mountain lion following them, but whenever they crossed their back trail, there were the fresh prints of the mountain lion over top their foot prints! And so it was as they tracked the ancient trail around the circumference of the gray and black mountain that the cat also tracked them.

★★★★

Molly, Sarah and Dancing Wind packed their Glocks on the top of their packs. They did not want to have to dig through all their gear to get to their weapons that they carried for self defense. The tracking went slower as their concentration was split between an awareness of the mountain lion and their awareness of the ancient trail that they were tracking. Mountain lions consider an ideal ambush as one where they can jump down from above onto the back of their victim. They use their one- to two- hundred pounds of body weight to knock their prey to the ground, and then they bite the neck breaking it, killing their prey. Their stalking may take hours or days. Their attacks are lightning fast and occur within just seconds! Therefore, whenever the dry washes or arroyos got over waist high as they tracked along the western slopes of the mountain, they would leave the arroyo for higher ground to have more visibility. They would not walk in a dry arroyo that was above their head, as it would give the mountain lion following them an ideal location to ambush them. Whenever there were high groups of boulders along the trail, they detoured around them as they did not want to give the lion the opportunity to ambush them. .

On the third day, tracking on the western slopes of the mountain, they encountered a stone map made on the flat surface of a massive boulder. The stone map gave three sets of directions. The compass-bearings, or lines of travel, were shown on this map as one inch high and one inch wide raised up straight lines, traveling the length and breadth of the massive thirty five ton boulder. One compass course or line of travel showed a trail off in the distance which led to a mountain far to the north. The second compass course showed a path of travel far to the south where one would find both water and a trail leading to a massive Spanish cache site a day's travel to the south.

The third line was the line which interested Dancing Wind, Sarah and Molly the most, as it showed them where in the round mountain they should travel should they want to locate or enter a stone door. This stone door was concealed among the rugged cliffs and faults of the mountain, among whose slopes they had been tracking. Dancing

Wind, Sarah and Molly were attempting to track the trail literally to the entrance, into the concealed stone vaults of the underground Spanish Treasure room. Late in the afternoon of the third day, they encountered a pointing stone, the pointer was giving a compass bearing into the mountains. In three days they had been able to find three fixed positions with compass bearings into the mountain.

★★★★

Upon finding the first sight stones guiding one into the mountain, some trackers would have rushed into the rugged mountains to attempt to find the location of the stone entrance immediately. And while it might have been possible to locate the entrance with just one, two or three compass bearings, this was not a path that the teenage trackers would choose to follow. As the girls tracked trails, they understood that they were also learning more and more about what they were pursuing. If they had been tracking elk, they would have observed what they like to eat and where they go to feed and get water. So the longer you follow the trail and observe their behavior the greater your understanding of the elk will be.

If you should track an outlaw, the longer you track their trail and the more you learn and research about the outlaw, the greater your understanding of them will be. As you track an outlaw you will learn about who he chooses to rob, as well as his method of operation. It is actually possible to learn his hide outs and how he performed his robberies and, sometimes, really top trackers may even recover his stolen loot!

So when Dancing Wind is tracking some California outlaws east from California towards Colorado to their camp on the Stolenmeyer and Piedra Rivers long before she reached their last camp she would have a feel for the character of the men she was tracking. Sometimes the men one is tracking are not very nice men. They may even be in the habit of having one man hold your attention or more correctly stated, the attention of the victims they plan to murder or rob, while his other two partners move around to your back to shoot or knife their intended victims. As you track the trail of an individual you should begin to understand how they think and act as well as where they make their camps.

Taking this a step further, as Molly and Dancing Wind tracked the trails into the mountains of Cañada del Oro they, too, began to understand the ways of the men they were tracking--even though they were tracking trails made centuries earlier. They learned about the sight stones they used to guide one into the mountain and how they varied each sight stone so as to prevent anyone trying to follow their trail.

As Molly and Dancing Wind tracked the ancient trails around Cañada del Oro, the teenagers focused on the trails made by the Jesuit (Order of Jesus) priest. When Sara asked them how they knew that they were Jesuit priests, Molly told Sarah that the two most common religious orders working throughout Mexico and the American southwest were the Jesuits and the Franciscan padres. The Jesuits had a certain arrogance they felt and clearly it showed up in the mathematics and engineering of the trail they were tracking. The Spanish often hid their treasures at cache sites protected by eleven false stone doors which worked as a security system protecting the twelfth stone door. The twelfth door had the most elaborate security systems of all and few individuals could survive the test of survival faced at the twelfth stone door unless they had an understanding of the security systems and how they worked. Dancing Wind told Sarah that because of the complexity of the monuments, they felt they were just a little bit too difficult for the Spanish or Franciscans to have constructed. While there were clearly numerous Spanish markers and caches here in Cañada del Oro,

Dancing Wind and Molly explained to Sarah that they were pretty sure it was Jesuits that they were tracking. These Jesuit priests who designed the markers and the traps were extremely intelligent and dangerous men who would not hesitate to kill their fellow man. These priests we have been tracking have deliberately created numerous false trails that would lead to death traps which would kill unsuspecting individuals who tried to track the priest to their treasure.

Just as the Jesuits had killed many Indians to obtain the treasure they possessed, certainly the priest's spirit had no intention of warning Dancing Wind, Sarah and Molly about the death traps they were responsible for creating. In life you will encounter individuals whose character is ruthless, treacherous, and lying, and who would murder another individual for a case of beer. Then you will also encounter the individuals whose character is, to the very core of their existence, dignity, honor, integrity, fair play. Both extremes, integrity or the lack thereof, are found both in the physical world and in the spirit world. Who you chose to work and associate with are your choices. If you do not like the choice you have made—change it. GOD literally gives you the right to choose as part of your free will and you are free to change your mind and choose again at any time in your life!

As Molly, Sarah and Dancing Wind tracked this trail through Cañada del Oro, they could feel the priest watching them from on top of the mountain and a good tracker can discern if the individual they are tracking is willing to warn them of the death traps they created or if he is perfectly happy to let the trackers be slaughtered in the death traps they created. These Jesuits were pissed off about the teenagers whom were tracking them. Certainly there was no love lost between the priest and the trackers.

★★★★

On the fifth day, as they were tracking on the northwest side of the mountain, they encountered numerous stone faces that were ten- to thirty feet tall, as well as thirty-foot stone hammers, eagles' heads, and even the number seven. When the stone hammer, stone faces and eagles' heads gave clear compass directions to a massive stone or face up on top of the slopes at the base of the cliffs, they noticed that these simple-to-locate stone marker lines or compass courses always guided one to the death traps.

Five times they followed the easily-seen trails or stone sight lines up the steep slopes to the base of the cliffs. Five times the trackers just observed the death traps designed to kill anyone following the priest's trail. On top of the gray granite mountain, the priest looked down upon the trackers. The three priest ghost were furious. There were five death traps that they created using hundreds of hours of forced Indian slave labor to erect, but not one trap was tripped by the female trackers. The priest thought that over the centuries dishonest men or thieves would try and steal their treasure and they had visions of their slaughter in the massive stone death traps they had created. Never had they ever even conceived of the idea that in the end, females would follow their century old trail and track them! They knew that the women were just the devil's temptation to man. They had been getting man into trouble since the Garden of Eden. Well those death traps the women found today would get rid of them and send them to Hell where they belonged.

The first sight stone they encountered guided them up the steep cliff slopes to a small six foot by six foot square hole in a soft clay or mud-like material that lay underneath the stone of the cliff towering above them. Clearly this location may lead them to the treasure the Spanish concealed centuries ago. The opening was probably just plugged or filled with soft mud or clay they needed to remove. The teenagers vowed to return the next day with shovels and digging bars. The teenagers then walked back to their jeep and talked about the tools and supplies they would need to recover the treasure. The next morning the teenagers were off to an early start at 6:00 am. They ate breakfast in a fast food restaurant and ordered a bag of roast beef sandwiches, which were made up for them for lunch. By ten they had the soft dirt flying out of their hole and down the slope. As they dug, they took turns breaking off chunks of dirt with the digging bar and removing it with the shovel.

"Quit horsing around and stop throwing dirt in my hair," Dancing Wind told Molly, after an hour of digging

Molly replied, "I am not throwing dirt in your hair."

Dancing Wind replied, "Well, whoever is throwing dirt in my hair better stop it unless they want a shovel-full of dirt in their face."

Thirty minutes later, as Molly was digging, she told Dancing Wind "Quit throwing dirt into my hair."

"I didn't." Dancing Wind replied.

Molly told her, "Yeah right."

As they looked at each other, a steady stream of dirt stated falling on Molly's hair from a crack over her head.

Each teenager's attention was riveted by the crack, which had only appeared after they had begun digging. Dancing Wind placed sunglasses on her face to protect her eyes from the falling dirt and walked over to examine the crack which had appeared over their heads. Looking up, she saw sunlight thirty feet above them. Time seemed to stop as Dancing Wind looked skyward into the rapidly increasing stream of dirt falling on her face. Suddenly, she grabbed Molly's arm, yanking her towards the entrance of their hole as she yelled "Run!"

Molly started to grab the tools and Dancing Wind pulled her, jerking her forward and out of the hole they were digging.

"Forget the tools!" Dancing Wind yelled, as she pulled Molly along beside her. As they cleared the hole, Molly started to run downhill.

"No! Along the cliff," Dancing Wind yelled.

Together the three girls ran for their lives as they raced away from their hole along the edge of the cliff. Sarah had taken the lead and when she had run fifty feet she sat down on a flat boulder and looked back. Dancing Wind, who was about three steps behind her, simply grabbed her arm and jerked her to her feet, yelling: "Run!" They all ran. Behind them they heard the roar of breaking rock as fifty tons of rock sheared off the cliff and rushed down the slope like an avalanche of boulders smashing through everything in their path of destruction.

Molly turned to Dancing Wind and said "What happened?"

Dancing Wind replied "We were in a Spanish Death Trap!" "When I looked up and I could see light above us I realized we were undermining the support of a group of massive boulder's designed to crush us in a trap!" "The dirt falling into our hair was from the ground above the boulder coming down the crack as the boulder was just beginning to shift its position as the crack was slowly widening." "We triggered the trap as we dug under the boulder undermining its support."

The three teenagers walked back to the Jeep. Their back packs and roast beef sandwiches were still where they left them before they had begun digging—just outside the hole. Of course now they were under twenty to thirty tons of stone! Molly said a not very nice word starting with: "S". She had just lost two-thousand dollars' worth of equipment in her back pack.

★★★★

Dancing Wind said, "Let's call it a day."

All three teenagers sat down on a large flat stone and thanked GOD that they had survived the lessons they were learning that day. Then they got up to walk back to the Jeep. Unbeknownst to the three teenagers, they were followed by a cat. The two hundred and fifty pound lion walked fifty to one hundred yards behind the teenagers as he observed them. He was capable of covering the fifty yards in six to seven seconds.

As they drove out of Cañada del Oro towards Tucson, Sarah and Molly suggested to Dancing Wind maybe they should talk to Dan and ask him to help us to track. I really want to live through the lessons we have chosen to learn at Cañada del Oro. Dancing Wind smiled and said when we get into cell tower range let's give him a call.

Sarah, Molly and Dancing Wind drove over to see Dan as they wanted his assistance. Dan had long silver hair, worn in two braids running down his shoulders and down his back. He had a brown, leathery face and a slow raspy voice. Usually Dan dressed in a comfortable flannel shirt, blue jeans and he wore cowboy boots. His wisdom always impressed the teenagers, whom he had taken a liking to, so he spent his free time teaching them to track. The wise medicine man was laying the ground work by first teaching the teenagers how to connect and develop a solid relationship with their Guardian Angel, or Spirit Guide, as Dan referred to them. Around a campfire at night Dan would tell stories in his slow raspy voice of the spirit work medicine men engage in. He would talk about how they work to set things back into balance in the environment as well as the spirit world. His raspy voice would hold the teenage girls spell bound as he explained the finer points of tracking an elk or tracking an Apache through the Malpais (badlands). Dan spoke with the authority of a medicine man who had been "up the creek and over the mountain" as the old timers say. He taught the teenagers survival on a physical level and a spiritual level, skills which few young people are willing to show any interest or effort in learning. Yet what he imparted into the students he taught were the skills to track a trail and to work with spirit forces to try and set things right or in balance again. Some skills were physical, such as how to stay alive in a wilderness or desert environment. Other skills were spiritual, such as communicating with spirits, taking lost spirits *home*. He also taught them how to work with the Wind, Rain, and Lightning Spirits as well as working with one's Guardian Angels or Spirit Guides, as the Native Americans called them.

A week later Dan, Molly, Sarah and Dancing Wind returned together to Cañada del Oro. As they hiked into the back country, they stopped for a breather and began drinking water. Dan pointed to the tracks of Molly and Sarah where they had walked out of the mountains the week before. On top of their track were the four paw prints of the mountain lion.

Dancing Wind said, "I know about the lion. It has been following us wherever we go. That is why we have our Glocks in our backpacks."

"We don't want to kill the lion but we both have the Glocks in our packs as we do not want to join the lion for his dinner," Molly added.

Sarah had a feeling the shit was just about to hit the fire, so she did not say a word.

Then the wise Lakota Indian asked them: "*So tell me, you have picked this trail to track into the Mountains of Cañada del Oro. And you tell me you have the weapons for self defense but you do not want to use them. You have chosen to track this trail with its dangers, which may have its rewards, or it may cost you your life. And you do not want to hurt a lion which has repeatedly tracked you.*"

"*So tell me, if your interest is tracking this ancient trail with its risks and rewards, what is the mountain lion's choice if he is following you every time he has you in view and he is maneuvering to get into a position where he can ambush you? Do you not realize what the mountain lions choice is?*"

Molly, Sarah and Dancing Wind looked at their feet; they did not want to look their dear Indian friend in the eyes as they realized they had been risking their lives foolishly. Dan was not finished with his lesson yet so he turned to Molly, Sarah and Dancing Wind and pointed to an old dead tree stump and told them,

"That tree stump is the lion attacking you; now kill it!" Then Dan started a slow count. "One", "Two." All three teenagers reached for the front snap to disconnect the strap holding the two shoulder straps together on their back packs.

"Three."

Then Dan jarred Molly's and Dancing Winds arms at the elbows so their hands slipped off the snap.

"Four." The teenagers regained the snap and released the short six inch strap connecting their front two shoulder straps.

"Five." As Dancing Wind started swinging the back pack off her shoulders Dan caught the back pack on the corner and gave it a shove. Dancing Wind lost her balance and fell over backwards onto her backpack. Dan's leg swept Sarah's right leg out from under her,and she let out a scream as she felt herself falling backwards.

"Six." Thrown off balance, Sarah and Dancing Wind tumbled over backwards on to the ground.

"Seven" Molly swung her back pack off and reached for her releases allowing her to open her flap over her pack. Releasing one snap, she got her hands on the second snap when Dan used a leg sweep and suddenly Molly lost her balance and went over backwards with her backpack landing on top of her. Molly shot Dan a dirty look.

Dan just shrugged his shoulders and said "That was just the rock you tripped over as the lion is attacking. Eight." Dancing Wind rolled onto her knees as she reached to release the snaps on the pack flap.

"Nine." Dancing Wind's hand reached into the pack and closed around her weapon. Molly reached into the pack and her hand closed around the Glock. Sarah was fumbling around in her pack, removing her sweater from around the weapon.

"Ten." Both teenagers had to use two hands to remove their Glocks from their holsters.

"Eleven." The Glocks came up pointing towards the old, dead stump. Sarah got her Glock untangled from her sweater and now her weapon was coming out of her backpack. Then both teenagers had to pull the slide back to chamber a round.

"Twelve." Both Glocks fired within moments of each other. Two puffs of dirt erupted three feet away from the tree stump. Clearly, both shots missed. Sarah was pulling back the slide of her Glock and then she took rapid aim. A puff of dirt erupted ten feet behind the old dead stationary tree stump. As Sarah fired at the tree stump, she corrected her aim, getting closer and closer until she began hitting the target most of the time. As Dancing Wind and Molly shot, the live fire continued down range towards the tree stump. On the fifth shot, fifteen seconds later, they both hit the tree stump. All three teenagers fired ten rounds through their Glock hand guns. Sarah had hit the tree stump with three of the ten shots. Molly and Dancing Wind had hit the stump four times. Nineteen bullets the teenagers had fired had completely missed the stationary target!

Dan looked at all three teenagers and said, "Had that been a real mountain lion attack, it would have been all over in two- to four seconds. An attacking lion will not be standing still like that tree stump was. During an attack it will be at a full run and a lot harder to hit! It would not be a little bump or bruise from me bumping you that would have occurred here. It would have been two inch claws ripping you apart or had it gone exactly as this lion wants, he would be attacking you from behind, and as his two hundred and fifty pounds slams into your shoulders and knocks you to the ground, he would quickly seal his victory by using his razor sharp teeth to break your neck!"

Dan told the two students, "Let's delay this trip until we can spend a couple of days working on your draw and aim so you can make your first shot count. Then we need to consider why you feel that you need to give an attacker trying to kill you, a fifteen second advantage over you! You need to realize that anyone trying to kill you does not deserve a fifteen second advantage over you. If you give that advantage to anyone, a mountain lion, a bear, a mugger, a rapist or murderer you may not survive the attack." He went on, "If you cannot rapidly access the weapon you need to stop an attack, then it is unlikely you will survive an attack."

For the next three days Dan instructed his three tracking students in the carrying of their weapons, drawing, aiming and firing their Glocks. Instead of carrying their weapons behind them in their backpacks, they switched to carrying their weapons where they were instantly accessible. They no longer carried their weapons without a shell in the chamber so that two hands were required just to put one in.

Dan showed them that they needed to keep the weapon's safety on, and how to use their thumbs to quickly enable the weapon to fire. He taught them the importance of keeping their fingers off the trigger, holding it straight against the side of the Glock instead.

"Never put your finger on the trigger until you are aiming or ready to fire your weapon," he told them. For three days they practiced firing five hundred rounds each day as they worked at hitting the targets they aimed for. Three days earlier, when trying to kill the dead stump, their firing time had been fifteen seconds; all three teenagers were now able to draw and effectively put live fire down range in two seconds. Only when Dan thought they were ready, did he follow them back into the Santa Catalina Mountains of Arizona.

As the old tracker followed along behind his students, he shook his head sadly as he saw the Death Traps they had triggered and barely escaped with their lives. To himself, Dan thought "Well, they certainly have plenty of room for improvement!" He did not want to lose his best students to a two- or three century-old security system, so Dan told them to come to him and he led the three teenagers to the very center of the tripped death trap. He had them all relax and then he told them to reinforce their white lights of protection.

"Next," he said, "call in your Guardian Angel. Hold hands with your Guardian Angel. Now feel the vibrations that these rocks and this site give off. Notice how it upsets your stomach, gives you a bad or uneasy feeling or makes you nauseous.

"Remember this feeling and it can save your life. Just as a dangerous death trap can give you this feeling, so can a dangerous or bad person. Do not judge someone by appearances; judge them by their actions and the feelings or vibrations they give off. I do not want you tripping too many of these Spanish death traps, as it is likely to ruin your day. The first Spanish death trap has cost each of you your backpacks and two thousand dollars in gear."

Neither Dancing Wind, Sarah nor Molly wanted to lose another pair of their backpacks with two thousand of their gear inside. As the teenagers selected a possible cache site and dug down, they thought, "Well, shortly we will find the treasure inside the treasure room." Eight hours later, as the sun was setting in the western sky, the teenagers climbed out of their six by six foot hole they had dug four-feet deep.

Molly said to Dancing Wind, "Apparently these treasures are not going to just jump out into our lap!"

Dancing Wind replied, "Well sometimes you must put a lot of sweat and labor into your job to achieve the results you want. Leave the digging tools here and let's call it a night."

So as Dan and the teenagers hiked back to the Jeep they had concealed in the mountains of Cañada del Oro, a hunter also followed them. This hunter had four legs, weighed two-hundred and fifty pounds and moved silently through the night. A jack rabbit saw the four hikers and circled around the hikers as they walked towards their Jeep. The jack rabbit which was staying out of their sight failed to realize the true threat to his existence. In three bounds the cat covered twenty-seven feet and landed on top of the rabbit, killing it. Because of its momentary lack of awareness of the true dangers it faced, the rabbit became the cats dinner.

Two weeks had passed before Dancing Wind, Sarah and Molly returned to Cañada del Oro in the Coronado National Forest. They were back looking at the next line leading up the slope.

Molly turned to Dancing Wind and told her, "Well I am ready."

Together, the teenagers walked over to a thirty foot tall stone face. The face had a "V" shape with the high point of the "V" running up the center of his face from his mouth to the top of his forehead. The noon day sun formed a shadow line along this line down the center of the gray granite stone of a man's face. Seeing this shadow line, they carefully followed this line up the rugged mountain slopes, carefully holding a straight line with their compass.

Here the cliff face seemed to have fallen over, crushing everything in its path. The longer Dancing Wind looked at the path of destruction, the more uncomfortable she became. It reminded her of the trap that she and Molly had accidently tripped, only this trap must have been tripped years ago.

Molly began digging in the center of the lines which guided her up to the base of the cliff. As Molly dug, she suddenly unearthed part of the skeleton of a man. Molly fell on her hands and knees and vomited. And she vomited again. There was nothing she could do to save this man. Dancing Wind and Molly refilled the hole. They sat down beside the remains and said a prayer to GOD for the man's spirit. Then Molly hugged Dancing Wind and told her dear friend,

"This is as far as I am willing to track this trail. For me, the trail on Cañada del Oro ends today. I have been stalked by a lion which could kill me in an instant, almost crushed under hundreds of tons of rocks, survived five Spanish death traps all intended to kill me, and now I encountered a fellow tracker whom I just reburied. I am sorry Dancing Wind; but for me the trail ends today!"

And so Molly had weighed the risk of the trail she was tracking just as you must weigh the risk of the trails that you track in your life. Molly chose not to follow this path any further. Dan, Dancing Wind and Sarah called it a day and walked Molly back to the Jeep. Even though Molly chose not to track this trail any further, she still had the respect and friendship of her friends.

★★★★

The next day, Dan, Sarah and Dancing Wind were tracking the trails along the northwest slopes of the mountain. There on the upper mountain slopes, just below the steep cliffs, stood a twelve foot tall stone heart with the bottom four feet of the heart buried in the ground. After observing the large stone heart for a few minutes the teenagers were looking around for other Spanish Markers and seeing none which held their interest, they started to walk on.

Dan had been letting the two teenagers track the trails while he watched, but he felt that they had missed an important lesson here so he asked the teenagers one question

"What is at the base or point of the heart? You know that sometimes the heart can mean a treasure, though it often is a trap to lure you away from the real treasure." Dan had observed the stone pedestal that the stone heart had formerly rested upon.

Sarah misunderstood the meaning of Dan's question; she assumed that there must be gold at the base of the heart. Sarah began digging beside the heart with her shovel. Dancing Wind watched Sarah dig. Slowly, a bad feeling came over Dancing Wind. It was the feeling of dread; this was not a place that they should be digging. Suddenly Sarah screamed and then she fell to the ground on her hands and knees and vomited. Sarah had just located a second tracker who had beaten the three teenagers to this site. Dancing Wind helped Sarah refill his grave.

Sarah was still shaking as they said a prayer over the man's grave. This was the first time Sarah had encountered a dead man in her tracking. Certainly Sarah hoped it would not happen again.

This tracker had come to this mountain seeking his fortune. At the base of the heart, standing up on a pedestal, he dug seeking treasure. As he dug deeper he had hit sand, which was used to hold the pedestal perfectly level. As the treasure hunter dug at the base of the pedestal and his hole got deeper, it allowed the sand to flow out from under the base of the pedestal. Suddenly the base became unstable and it tipped towards the hole. As the pedestal tipped towards the hole, the twelve foot tall stone heart slid off its pedestal and slid onto the man digging the hole, killing him instantly.

Suddenly, Dancing Wind turned to her Spirit Guide and asked her what lies under this trap. Her Spirit Guide replied that *"She is not the first tracker to come here seeking the treasure here in Cañada del Oro. One of the trackers who was trying to recover the treasure here lies under this trap at the base of the cliff."* Then her Spirit Guide told her, *"You will need to take his Spirit home; you can ask him if he is ready."* Dancing Wind then spoke with the spirit of the tracker and asked him his name and if he was ready to go *home* now. The spirit told Dancing Wind,

"My name is Señor Rivera. I would like to go home as long as you will help my friends go home too."

As Dancing Wind and Sarah walked by the large stone heart; Dancing Wind stopped and turned again to her Spirit guide.

"Did you say: 'one of?' and 'who were?'"

Sadly, the angel nodded 'yes'. Dancing Wind realized the angel was using the plural tense—there were more than the two treasure hunters who had preceded them into Cañada del Oro and were still here. Dancing Wind asked her Guardian Angel if there were more trackers or treasure hunters who came here first were still here.

Sadly, the angel replied, *"There are many spirits here within Cañada del Oro who will need your help going home. My darling Dancing Wind, there is much work for you to do here but there will be many sad trails you will track, should you be aware enough to hold on to your physical form. If you chose to walk, certainly there is no shame or dishonor for making that choice."*

As they walked back to their Jeep, Sarah and Dancing Wind were lost in thought. Dan was ensuring their safety as he realized both teenagers were not paying attention because of today's events. When they got to the Jeep and were driving back to Tucson, Sarah turned to Dan and Dancing Wind and told them,

"I am sorry, but for me, this trail ends now! That could have been me under that stone heart. This is not a trail I am willing to track any further. I hope you understand."

★★★★

A week later, Dan and Dancing Wind left Tucson walking north east along the Pima Canyon Trail. For two hours they walked in silence, and Dan knew that his student was lost in thought. Dan just waited for the questions that he knew would come in time.

As they walked Dancing Wind turned to Dan and said *"What am I to do? My friends are no longer with me; I am afraid that you, too, will leave me."*

Dan smiled at his student and he told her *"Not every trail will you have companions along to help you. Sometimes in life, there are very tough paths that one must walk alone. Certainly you have picked a difficult trail to track."*

"Well then, you pick a better trail for me to track," she told Dan. Dan told her he could not do that as this was her path.

Dan told Dancing Wind, *"You have picked this trail. I cannot pick another trail for you."*

They walked in silence for a few minutes and then Dan asked her, *"Tell me about the women."*

Dancing Wind replied, *"I do not see any women around us."* Dan told her to reach out with her senses and locate the women.

A few minutes later Dancing Wind told Dan, *"I do not detect any women—I would have to lie to you to say I know about them—and I can not lie to you."* Dancing Wind walked over to Dan and he held her in his arms as they hugged each other. Then Dan told Dancing Wind to start over and find the woman. Dancing Wind began again, putting a white light of protection around herself. Then she asked GOD for a golden light of protection and then finally a violet or indigo light of protection to flow all around and about them.

Dancing Wind said, *"There is the couple who were murdered in their car. It was a senseless murder. The two men murdered the couple who were on a drive to have sex simply because they were there and they felt like murdering someone."*

Dan replied, *"You need to move further east."*

Dancing Wind said, *"The young teenage girl who is coughing up blood?"*

"No not her," Dan replied, *"she is an imprint; her spirit has already gone home."*

"There are the Mexican outlaws in the canyon kind of north of us," Dancing Wind said.

"Not them. How about the two woman murdered near here? When were they murdered?" *"Say around 1900-1920."*

Dancing Wind replied, *"I have them now. Their hands are bound in rope, tied tightly in front of them. They were kidnapped! The first was about 1895; they were kept here as a slave and for sex, then they later murdered her.*

The second was kidnapped about 1908. Her husband was murdered and they stole his cows. It is the same manner of tying her hands in front of her with rope."

Dan asked, *"Did the Mexican bandits in the canyon to the west have anything to do with their kidnapping and murder?"*

Dancing Wind replied, *"It is the same two Mexicans who kidnapped her; they later murdered her, too. It was not the Mexican bandits who are further west and north of us in that canyon--these are different ones. The larger group of Mexican bandits had nothing to do with kidnapping the two women."*

Dan asked Dancing Wind, *"Where are the Indians that have been watching you for awhile, and they are watching and observing us now?"*

"I do not know where they are hiding," Dancing Wind replied, *"I feel they are watching us, but I do not know from where."* She added, *"The Indians are not up on the mountain peaks of Cañada del Oro, as there are three priests up there. There is no love lost between the Native Americans and the priests."*

Dan said, *"Where are the Indians?"*

"I do not know," Dancing Wind said, *"There are three Indians to the southeast of the high mountain—they fell to their deaths making the Spanish Markers on the cliffs above them."*

"Where are the three trackers or treasure hunters that beat you here first?" Dan asked.

"They are on the northeast side of the mountain. It looks to me like the first three Spanish death traps that they encountered put the treasure hunters all into spirit," Dancing Wind replied.

Dan said, *"As you track these slopes, how many Spanish or outlaw caches (treasures) are here in the Coronado National Forest?"*

"Here total or here now?"

"Here now."

She said, *"There are six caches here now."*

Dan asked, *"Can you recover them?"*

Dancing Wind replied: *"That there are six caches currently here, I am positive. That I can recover them is a different story. Some are not for me—so they are not a trail I am to track. Some are too difficult for me to recover. Certainly the cache that the stone shelter bird speaks of would be very difficult to recover. The Mexican outlaw cache would be of great difficulty—they (the outlaw spirits) would tag team me like those wrestlers on TV. One spirit would slam me and just as I was knocked off balance another would slam me. That is a treasure I will certainly pass on. The other Spanish cache on the cliff to the west is awfully deep for me to dig a hole—besides there are traps on the way down. I guess I will pass on that one, too."*

Dan asked, *"Where are the Indians?"*

"I do not know," Dancing Wind replied.

Then Dan asked, *"Where are the two woman's spirits?"*

Dancing Wind replied, *"To the northwest, by the water."*

"By the caves?"

"Yes by the caves. They got water from the spring," she said.

Dan said: *"This was a remote area a century ago. There were a lot of outlaws and not very nice people here then. Where is the cattle rustler?"*

"By the corral."

He asked, *"How did he die?"*

Dancing Wind paused, then she said, *"Give me a couple minutes."* Dancing Wind used this time to talk with her Guardian Angel and she asked her Angel the questions she anticipated that Dan was going to be asking her shortly. Then she said, *"His name was Juan Poncho Hernandez Cabez de Vaca. He had come into this area as a cattle rustler to make the easy money which results when you steal other people's cows and then resell them at a profit. Juan had been holding the cows together by the water hole while his partners found a buyer for the stolen cattle. When the buyer was found and the cattle sold the four cattle rustlers were paid six silver coins. This presented a problem dividing the loot, as they did not know how to divide the six silver coins among four men. One outlaw realized the solution so that each outlaw would get man two coins each. The gang leader simply walked behind Juan Poncho Hernandez Cabez de Vaca as he sat around the fire and shot him in the head, killing him. Now there were two silver coins for each outlaw. For over two centuries Juan Poncho Hernandez Cabez de Vaca's spirit stayed by his campfire, watching over the cattle in Cañada del Oro. Juan did not realize he was dead, nor did he understand how to go home."*

Dan said, *"Look east; out near Catalina Highway: Where is the woman?"*

"Northeast of the shelter."

"Why has she not been found?"

"She is buried!" After a moment's pause she added, *"Less than two feet deep."*

"How old is she?"

"In her upper twenties, close to thirty."

Dan asked, *"Who murdered her?"*

"One or two men in a high raised up truck; with big wide tires," she said. *"They murdered her near the shelter / within sight of the shelter, and then dumped her body."* A moment later, Dancing Wind added, *"They came back and reburied her."*

Dan's questions jumped to the mountain tops of Cañada del Oro, *"Why do you call the priests Jesuits?"*

"Their arrogance," she replied, *"they helped the Spanish hide their gold and then they hid the gold they mined at the same site, and used the Spanish death traps to protect their treasure site too. The Jesuits could recover their gold whenever they wanted and take all the Spaniards' gold, too, if they wanted. The Jesuits just did not count on the ruthlessness of the Spanish in double-crossing the priest and murdering them too!*

"The Spanish were Catholics, so the Jesuits did not believe the Catholics that were in their congregation and prayed in the church with them would commit an act of treachery like murdering hundreds of priests throughout all of Central America, Mexico and New Spain. They underestimated King Charles of Spain's

greed and the treachery towards their good fathers, the priests. They never believed the king would order their arrest and torture."

"How many ways do you have out of here?" Dan asked.

"Two," Dancing Wind replied.

"Do you have a line of supply?"

"Yes," replied Dancing Wind.

"Do you have a cache of food and water?" He asked.

"North of here, at the junction of Forest Trail numbers two and four," Dancing Wind replied.

Dan asked: *"Are the priests who are watching us in brown robes?"*

"Yes," Dancing Wind replied.

"Are their heads shaved?"

"How am I supposed to know if the three priests, two thousand, five hundred yards away from us have shaved heads under their robes?" Dancing Wind replied in frustration.

Dan patiently replied, *"Just look!"*

Dancing Wind replied, *"I do not know."*

Dan calmly replied, *"Their heads are shaved,"* then, *"if your escape through Cañada del Oro to the north is blocked, what is your back up?"*

"I have a cache by the junction of the Forest Trail number 24 and Forest Trail number 72 on Sabino Canyon," Dancing Wind replied.

Dan asked: *"Then you can head east or south?"*

"Yes, I can head east or south as well as west or north," she replied.

"Do you have food and water there?" Dan asked.

She said, *"I prepositioned three gallons of water, and five MRE's (meals ready to eat)."*

"Why do you call them Jesuits?" Dan asked.

Dancing Wind replied that *"The only priests I have ever heard of are Jesuits or Franciscans, and the three German priests who we took home. (The German priest story is told in The Treasure of Francisco Martinez.) I just never heard of other priests being here two- and three centuries ago."*

Dan replied, "*The priests up on that mountain are Dominican priests.*"

She said, "*I will take your word for it, since I certainly would not know the difference. All I can tell is their energy levels are a lot higher than anything I have ever encountered, so I would like to avoid them.*"

"*You are correct about them having a very high energy level,*" Dan said.

Dan asked: "*So where are you planning to look up upon Cañada del Oro?*"

"*There are four slot canyons, running east to west. The northerly slot canyon is number one while the southern most slot canyon would be number four.,*" Dancing Wind replied, "*I was planning on looking in the second, third, or fourth slot canyon.*"

Dan asked: "*Where are the Dominican priests on that mountain?*"

Dancing Wind replied: "*In the first slot canyon.*"

"*Where is the treasure up there on the mountain?*" Dan asked.

Dancing Wind replied, "*In the first slot canyon.*"

Dan then asked her: "*Then why are you planning to look in the second, third or fourth slot canyons?*"

"*I was trying to avoid the priest! I think there is no love lost between us! I did not especially want to go into the first slot canyon or the three priests may lift me up and carry me over to the cliff's edge and give me a free flying lesson off the high cliff!*"

Dan told Dancing Wind: "*Here is what you do: First, constantly keep a solid white light of protection around you; second, make a handmade wooden cross and always carry it with you. As you hand-make the cross, ask GOD to fill it full of his unconditional love. Third, since they are priests, remind them of the 10 directives. Ask them if they follow the ten directives of the Lord. You know the one, if they are a little slow… 'Thou Shall Not Kill.'*"

And so, as the teacher and his student sat in Cañada del Oro, they discussed the numerous trails that were available for Dancing Wind to track. Dan told her,

"*The man who wants to go with you and you have in the back of your mind, does not have any dignity nor honor. The only reason he wants to go with you is to steal anything you should recover. Because he and his friends have no integrity, they will shoot or knife you in the back!"* Dancing Wind talked about tracking the two women with their hands bound in front of them, as well as the woman who was murdered by some evil people along the Catalina Highway at the camping sites. They talked about the lion and how the mountain lion had already made his choice. Dan spoke of the evening that Dancing Wind walked back to her Jeep as the sun set.

"The lion was within seconds of making his kill," he told her, *"You were his prey."* They talked about the sheer cliffs she must climb to get up to where the eagles fly, and they spoke of the choices one made in life.

Dan hugged his student as he told her that these were not his trails. Sadly, Dancing Wind knew that if she was to track these trails, that her dear teacher would not accompany her. Tears ran down Dancing Wind's face as she realized that if she continued upon this trail, that it was hers to track alone.

Throughout the day, the teacher and his tracking student walked. Sometimes there was a steady stream of questions; sometimes there was thirty minutes to an hour of silence as Dancing Wind was lost in her thoughts. Dan was simply enjoying the silence, giving his student time to sort out her thoughts and questions in her mind. With the coming of nightfall, they made a camp and built a small campfire. Then, as they sat around the campfire, the barrage of questions began.

"Should I joke with the priests when I arrive at their side? Should I tell them 'Boy, I am sure happy I found you,'?" Dancing Wind asked,

"I would not joke around with the priest at first; maybe later on," Dan replied.

"If I track the woman who was murdered at the camp site, can I ask her spirit to help me track her?"

"Of course you can ask her for her help," Dan replied.

"*Should I take her home?*" Dancing Wind asked.

Dan said, "*You can take it one step at a time. Why don't you find her first?*"

"*Ok,*" his student replied, "*Then I will find the two women who were kidnapped. I am sure the spirits of the men who did it will be there too.*"

"*So far you are fine,*" Dan said.

"*I am going to piss those two kidnappers off,*" Dancing Wind replied.

Dan said, "*That's ok; you will be doing them a favor when you piss them off---though they will not realize it.*"

"*Are you overlooking something?*" Dan asked.

"*What?*"

"*What sometimes live in caves?*"

Dancing Wind replied, "*I guess I forgot the cat for a moment.*"

"*When you run into the kidnapped women—your guard may come crashing down like the flood of tears on your cheeks, but you cannot let your guard down— you must be tuned to your Spirit Guide. You must be aware that the lion could be in the cave or returning to the cave. So the lion may attack you from the front or your back.*"

Dan then asked Dancing Wind, "*What are you going to do about the cattle rustler?*" For as Dancing Wind, Molly and Sarah explored these trails they often encountered the spirits or ghosts of the men and women who had died here over the centuries. So with tracking the trails came the obligation to help the spirits who would accept their help, and choose to go *home*. Certainly not all the spirits here were friendly. Nor would all the spirits choose to go home. So Dancing Wind accepted the reality that the spirits she would help would be the spirits who would be open to love and light, peace and unity. These spirits would be the ones who chose to leave this reality and enter GOD's house (heaven).

So after thinking about her reply for a few minutes, Dancing Wind told Dan, "*I figure that every time I walk by his camp I will invite Juan to accompany me. The two reasons why I will do this are that, by inviting Juan to travel with me, I want to gain Juan's trust over time and then I hope I will be able to help him return home. Juan now knows that I am here tracking and so to hold his interest as we walk together I will discuss tracking, as well as cattle, the grass, the weather and water with him so I can hold his interest as we spend time together."*

"*What are you going to do about the Mexican outlaw gang?*" Dan asked.

"*Pray for them, like the ocean waves crashing on a sandy beach, I will be asking GOD to let wave after wave of Divine Love to wash over them and through them and fill them to over flowing,*" Dancing Wind replied.

"*What are you going to do about their loot?*" Dan asked.

She said, "*Sometimes you can help spirits; sometimes you have to walk. Sometimes a spirit will work with you, like the three women—so I will go out of my way to help them, but those Mexican bandits will attack me and try to hurt me, so I will leave them there, and their loot with them. I am certainly not going to force my will upon them. Should they choose to go home, I will certainly call in some Angels to help them follow that path.*

"*I am sorry, Dan. I am sorry if I get cynical. I will help them if I can, and if they are willing to accept my help; but that is where I will draw the line.*"

Dan replied: "*You are doing fine kid; I will certainly never pick up a stone and throw it at you.*" (The conversation was referring to a passage in the Bible about the crowd wanted to stone a prostitute as she had committed a sin. Jesus said: "The man whom was without any sin to come forward and he could cast the first stone." Since no man was without sin, no one threw a stone at the woman). So what Dancing Wind was saying what that she was cynical about the Mexican bandits and she did not think she would be able to help them go *home*.

Dan was replying that he was not going to criticize his students decision nor say she was making any mistake in her actions by not doing more to try and help the Mexican bandits, as he knew, as well, that they would do their best to violently attack Dancing Wind should she get very near their hideout.

"Sometimes when we track a trail, we can help the spirit; sometimes there are trails like the Mexican bandits or the Apache where I see no path to follow other than to walk away. Good intentions will not cut it with the bandits, nor the Apache, so I will walk away. It is not my path to track that trail."

Dan then asked Dancing Wind about the murdered couple. *"What are you going to do about the lovers, the man and the woman (male and female spirits) whom came (drove to a remote location) to have sex?"*

Dancing Wind replied, *"They will be in my prayers. They will have several months to decide."* The wood in their campfire had burned down to reddish and gray coals. Occasionally, Dancing Wind or Dan added a small stick.

Dan spoke to his student, *"What are you going to do about the Indians?"*

Dancing Wind flashed a quick smile and said, *"As you know, the Indians are already in my prayers. Every night I ask the Great Spirit, who moves through all things, to let wave after wave of unconditional love to wash over them throughout the night. Like the gentle waves washing up on a sandy beach, I ask GOD to have wave after wave of unconditional love wash over, around and through the Indians until it fills their spirits to overflowing. Then I ask for wave after wave of honor to wash over them and fill them to overflowing. Then I pray for wave after wave of integrity to wash over them and fill them to overflowing. Then I ask for wave after wave of courage to wash over them throughout the night. Then I pray that wave after wave of unity wash over them and fill their hearts. Then I ask for wave after wave of joy to wash over them, filling their spirits to overflowing. I will take them home, of course. I think they are ready to go."*

"You know you will have to find them," Dan said.

Dancing Wind flashed a longer smile, and then replied, "Will I? You know it is very difficult for me to find one or even a hundred spirits or ghosts who choose to hide from me."

"Well what do you plan to do?" Dan asked.

Dancing Wind was quiet for a moment lost in thought, then a sly grin formed across her face which turned into a smile, and she replied mischievously: *"I figure that the Native American Indians have been watching me for weeks now. They are perfectly capable of reading both my thoughts and intentions, so they know exactly what I am planning."* Dancing Wind replied with a smile, *"I will just say: ALLY ALLY IN COME FREE—Ally ally in come free! --Then they will come out of the gullies, washes, boulders and mountains they have been hiding behind as they watched me all these weeks."*

Dan doubled over with laughter.

"So that leaves one final question," Dan said, *"What are you going to do with the Dominican priests?"*

Dancing Wind replied: *"I am not going to do anything to them; I will simply track the trails where they lead. Then I will point out their options to the Dominican priests. What options the priests will choose to take is up to them. The option I hope they take will be to travel the path of the Angels, for that is where I feel they really belong. But I suspect they will want to ensure I keep my promise to them, and that is ok, too. I kind of feel that they will be much more willing to travel with the Angels after they travel with me awhile. Besides, I plan to pull a trick on them—I will tell them they need to accompany me to ensure I completely keep my promise to them—and as they will have suspicions and doubts in the back of their minds, they will follow me everywhere to ensure I keep my promise.*

"See, by following me they will have to leave their mountain—and so after they see I keep my promise to them, well, they will just have three options left to them: the first option is to go back to an empty mountain, and there is no point of being there any longer. The second option is to follow an imperfect woman, me, all day, and how long do you think three priests will really enjoy doing that? Finally, the third option I will point out to them is to follow The Path of the Angels."

Dan smiled at his student, he liked her logic.

And so night fell around the Lakota Indian and the Arapaho teenager he was teaching to track. In the morning they walked towards the east as Dan's old diesel pickup was parked along the Catalina highway. Dan invited Dancing Wind for breakfast. They ate breakfast in silence. A quiet sadness had come over Dancing Wind, as she knew that this trail was hers alone to track.

She knew where the slot canyons were. She knew where the Dominican priests would be standing, on the high escarpments of the rugged gray cliffs of the slot canyons, as they watched and waited for her arrival. For the priests knew on which days she was hiking out towards their mountain. For the next four months the priests' spirits would always be at the same location looking down on the teenager as she tracked the ancient trails towards them.

★★★★

"God help us," they prayed every day, "Why did you send an Indian woman here?" Possibly GOD just has a sense of humor. Certainly the Indian spirits hiding nearby watching Dancing Wind as she tracked the trail into the first slot canyon thought it was funny. For certainly the Indian spirits hiding nearby) could read *all* the priests' thoughts.

At dawn on the second day of February with climbing gear in her back pack, Dancing Wind climbed up into the high mountain peaks of Cañada del Oro. Removing her climbing gear and rope, she slowly climbed up into the highest peaks where the eagles and hawks' nested. As she climbed into the first slot canyon, she removed a handmade wooden cross she had made out of a piece of 2" X 6" redwood. The wooden cross was about eight inches tall and 5 ½" wide. The arms of the cross were about 1 ½ inches each. Before her was an empty slot canyon, or it had that appearance, until suddenly, before Dancing Wind's eyes, the spirits of three Dominican priests suddenly materialized out of thin air.

None of the priests were very happy about the appearance of the Arapaho teenage girl who appeared in their sanctuary. There were no smiles, handshakes or greetings. To remove her from their mountain would not be an easy task; especially as she held the white light of protection firmly around her.

Dancing Wind looked at the three priests then she picked up her cross and turning to the Priest said "Maybe you can help me with the Lord's Prayer for I am a little rusty." Then, to the priests' surprise she began:

"My Father, Most Holy is your name. May your kingdom come to us now; as it has already come to us in Heaven. Forgive me and my partners here of our sins; and help us not to mess up and sin too often…"

The priests shook their heads sadly; she sure needed a lot of work, if she was even going to come close to the proper words in the Lord's Prayer.

"GOD help us!" the priests prayed.

When the prayers ended, Dancing Wind carefully replaced the cross inside her backpack and then removed her digital camera. Placing the backpack with the wooden cross back upon her shoulders, Dancing Wind slowly moved through the canyon with her camera as she captured the slot canyon in dawns breaking light. She captured the images and shadows from every possible angle as the sun played across the canyon walls. Then she captured the skyline from within the slot canyon, and finally she climbed to the highest adjacent peak and captured the slot canyon from above.

Every hour she repeated this sequence of photographing the slot canyon from every possible angle. These photos would be developed and plastered upon her living room and bedroom walls as she attempted to track the century's old trail of the padres. The trail was approximately two centuries old. The Padres had left Dancing Wind eleven doors in the slot canyon leading to ancient but fully operational death traps. It was the twelfth door, which the padres had carefully concealed, that Dancing Wind sought. For it was within the twelfth door that the Dominicans had concealed the wealth acquired from the secret mining operations the church had conducted. It was this wealth that the Dominican priests' spirits watched over and the reason they remained earth-bound.

And so began the first day of many months, the Dominican priests and the Indian teenage tracker would spend in the mountains. They would often try each other's patience. The priests would point out the eleven different doors, and Dancing Wind would simply walk by the death traps, which she had no interest in entering. She would question them about their motives for trying to lure her into the eleven doors they had shown her. They often got angry with each other. The priest wanted the Indian girl to give up and leave their mountain, but Dancing Wind was determined to break the codes of the priests and enter the twelfth stone door. It was her persistence and her ability to recognize a 3, 4, 5 right triangle that finally enabled Dancing Wind to locate the concealed entrance into the twelfth stone door. The entrance to the twelfth door was under a boulder marking the position of the ninety degree angle of the 3, 4, 5 right triangle.

Once Dancing Wind was able to find the twelfth stone door, she had to remove a boulder which stood over top the opening. The boulder weighed one thousand pounds! It was nine times heavier than Dancing Wind! The priest smiled, as they knew that the lone Indian girl would never be able to move a one thousand pound boulder.

Two days later, Dancing Wind returned to the mountain with a Come-A-Long and some wire cables. As Dancing Wind began laying out the Come-A-Long, the wire cables and slings, the priesst were filled with mixed emotions. They first felt anger at the fact that she had figured out a method of entering their twelfth door, yet they also admired her persistence and her logic in overcoming insurmountable obstacles. The half-ton boulder required a Come-A-Long attached to a sling around the boulder, so as to enable her to remove the stone boulder which blocked the door. After removing the boulder and moving it about ten feet from the entrance, she faced the next task of digging down one meter to the stone door entrance. The entrance consisted of a solid stone door fitted into a rock frame.

Uncovering the stone door brought a smile to the Arapahoe girl's face. She just knew that she had properly broken the codes of the Pictographs her people used centuries ago, for there were two shadow Eagles guiding her to the position the boulder had sat. Then there was the turtle facing the stone. There were two small "U" notches directing her also to the same spot. She had also seen the face of Janus from Greek mythology glancing towards a shovel made of stone. The ten foot tall stone shovel was positioned as if to dig up the boulder. Below her was a fifteen foot shaft dug into solid rock. Dropping down the shaft, she observed a treasure chest ten feet down into the tunnel. Here Dancing Wind encountered the first death trap in this tunnel. The three Dominican priests watched Dancing Wind to see if she would remove any of the chunks of high-grade wire gold ore or bars of silver, which they had placed inside the small treasure chest. Instead of reaching for the high grade gold or silver bars, Dancing Wind instead looked for a position to block the trap from working with a 4 X 4 piece of timber. Using one of her Pursiks, she measured the correct length of the timber to prevent the trap from activating; then she placed a knot in the pursik's at the proper length. Then using four additional pursik's she slowly climbed out of the shaft. Leaving the slot canyon, she walked the trails back to Tucson as she would have to cut a 4 X 4 timber the correct length, to block the first trap.

Had Dancing Wind removed any of the rich gold ore or silver bars from the treasure chest, the trap would have killed her like a mouse trap when the mouse takes the cheese. By blocking the death trap with a 4 X 4, she was preventing the trap from working.

Upon Dancing Wind's return, she blocked the first death trap and descended to the bottom of the ancient stone shaft. In the bottom of the shaft she was faced with her second life-or-death test. Before her were two tunnels: one tunnel headed south. This tunnel was wide and clear and had a treasure chest in plain view of her million candle-power spotlight. The second tunnel, to the north, seemed to run about five or six feet and was piled high with old mining timbers and digging tools. Dancing Wind remembered Dan telling her, "When one makes life-or-death decisions, should you have the opportunity, ask the Angels for their advice." And so Dancing Wind sat down and prayed and then, after completing her prayers, she asked her Guardian Angel for advice, while the three Dominican priests stood beside the teenage girl, watching her . Dancing Wind's Guardian Angel told her charge to move carefully North into the alcove where the tools and timbers were stored. The Angel told her never to go into the second tunnel, as it was a trap designed to kill all intruders.

As Dancing Wind moved carefully into the small adit where the timbers and digging tools were stored, she was faced with a solid stone wall in front of her. Standing with a wall in front of her, Dancing Wind looked to her right at the Angel standing beside her. The Angel told Dancing Wind to open the stone wall. In front of Dancing Wind, the wall appeared to be solid, but if her guardian Angel told her to open it she intended to open the rock wall. Looking for levers or something to pull or grab, there was nothing. Dancing Wind then began systematically pushing against the wall from as high as she could reach, moving from left to right. Suddenly Dancing Wind fell forward as the wall began pivoting. The solid stone wall contained a stone door shaped like an oblong egg which pivoted on a top and bottom socket. As she opened the stone door, a portion of the wall opened, giving an eighteen inch opening into the hidden room. Blocking the door open with an old piece of timber from the adit she was in, Dancing Wind moved into the concealed chamber. Inside was a room carved out of solid rock about 15 X 15 feet. There before her, stacked in a row along one wall she saw hundreds of black bars. Each black metal bar was about one inch square by a foot long. Upon every bar was the church cross. Walking over to the bars, she lifted one up. Yes! They were heavy like she thought. She removed her knife and scratched the metal bar and the black coating of tarnish gave way to a bright silver color! Before her was a treasure of silver! She placed five of the small, silver finger bars of silver into her back pack. Then she headed out of the tunnel with her treasure.

For months, Dancing Wind hiked the trail and then climbed the cliff face into the first slot canyon. During the first month her backpack was heavier going in than coming out. For the next three months, her back pack was always thirty pounds heavier when she walked out than when she hiked in. Finally the day came when Dancing Wind and the three Dominican priests sat down for a long talk, as Dancing Wind came to lay out their options.

"Since there are three of you here, I have left each of you three small 1 X 1 X 12 finger bars of metal (silver). I have left it here to show you I am not affected by an overwhelming greed for money or silver. You can stay here and watch it for a couple more centuries if you like – it is simply one of your choices. Another choice is to follow me off this mountain. Now if you follow me—and it is your choice, of course-- you can ensure I keep my word to you that 25% of everything I have taken off this mountain goes to feed the poor or goes to charity. If I start to slip up you will be there to show me how to walk a camel through the eye of a needle (…it is harder to get through the gates of heaven than to walk a camel through the eye of a needle-Bible). If you don't go with me, you will always be wondering how many dresses and pairs of shoes I purchased with your bars of silver, but if you tag along with me, you can always explain the finer points of feeding the poor to me, or how Jesus fed the people when he gave the Sermon on the Mount."

When Dancing Wind left the high mountain peaks in Cañada del Oro, three Dominican Priests followed her off the mountain. As Dancing Wind hiked towards her Jeep parked in Tucson, she glanced behind her at the three priests walking behind her. Smiling to herself, she started to hum a song called *Green Sleeves*.

★★★★

As Dancing Wind walked out of Cañada del Oro, the mountain lion watched from his vantage point among the high cliffs. He knew the path she took towards her Jeep, for he had followed her many times. He had selected his ambush point along the trail to catch the lone Indian girl by surprise as he sprung his ambush. The cat silently crept into his ambush position. He heard her singing a tune, but this time she was not alone as the mountain lion had expected. Beside the skinny Indian girl, there were three big priests singing *Green Sleeves* along with her. One of the priests carried a rifle. Although the lion would not have realized the rifle was a wheel lock rifle that was made four centuries earlier, the lion did realize the danger that a hunter with a rifle represented. The mountain lion quietly slipped away to avoid the man with the rifle.

★★★★

Ninety days later

Dancing Wind was walking east along the shores of Padre Island, Texas. The island is a vacation spot for thousands of people. There are shipwrecks here and occasionally a Spanish coin is found along the sandy beaches which stretch for miles. She walked on the firm sand, which was moist from the sea water as the waves washed ashore. The waves frequently washed over their feet as they walked. As Dancing Wind walked along the beach, three Dominican padres accompanied her. Then a sly, crooked smile crossed her face as she listened to the advice of the angel beside her, for it was upon the advice of the Angels she had come to walk upon the lonely sandy beach.

Dancing Wind turned to the priests and asked them a question whose answer she already knew.

"Have I kept my word to you?" She asked the three Dominican priests. They replied, "You have kept both the spirit and the letter of your promise to us."

Then Dancing Wind broke into the last song she would ever sing with her friends. Dancing Wind began singing "Oh God Beautiful" by Paramansanda Yoganda as the padres sang along with her. As they finished the song praising GOD, Dancing Wind asked the Padres how baptisms go, and the three priests happily immersed Dancing Wind in the ocean surf. Then Dancing Wind turned to the three priests: one at a time she immersed the three priests in the ocean water.

As she lifted the first priest's head out of the water, she asked "Can you see the light now of the Holy Spirit?"

But he never replied, as the padre was already gone; he sped down the white tunnel of light. The second padre then let Dancing Wind immerse him in the ocean surf. When she asked him if he could see the light of the Holy Spirit, he was already gone as well. The oldest and wisest of the Dominican Padres knew that Dancing Wind had called in the Angels from heaven. He had tears running down his cheeks as he walked up to Dancing Wind. But instead of immediately allowing the teenage girl to immerse him in the sea water, he reached out and circled his arms around her back as he gave her a hug. Then he whispered into her ear: "Vio Con Dios Mi Amiga." (Go With God My Friend) Dancing Wind hugged the elder priest then immersed his head under the water. Then she again said: "Can you see the Holy Spirit?" But the priest was already gone. One of the two Angels of the Lord turned to the teenager and said

"Well done."

The Angel smiled at Dancing Wind and she flashed a return smile to the two Angels. Then, in a flash, the two Angels of the Lord were gone. Dancing Wind was then alone on the beach. She heard the waves crashing ashore all around her. Dancing Wind felt so…at peace.

Dancing Wind walked out of the surf and turned back, walking towards the hotels and the condominiums whose lights she saw in the distance. The water dripped off her wet body and clothes. The sand covered her bare feet. She felt the cool ocean breeze on her body under her wet clothes on her bare skin. As she walked along the beach, she looked over the ocean and she could see the red, green and white lights of the fishing boats offshore. The stars were coming out to grace the firmament of the night sky. As Dancing Wind walked along the sandy beach she thought,

"One down; by GOD's grace she had five more trips to make back into Cañada del Oro."

★★★★

Dawn, four weeks later found Dancing Wind hiking into the canyon known as Cañada del Oro. She hiked to a large flat stone over one hundred feet wide by one hundred feet long, to the East of the mountain where she had been working. There she sat down on the big flat stone and said her prayers, asking for the help of the Angels. Then she asked GOD to surround herself and the area about her with a White Light of Protection. Then she took sticks of incense and placed them about in the pattern of a large circle. In the center of the huge flat stone she lit three candles. Next, she lit the incense and then she smudged herself with sweet grass and sage. Then Dancing Wind sat down upon the immense flat stone and slowly started drumming. The sound of the drum carried all across and around Cañada del Oro.

Then, speaking loudly, she hollered for all the spirits to hear: "Ally ally in come free! Ally ally in come free!"(from a children's game of hide and seek she played when she was a little girl) This she repeated three times, for Dancing Wind wanted the Indians to come into her circle.

Certainly the words Dancing Wind said did not actually mean anything in the language of the Native American Indians, but they fully understood her intent and her pure heart. As the Indians came out of hiding, she greeted them and welcomed them into her circle.

Slowly at first, several Indians came out of their hiding locations from which they had watched Dancing Wind for many months. Gradually more and more Indians appeared, walking towards the circle. Slowly Dancing Wind drummed on her old wooden and leather drum which had been a gift from her old and dear friend and teacher Dan, to give all who wished to return *home* time to arrive. Soon, Indians began arriving into her circle from all directions. Some of the spirits who had been crushed as they were forced to make the giant stone images for the Spanish, were dragged by their family or friends into the circle. Some of the Indian spirits were carried into the circle. Elders and mothers with infants also began to approach as they arrived from the directions of the four winds.

For an hour Dancing Wind drummed and when an Angel told her that all were here she asked the spirits to form a circle. Dancing Wind then asked the spirits to move around her in a large circle as she drummed.

Dancing Wind drummed very slowly at first and then she gradually sped up. Dancing Wind drummed on as The Wind Spirits arrived and her hair blew into her face. The Rain Spirits arrived and soaked the dry earth and Dancing Wind drummed on. The Lightning Spirits played across the sky and Dancing Wind drummed on. Then the two angels of the Lord arrived and between them was a door of light. As the Native American Indians danced around the circle, first this Indian or that Indian, a child or a crippled man looked into the light of the tunnel leading to heaven. Their infirmities, injuries, pain, and uncertainty instantly disappeared and the spirits flew down the tunnel into their loved ones' arms. Dancing Wind saw the last of her guests enter the tunnel of light. The Angel on each side of the door entered the tunnel and instantly they were gone. Dancing Wind stopped drumming and placed her drum inside her backpack. She removed a bottle of water and drank from it. The rain came in sheets and washed over her. She smiled to the Rain Spirits, the Wind Spirits, and the Lightning Spirits and thanked them for coming.

Dancing Wind walked through the rain towards her car, which was parked along the Catalina Highway. As she walked along the muddy trail, her boots got heavy with the mud. For hours she walked through the mud as she hiked towards her car. Sometimes she slipped and fell. Her body became covered in mud from her falls. I am tired, she thought. I am so very tired. When she finally reached her Jeep she was unrecognizable, as she was covered in mud from slipping and falling on the trail out of the mountains. She drove home to where she was staying. When she got back to her room, her muddy clothes fell onto the bathroom floor. She took a hot shower and got into some dry clothes. After walking into her bedroom she collapsed in exhaustion, falling face first on top of her bed, asleep. She snored in peace upon her bed. Beside her, her Guardian Angel watched over her charge and smiled, turning her eyes upward towards heaven she simply said: "Thanks GOD; that was a beautiful lesson."

★★★★

Dancing Wind had been tracking the band of Mexican Outlaws for three weeks. In a steep, high-walled canyon she sat down a hundred yards from them. She would not approach any closer, as she did not want them to attack her. As a safety precaution, she kept a solid white light of protection around herself. By a large boulder near the center of the wash or dry arroyo, the outlaws stood facing her. The outlaws stayed near the boulder to watch over their stolen loot of gold, silver and paper money. The paper money had long ago rotted away. Had Dancing Wind approached any closer, they would have immediately taken overt hostile measures against her. Dancing Wind spoke aloud and clearly so there would be no misunderstanding, even though all the bandits could and did read her thoughts. Should any of you choose to go *home* I will help you. The men replied, saying not very nice things to her. Dancing Wind then got up to leave.

Her last words to the men were, "The door is always open should you choose to knock."

Then Dancing Wind walked away. She was never to see these spirits again and they had no interest in leaving their stolen loot. We are all trackers who must accept this fact sometimes you can help a spirit return *home*, sometimes the spirit wants nothing to do with you. As a tracker, you must accept the fact that sometimes you can help the individuals you encounter along the trails you travel. Sometimes individuals as well as spirits, want to be exactly where they are; doing exactly what they are doing. So as a tracker you must accept their choice and leave them alone.

★★★★

For a teenage girl going out for a walk she went pretty well-armed. Dancing Wind had a Glock semi-automatic on her right leg in a swat holster. The shell was in the chamber. The weapon was cocked and locked. With one finger she could remove the safety and fire. She had bear spray hanging off her left leg. She was wearing a light backpack andhad a shotgun hanging on a rapid-fire sling in front of her chest. In her pack she carried a metal detector, her lunch, and water. She had a bad attitude, as it had taken five weeks for her to work out the trail, but eventually her persistence had paid off and she had worked out the trail. In Cañada del Oro, she was going to the caves where two outlaws spirits hung out. She fully intended to piss them off, and she was pissed off enough she would enjoy what she was about to do, for she intended to steal the outlaw-kidnappers' stolen money, and that is why she brought along the metal detector. Even though she was mad as a hornet, she worked to keep a white light of protection around her. Constantly she turned to the Angel beside her for guidance as she did not want to blow this tactical assault she was making upon the kidnapper's stronghold. The kidnappers knew she was coming and they were waiting for her. For these kidnapers as ghost could easily read Dancing Wind's thoughts and intentions. When she approached their cave, the attack began. Both men ran towards her with knives drawn. Surprisingly, this woman showed no fear. Repeatedly they attacked her with their fist and knives as she walked into their camp. But the assaults against her failed as the men could not hit her through the white light of protection she kept around herself. The knives they used to attack her and try to slit her throat, and knife her in the back, as they had done murdering individuals before; simply would not penetrate the white light of protection she held around herself.

Outside the cave, the two terrified women watched the outlaws repeatedly attack the teenager. Both of the women had died in such a similar attack. The first woman was murdered about 1895. The second woman was also murdered by the caves about 1908. Both women were in Spirit, or what some individuals call ghosts. The women's fear of their murders and the violent attacks had so terrified the two women that they remained at the site where they had been murdered, yet as the two women's spirits watched in awe, none of their attacks by the assassins were effective. Their fists could not penetrate the white light she kept around her. In the middle of the knife attack the two women noticed the teenager turned and winked at them. Then suddenly there appeared a white light of protection around them, too. When the two outlaws and kidnappers were unable to hurt her, they retreated to the cave where they kept their loot.

When the men fled into the cave, Dancing Wind turned to the two women and told them;

I will be coming for you in a few minutes. Then she pumped a round into her shot gun and walked into the cave. Certainly, firing the shotgun at the two spirits would not have hurt them in the least. Dancing Wind was just being cautious about the mountain lion, should it be inside the cave. Cautiously examining the interior of the cave, Dancing Wind saw the two spirits standing on one side of the cave. Walking outside the cave, Dancing Wind picked up her metal detector. Scanning the caves interior, she got a reading at only one location— directly under the two kidnappers. Using her boot to kick the dirt at their feet, Dancing Wind bent down and removed a rotten leather pouch from the ground and dropped it into her front pocket. Then she scanned the site with the metal detector to see if there was not a second target. Her metal detector was silent. She had taken all the two men's loot, and in doing so she pissed them off.

Carefully walking out of the cave, Dancing Wind scanned the terrain around her carefully. For in the cave were the remains of many animals the mountain lion had killed and brought back to the cave to eat. As the tears ran down Dancing Wind's cheeks, she hugged each of the women's spirits. She told them there was no reason they need to stay here any longer. As she smiled at them she said,

"You saw them do their best to hurt me and they failed. They can't hurt you anymore. Follow me!" Then Dancing Wind walked away from the cave of the kidnappers, taking their loot with her in her front pocket. Beside her walked the two women who had been kidnapped in 1895 and 1908 and were later murdered at the cave.

As they walked through the mountains Dancing Wind said"They cannot hurt you anymore. It is time for you to let go of your anger and fear. You did nothing wrong," she told them. "It was not your fault that those two animals attacked and kidnapped you, and as long as you hold GOD's white light of protection around you they will never hurt you again."

As they walked Dancing Wind scanned the terrain for the mountain lion while she also listened to the three Angels walking beside her for their advice and suggestions.

To Melanie she said: "Your parents are waiting for you around the bend just ahead."

To Mary she said: "Your husband has been waiting a hundred years for your arrival."

The two women were in disbelief that their ordeal was finally over. Tears streamed down all three women's faces and suddenly in the trail just ahead of them they saw a golden tunnel or door. Melanie looked inside and saw her parents and she rushed into their arms. Mary saw her husband and as he called out to his beloved wife, she flew into his arms. Two Angels smiled at Dancing Wind, then as suddenly as they had appeared, without saying a single word, they were instantly gone.

Dancing Wind was alone as she walked south out of the mountains. As she arrived by her, car a homeless man stopped and asked if she could spare any money. Reaching into her pocked she pulled out a rotten leather pouch. She handed it to the homeless man. The man looked perplexed by the rotten leather pouch but he could feel the weight of something inside. As Dancing Wind walked on by, he hollered out thanks as the ancient coins spilled out of the leather pouch into his hands.

★★★★

A month later, Dancing Wind walked near the site where the couple of lovers had been murdered. In a clearing about two hundred yards away she lit three candles. Into her prayer circle she invited the couple who had been murdered years earlier, she invited the three treasure trackers (Señor Rivera and his two friends) who had died on the northwest side of the high mountain of Cañada del Oro and she also invited the two outlaws and kidnappers whose loot she had taken and given to a homeless man. As the sun set in the western sky, she asked them to join her in a prayer to the Lord. As Dancing Wind prayed, she poured out her heart to GOD that he spread his love and grace around her prayer circle and help her companions return home. She asked them to forgive those who had hurt them and let GOD's love fill their hearts. As the tears poured down Dancing Wind's cheeks she poured out her troubles, her fears, and worries to the Lord and she asked him for his help. As she ended her prayer and said amen, she looked up and there was no one at her prayer circle but herself, for the seven spirits had gone *home* with the Angels as Dancing Wind prayed. Across from Dancing Wind sat her Guardian Angel. As her attention focused upon her Guardian Angel, she said to Dancing Wind, "I think you handled it nicely."

★★★★

In the Catalina Mountains on the east side there are some camp sites / picnic areas and it was here that Dancing Wind could be found walking in the early morning hours and at sunset, for she was tracking a woman's spirit who had been murdered here. This trail was difficult for Dancing Wind to follow, so she had been asking the women to help track her too. The Spirit would have to guide her in to her. In a dry wash on the east side of the Catalina Highway, Dancing Wind found the hidden grave site of the murdered woman. When evening came, Dancing Wind returned and set flowers on the unmarked grave site. As she sat by the grave site, she relived the terror the woman experienced at the hands of the man who murdered her because she refused to have oral sex with him. He had ordered her at gunpoint to go down on him, and when she refused, he angrily put the gun to her head and pulled the trigger! No man has the right to murder another person. Dancing Wind said a prayer to God, asking for justice. She prayed that he send his angels to accompany this woman *home*. As Dancing Wind prayed out her heart to GOD, several Angels appeared and surrounded the murdered woman and poured their love upon her. She smiled at Dancing Wind and thanked her for taking the time to find her and help her return home. Dancing Wind smiled at her, and an instant later she was gone with the Angels who accompanied her. Dancing Wind then got up to walk back to her Jeep. A smile suddenly crossed her tear-streaked face, as she saw a tall Indian in cowboy boots, blue jeans and a leathery face with his gray hair wrapped in two braids running over his shoulders and down his back, leaning against her Jeep. She ran into Dan's open arms and as he hugged her, she cried.

Some Friends are Beyond Price;
Some Friendships are Beyond this Life;
Some Friends you have known in another time and place;
Some Friendships you have had in another Life!

Three Barrels: One Of Courage, One Of Honor, And One Of Integrity

O ne *Cheyenne and two Lakota* warriors were on top of the cliffs looking down upon the camp of the three teenage girls down by the river which ran below. The warriors seldom traveled this far to the north since their murders in 1680. They would not have been here, but for the Wind Spirits.

"*You may want to journey to the north along the Rio Grande and see if any warriors were traveling south along the Rio Grande towards you,*" The spirits said.

The three warriors' spirits listened to the Wind Spirits advice and within moments they were flying to the north, scanning the terrain to locate the warriors. In moments, they had traveled to the head waters of the Rio Grande in the San Juan Mountains. Not once did they see any Indian warriors. So the three Warriors stopped to talk on top of a tall mountain adjacent to the headwaters of the Rio Grande. Here, on top of the 13,821 foot-tall Rio Grande Pyramid, the warriors stopped to discuss their failure to discover the warriors. The warriors felt that in the sixty seconds they had spent searching the last hundred and twenty miles of river they certainly would have seen any party of Indian warriors traveling down the river to the south. (They had actually taken sixty seconds to search over four hundred and eighty square miles as their search path was four miles wide.) But the Lakota and Cheyenne spirits knew that the Wind Spirits would not have lied to them, so they searched the river a second time to find the Indian warriors. They found no Indian warriors approaching them! From Creede to just south of Santa Fe on the San Cristobal Pueblo, the Lakota and Cheyenne again searched for the Indian warriors.

South of Santa Fe, on the San Cristobal Indian pueblo, the three perplexed warriors discussed the events that had just occurred. They had failed to find any Indian warriors approaching them on the Rio Grande, even though the Wind Spirits had told them that they may want to journey to the north along the Rio Grande and see if any warriors were traveling south along the Rio Grande towards them. They had found no Indian warriors approaching from the north and yet the Wind Spirits told the three Native American Indian Spirits that warriors were approaching them, and the Wind Spirits would not lie to them. They did not understand how this could be so, so they asked the Wind Spirits again to repeat what they had told them.

The second time the Wind Spirits spoke to the Lakota and Cheyenne warrior's spirits they told them *"You may want to journey to the north along the Rio Grande and see if any warriors were traveling south along the Rio Grande towards you."*

Then the Wind Spirits added another sentence, *"We thought you have been looking all theses centuries for warriors with Courage, Honesty and Integrity. Now Courage, Honesty and Integrity are not found exclusively in one race of people; nor are these characteristics found only in males of a race and not females."*

The three warriors then realized their mistake and thanked the Wind Spirits for their help. This time, when they traveled to the north along the Rio Grande; they came to stop at the top of the rim of the Rio Grande Gorge and look down upon the camp of the three women.

★★★★

The Rio Grande River begins in the San Juan Mountains of southwestern Colorado. Then it flows through the center of the entire length of New Mexico. The Rio Grande continues along the southwest Texas border flowing from El Paso to Brownsville, where it flows into the Gulf of Mexico. The river flows through 1,885 miles of the American southwest providing her life giving water to the plants, animals and people. Few individuals realize what a precious gift Mother Nature provides with her life-giving water and even fewer take the time to thank Mother Nature or the Water Spirits before using the water. Most people take the right to use water and even waste the water, for granted. It was along this river that Sarah, Molly and Dancing Wind decided to take a vacation, canoeing and camping.

The three teenagers canoed along through the river past the steep canyon walls. As the sun sank low the three women found a place to make a camp and build a campfire out on a gravel sand bar along the river. They tied their canoe securely to the shore. Then Sarah and Molly set up their camp and rolled out their sleeping bags upon the brown canvas tarp. Meanwhile, Dancing Wind gathered fire wood with which she would build a fire. Then she started cooking the bratwurst. They fixed a dinner of brats, sauerkraut, mustard and tortillas. With the meal they enjoyed the life-giving water Mother Nature provides.

Around the campfire, as darkness engulfed the canyon, the three women talked about the events of the day and some of the challenges they encountered on trails they had tracked. Unknown to the three women, they were also being tracked by one Cheyenne and two Lakota spirit warriors.

★★★★

This was certainly not what they had been expecting—three teenage girls! If this was to be, then the GREAT SPIRIT certainly had a funny sense of humor! For over three hundred and twenty-five years, the warriors had waited and watched along the Rio Grande, expecting to see the arrival a war party of Lakota or Cheyenne warriors with courage, honor and integrity. After a hundred years had passed they decided they would settle for warriors of any tribe. After two hundred years of waiting and watching, the two Lakota and one Cheyenne warriors wondered if they would ever encounter the warriors they were seeking. Never did they think the Great Spirit would send women!

"This could not be—women!" The first Lakota warrior Fast Runner told his two companions, "I do not think they have the courage of a warrior."

So Fast Runner turned himself into a Snake. Fast Runner decided that a ten foot Rattle Snake would scare the women and send them fleeing. Sneaking up to the camp, the Rattle Snake positioned himself to strike Sarah. Rattling the rattles on his tail, Fast Runner knew the three women would be sent in scared flight.

Hearing the rattling of the enormous rattle snake posed to strike Sarah caused an immediate reaction all right; but certainly not the reaction Fast Runner now holding the form of a snake anticipated. Dancing Wind and Molly both immediately pulled Glocks from their holsters and they told Sarah to freeze.

Dancing Wind told Sarah and Molly they would fire on 'three'.

"Sarah," Dancing Wind said, "when we fire you run."

Molly told Dancing Wind, "I am ready."

Dancing Wind rapidly said, "One, Two, Three!"

Both Glocks fired simultaneously, and over a period of two seconds, six 9 mm rounds flew to the location of where the head of a snake had been, but it was nowhere to be found. The snake had simply vanished!

Sarah stopped running as soon as she reached her backpack. After grabbing the Glock out of her pack she pulled the slide back and chambered a round. Immediately she used her index finger to push the safety off. Within seconds of having reached her Glock, she pivoted around and brought her Glock up to aim where the snake had been only a moment before. To her surprise, where she had just seen the snake, now nothing was there! This she could not understand; one second she had been facing death and the second the weapons discharged there was nothing there. Dancing Wind and Molly carefully scanned the area about them. It was as if the snake had never existed! Dancing Wind was the first to actually say what she thought.

"It must have been a spirit holding the form or thought form of a snake for I do not see the dead snake, or even any tracks of the snake on the sandy shoreline by our camp," Dancing Wind said.

★★★★

On top of the cliff, the two warriors' spirits were rolling in laughter as Fast Runner instantly materialized beside them.

"I see they passed your test of Courage! But tell me again Fast Runner; were you showing us how fast they would run when you scared them or showing us how fast you can run when the two women pulled the Glocks and began firing at you?" Red Fox told Fast Runner.

Fast Runner's face turned redder than the dark red it normally was, as he was embarrassed at how he had clearly underestimated the courage of the three teenage girls. All three warriors agreed the three teenagers had passed Fast Runners test of Courage.

Strong Bear decided he, too, would test the women's courage for himself. That night after the teenagers were fast asleep, Strong Bear took the form of a Grizzly Bear! Then he appeared in each one of their dreams. In the dreams he would appear as a charging Grizzly Bear going straight after them.

First he attacked Dancing Wind: she instantly rolled out of her sleeping bag and snatched up her Glock, pointing it at him. Instantly he disappeared, only to repeat the events with Sarah an hour later. She, too, grabbed her Glock and brought it up to fire upon him. An hour later, he again appeared in Molly's dream as an attacking Grizzly Bear! Molly also scooped up her Glock and began aiming her weapon at him. The Lakota warrior Grizzly Bear, had personally satisfied himself that all three of the women had courage!

All three women were now wide awake. They were all discussing their dreams and how strange it was that all three had dreamed that they were being attacked by a charging Grizzly Bear. They spoke of how vividly real the dream seemed with the charging Grizzly bear running right for them. Molly said it is possible for one of us to have a nightmare about a charging Grizzly Bear but it is impossible for three of us to have the same dream unless spirit forces were at work.

Molly said "I had a White Light of Protection around me, and I cannot see that Grizzly Bear coming in like it did unless it is one of two things: It is warning us of the danger of a Grizzly Bear attack, or it is giving us a spiritual test prior to having us do something important."

Dancing Wind said, "I do *not* think this is an actual spiritual attack against us, or my Guardian Angel would be clearly warning us of the danger. To have this spirit move in so close to all three of us is highly improbable, unless our Guardian Angels are supervising what is occurring. So my best guess is this is a spiritual test."

Red Fox told Strong Bear that it was his turn to devise a test for honor!

"Then we will put the three young teenagers to the test," Red Fox said, "It is said that greedy people will do anything for gold. Let us see if their honor is compromised by greed."

So when Sarah dug a hole to go to the bathroom in, she hit a pocket of gravel as she scooped out the dirt. The gravel was full of gold nuggets. Red Fox wanted to see if Sarah's greed would cause her to keep it all to herself or if she would share her discovery with her friends.

Sarah looked with astonishment into the hole she had just dug, for there appeared dozens of small gold nuggets in the hole.

Red Fox watched Sarah to see if her greedy nature would cause her to keep the discovery all to herself or if she would show her two friends what she had found. Red Fox knew that gold caused many individuals to compromise their honor. As Red Fox worked hard to give the gravel the color and appearance of gold, he had to work even harder when Sarah picked up one of the rocks, as Red Fox also had to give the gravel the heavy weight of gold. Sarah had picked up one gold nugget and with it she walked over and showed Dancing Wind and Molly what she had found. As Dancing Wind and Molly looked at the gold nugget, it suddenly changed back to its normal color of a small quartz rock as the three teenagers looked at it.

Sarah said, "I could have sworn a minute ago it was a gold nugget. I do not know what happened. Here, let me show you the hole I dug; it is full of gold."

When the three girls looked, there was only normal gravel.

"Well," Molly replied, "as you first showed it to me, I too thought it was a gold nugget, and while you held it, it changed color from gold to white quartz. I think this was another spirit test."

Dancing Wind agreed; she too thought it was a spiritual test for Sarah, to see if she was affected by greed. When you showed the gold to us, you passed the test and the Spirit who was testing you then dropped the illusion he had created, which gave the stone the appearance of gold.

Then Molly added her thought: "Well, if the Grizzly Bear attack came to all three of us, then Dancing Wind and I will be tested next."

Dancing Wind was beginning to wonder what these tests were leading up to. Certainly the amount of energy the Spirits were utilizing to create their test was way above anything a normal ghost or spirit utilized or had available. All three women were already keeping very intense white lights of protection around themselves. Dancing Wind knew she could try and prevent further tests by instructing her Guardian Angels to not allow the Spirits to get in close to them. On the other hand, she felt that her Guardian Angels would have clearly warned her if danger was approaching. All three teenagers had worked with their individual Guardian Angels to give them a clear personal signal that the Angels would send them when danger is approaching.

Since her Guardian Angel had not clearly told her that danger was approaching, clearly her Guardian Angel was in on what was occurring or recognized the test as coming from spirits of the "Light" or " Good" and so was not interfering but simply watching or observing what was occurring.

On the second night, the Cheyenne warrior Red Fox came to Dancing Wind at 2 am in the morning as Dancing Wind was fast asleep. Red Fox appeared in Dancing Wind's dreams as a beautiful red fox with a long fluffy tail. At first Dancing Wind was just observing the red fox, but then to her surprise, the fox walked up to her and told her:

"I can make you rich; in the morning you will see a red fox along the shore line. You will need to make an excuse as to why you need to be alone with me on the shore. Then, ditch your friends. I will take only you to a small chest of Spanish coins. They will be just for you. There is no reason to share what you earn with the other two girls. All the gold coins will be yours, without them knowing anything."

As suddenly as Red Fox had appeared in Dancing Winds dream, he promptly disappeared after leaving a message.

In the morning Dancing Wind told Molly and Sarah about her dream. When, an hour later, they all saw a red fox on the east river bank, they observed the fox and then all three teenagers simply paddled their canoe right on by the red fox. No one made any effort to stop or follow the fox. They were partners and would stick together and share what they found equally between them. Their Honor required them to treat their friends the way they themselves would like to be treated. They would share anything they found equally, or they simply would not touch it; their honor gave them no other choice.

When they stopped for lunch, the three teenagers stopped on a gravel bar to make lunch. Again they decided to build a fire. All three teenagers began gathering sticks from dead trees killed by the tiny black tree borers which were killing millions of trees throughout New Mexico. As they gathered the smaller sticks to get the fire started, Molly wandered off by herself.

Suddenly, there in front of her, was the red fox Dancing Wind had told her about. Molly paused a moment, looking at the fox.

"I can take you to a treasure of gold coins as long as you do not share it with the others," the suddenly fox told her. Then the fox slyly told Molly, *"It is only fair that you keep all the gold only for yourself as you have a greater need for the gold. They do not have big bills like you, which you need to pay soon."*

Molly promptly gave Red Fox her response as she scooped up a handful of rocks to throw at the fox. As Molly wound up her arm for her best baseball pitcher's hard throw with the rocks in her hand, the fox disappeared! Molly, too, had just passed her test for honor.

On the third evening all three teenagers realized the spirit test would start again. They stayed up late around the campfire speculating on the reason for the spiritual tests they were encountering. Around eleven that night, the teenagers turned in to sleep; all were nervous about what would happen next. That night Strong Bear appeared in all three teenagers dreams he began showing them about his life as a free Indian and how that all changed when he was invited by the Spanish to enjoy some whiskey. He began drinking, and when he awoke, he found he was bound in chains and was now a slave of the Spanish. The Spanish had invited Strong Bear and the other Indians with him to try the Whiskey. This was a special whiskey, as it was generously laced with opium from China. He showed them how he was beaten with a whip, he often he slept with no blankets on the cold ground, and the food he was given was often not fit for human consumption. He showed the teenagers how many of the Indians were forced to work in the Spanish Mines, half way up on the east side of Taos Mountain. Here the average life of the Indians forced to work in the mines was four to six months. The hard work, malnutrition, cave ins, poor air, mine accidents, and brutal beatings by the cruel Spanish guards resulted in daily deaths.

The Spanish had a lust for gold which resulted in the deaths of thousands of Indians who worked to their deaths in the Spanish gold mines. It seemed that none of them had any hope they would live or ever see their family's again.

And then the impossible occurred: hope arrived. On August 8, 1680, an Indian from the Taos Pueblo arrived, bringing supplies for the Spanish miners. The slaves were ordered to help unload the supplies from the pack mules. Unseen by the Spanish guards, the Taos Pueblo Indian signaled to the other Indians that in three days Indians everywhere would kill the hated Spaniards who had held them in slavery. The Taos Pueblo Indian indicated that one hundred feet down the trail, on the side of the rising sun were three bows and arrows. That was all he could do to help these slaves.

On August 11, 1680 no help arrived to free the Cheyenne and Lakota

Indians from their chains. They were on their own if they wanted to achieve their freedom. Freedom often comes at a high price, and such was the case with the Indians that the Spanish had enslaved by force or trickery. The manner of the Indians had changed on the appointed day. They walked taller and they seemed to have regained their spirit as they even watched their Spanish guards instead of being subservient and looking away or at the ground.

July 13, 1680-27 days earlier

Sergeant Juan Solorzano was summoned to the Palace of the Governors in Santa Fe. As he responded to the governor's orders he hoped it did not involve the small inconsequential matter of his soldiers not being paid. He had told his men the reason that they had not been paid in three months was that the payroll had to come up from Mexico City. Sergeant Solorzano rehearsed what he would say to the governor; that he had not stolen his men's money, he had just borrowed it. He was sure he would be able to win his lost money back the next time he played cards in the cantina.

Sergeant Juan Solorzano had volunteered to come to this frontier outpost as he realized that the men he owed gambling debts to in Mexico City would never follow him a thousand miles to the north just to try and collect the money he owed them. But most importantly of all; Sergeant Solorzano thought of the frontier as the land where opportunity combined with good fortune could enable him to make the fortune he needed to return to Spain and retire, living the life of luxury. As the effective commander of this Presidio, he regularly escorted the king's gold and silver which he and his men collected from the numerous mines. One fifth of all the gold and silver mined went to the king of Spain. He just had not yet figured out how to make some of the king's gold his own gold yet! Somehow, he needed to figure out a way to lose a couple of hundred pounds of gold, and not be held responsible for the loss. Two pack mules of gold was what he wanted to steal from the king, and that would provide him with the wealth he desired for his retirement.

★★★★

Usually out in the field he had a completely free hand to do whatever he chose to do. Seldom did his commanding officer, Lieutenant Juan Tories, leave the fort except to chase the señoritas. Lieutenant Juan Tories liked the women, the parties, and the dances, in that order of preference. The Lieutenant only went out riding so as to be seen escorting the gold and silver into the capital. Then he heard that the king's soldiers were riding into Santa Fe so he would ride out of the capital city and for an hour to meet his men. Then, leading his command back into the Capital of New Mexico, he showed his leadership to all the señoritas and bystanders. The governor no longer relied upon the lieutenant, except to be a gracious host, or pompous ass, at the official functions at the Palace of the Governors.

★★★★

The Governor did not keep Sergeant Solorzano waiting as he usually did. As soon as he arrived in the Governor's office, the Governor got straight to the point. There had been a rebellion of the Indian slaves at the mine high up on the north side of Taos Mountain. Three days ago the slaves had revolted and killed their guards and then strangely enough the Indians had loaded up the pack mules and stolen the gold too! The Governor was sure the Indians could not have gotten far, as they were all in chains. The Governor ordered Sergeant Solorzano to capture all the Indians and make an example of them by slowly torturing them so no other slaves even think of revolting against their masters. The thieving Indians had stolen 4,000 pounds of gold! Never had this happened before anywhere in New Mexico; never must this be allowed to happen again.

"Most important of all," he said, "you must recover the king's Gold!"

Sergeant Solorzano left the governor's office in a run. Opportunity knocked, and he must respond at once. If he was first on the scene and recovered the gold, this would be the perfect opportunity for the loss of 400 lbs of gold to pass unnoticed into his hands. Carefully handled, this could mean a retirement in luxury instead of poverty. First, he must notify Lieutenant Tories about the Indian slaves revolting. It would be best not to let the lieutenant know about the lost gold, or he would want all the glory of recovering the gold and would insist on accompanying the men into the field after the rebelling Indians.

Sergeant Solorzano told his Lieutenant Juan Tories that the Indians had revolted up at the mines on Taos Mountain. Lieutenant Tories told the Sergeant that his first duty was to protect the people of Santa Fe; so he must guard the Presidio at Santa Fe in case further troubles erupted and he required five men. Lieutenant Tories ordered Sergeant Solorzano to take the remaining thirty soldiers with him to kill all the escaped slaves.

Sergeant Solorzano ordered the drummer to drum out a call to assemble. As the men ran out of the barracks Sergeant Solorzano quickly briefed his men.

He said, "The Indians up upon Taos Mountain have revolted. The Governor is depending on you to ensure that the slaves are promptly brought to justice and killed. The people here are depending upon us to protect them from the hostile Indians. Grab your weapons, food, and water and we ride for the glory of Spain!"

Fifteen minutes later, Sergeant Solorzano led his men past the

Governor's Palace at a trot. Sergeant Solorzano wanted the Governor to remember how he bravely led his men into battle against the Indians who had revolted. Maybe there would be a promotion for him after his glorious victory against the wild savages.

At nightfall the Sergeant and his men camped at Española. Another two days of hard riding would bring him to Taos. Hopefully in the four days it took to get to the north side of Taos Mountain, none of the gold would have been recovered. Sergeant Solorzano needed to be the man who recovered the gold as well as the man who inventoried all the gold they recovered! Let me see, he thought to himself, who are the most stupid men in his command? He would need men who obeyed his orders without question and had no ability to count. These would be the men who he would place in charge of inventorying all the gold they recovered.

Late at night on July 15, 1680 Sergeant Solorzano and his command of thirty men rode into Taos plaza. His men watered their horses and then ate beans, chili, and tortillas, which had been prepared for their arrival. It was here that he learned that the Indian slaves were last seen at Valdez. At daybreak he would ride for Valdez.

July 16, 1680

Sergeant Solorzano reassured the people of Taos that he was here to restore law and order in the name of the king. He assured the people of Taos that justice would prevail and he would personally execute these Indian slaves. The people of Taos could sleep well knowing he was here on the king's behalf to ensure their safety. Sergeant Solorzano thought that should there later be an inquiry about lost gold, that no one would question his loyalty to the Crown and his dedication to duty. Secretly, Sergeant Solorzano was pleased that none of the gold had been recovered prior to his arrival and his taking charge.

Six hours after leaving Taos, the column of Spanish soldiers arrived in Valdez. Here the King's subjects told him that the Indians had taken the mules loaded with gold and ridden north. But they added that a small group of the slaves may have taken the logs they had drying for vegas and floated down stream. Sergeant Solorzano then split his command. He would send twelve soldiers to search down river for any slaves.

He ordered Corporal Valdez to take eleven men and search along the Rio Hondo from Valdez to the hot springs at the crossing on the Rio Grande.

"You are to properly torture all the slaves you encounter, and then execute them." He ordered, "If you have extra time, make a search up to the headwaters of the Rio Hondo hunting down and killing any escaped slaves you encounter.

As Corporal Valdez led his eleven men down the Rio Hondo they encountered the drag marks of the chains the Indians' leg- irons were shackled together with. Because the Indians' legs were connected by a short chain, the fastest an Indian could move was about one mile per hour. If the slave attempted to move faster, the chains would cause the Indian to trip and fall. The escaped Indian also had to avoid all vegetation and branches which would grab or entangle the chain and cause him to fall.

As the first Indian came into sight, Corporal Valdez ordered his men to use swords only. Then each of his men in turn rode by the fleeing Indian, slashing him with their swords. The game they enjoyed themselves by playing was to slash the Indian repeatedly with their sword. Yet to prolong their pleasure and the sport of the hunt, the intent was not to immediately kill the poor fleeing Indian, but to inflict the maximum amount of pain and suffering while not inflicting a fatal wound. After two hours of sport, the Indian no longer moved or provided any more entertainment, so Corporal Valdez got down off his horse and walked up to an Indian who was dying on the ground, and using his knife, he slit the slave's throat.

When Corporal Valdez and his men encountered the next escaped slave, he ordered his men to use Pikes, which are a type of spear/hatchet weapon on a five foot wooden pole, only. So as his men rode by the poor fleeing slave, they repeatedly drove their Pikes into the defenseless Indian's body, tearing off chunks of flesh or hacking the Indian's body with the hatchet blade. When the Indian lay dying on the ground and could no longer move then Corporal Valdez got off his horse and walked over to the Indian and slit his throat, too. All day long they hunted down the Indians who had tried to escape the slavery in the Spanish mines. By evening, Corporal Valdez and his men camped at the small village of Hondo on the Rio Hondo. Tomorrow he would reach the crossing at the hot springs.

July 17, 1680

Down on the Rio Grande, within sight of the Cave of Gold of the Rio Grande, Wild Buffalo, Fast Runner, and Red Fox had just finished burying four-thousand pounds of gold that they had stolen from the hated Spanish. They buried it in small caches along both sides of the Rio Grande in hundreds of locations. Then they had carefully concealed all evidence of their tracks and their digging, all three Indians knew that nothing would get the Spanish more furious than losing their gold, for the Indians realized that the gold was the reason the Spanish enslaved them and forced them to work in the mines.

Now Wild Buffalo began shaping a bow while Fast Runner began taking the strands of bark from the Juniper tree and making a bow string. Red Fox had begun making the arrows using a dozen straight red willows he had cut down along the Rio Grande. If they could at least make a bow and some arrows, they stood a small chance against the men who would be sent to torture and kill them.

With the help of several Indian guides from the Taos Pueblo, none of the escaped Indian slaves were able to flee. The few Indians who had been able to conceal their tracks made by the chains and shackles which imprisoned them from the Spanish Conquistadors under the command of Corporal Valdez, were located by the Taos Pueblo Indian guides. Corporal Valdez made sure the escaped Indians suffered a horrible and painful death.

Corporal Valdez would have missed the three escaped slaves concealed among the numerous boulders, but his Indian guides did not. Corporal Valdez was a man who literally carried out his orders without question. And so when he captured Wild Buffalo, Fast Runner, and Red Fox as they were attempting to make bows and arrows, Corporal Valdez personally, clearly establishing the law and order of Spain, carried out his orders from Sergeant Solorzano. He ordered his men to bring the three escaped slaves up to the top of the steep cliff on the East side of the Rio Grande Gorge. Here, Corporal Valdez personally took great pride in carrying out his orders as he had his men hold the three struggling and helpless Indians. First, Corporal Valdez used a heavy wooden club to break the Lakota and Cheyenne warrior's arms. Next, he broke the Lakota and Cheyenne warriors' legs. He saw the anger in Wild Buffalo's eyes so he drove a spear into his lower left side. Then he heaved the disabled Indian over the cliff to die as they smashed in the rocks below beside the Rio Grande. It took only minutes for Corporal Valdez and his men to murder the two Lakota warriors and one Cheyenne warrior who had done their best to steal the gold they had been forced to mine and who were trying and escape so they could regain their freedom.

As she had been at the base of the cliffs down by the Rio Grande getting water for herself and her baby, Wild Flower saw her husband's murder as the Corporal drove the spear into her husband and the Spanish soldiers threw him off the high gorge cliffs. She ran to her husband's side and removed the broken spear from her husband's side, but it was no use; she could not save Wild Buffalo, as he was dead.

Above her she heard the Spaniards cry out in excitement as they saw another Indian that they could torture and kill. Grabbing the broken spear point in one hand with her baby in her other arm, she fled south along the east bank of the Rio Grande. She fled south of the hot spring among the black basalt cliffs with the Spaniards descending the cliffs on a trail leading to the hot springs that are now called Stage Coach hot springs. The Corporal led his men and accompanied by Indian tracks, they pursued an escaped Lakota woman named Wild Flower. Wild Flower was carrying Wild Buffalo and her baby as she had been fleeing south towards another old Indian trail crossing the Rio Grande north of the present Rio Grande gorge bridge.

Wild Flower was unable to outrun the Spaniards mounted on horses and they quickly closed the gap separating them. Upon finding her, the corporal had his men promptly seized Wild Flower's baby from her arms and murdered the baby, as they knew nothing would upset the Indian woman as much as murdering her baby in front of the mother. There were many men, both Indian trackers from the Taos Pueblo, as well as Spaniards, who knew that what they were doing was wrong in their eyes, as well as GOD's eyes, yet they did not have the courage nor honor to stand up for what was right. So they kept silent, as a few bad men had a free hand to do their evil work. Then they proceeded to hurt and then murder Wild Flower.

★★★★

One man who lacked the courage to stand up for what was right went back to the site of the baby and her mother's murder and buried them. Later, he climbed the cliffs. He realized what he had allowed to occur in front of his eyes was wrong but he had been afraid to stand up against so many evil men, as he too would have been instantly murdered.

As the man looked down from the top of the east side of the Rio Grande Gorge, he took a last look at the burial site. It was on the south side of the east-to-west trail on the east side, about a hundred feet above the river. He saw the black shadow of an Indian with a feather in his hair twenty feet to the northwest of the burial site, and beside where he buried the mother and her baby was a stone figure of a man with his feet towards the northeast and his head towards the southwest and he was about three meters tall. He felt that the least he could do was place the woman and her child beside a man who could protect her in the spirit world since he had been unable to help her in this world.

★★★★

Wild Flower was extremely angry and upset over the murder of her child. She had watched one lone man later return and bury her. Beside her body, she saw where her murdered baby was buried. For centuries Wild Flower would return to the site her baby lay and she cried in the anguish that only a mother could know. She mourned the loss of her child and many tears were shed upon her baby's grave.

★★★★

As Corporal Valdez and his men mounted their horses, they rode hard for Taos to make it by nightfall. It had been two days since they had eaten. They wanted a hot dinner in the Taos Plaza. Corporal Valdez and his men were proud of the work they had done this day. They rode for the glory of Spain! Yes, Corporal Valdez thought, I deserve a promotion for all the good work I have done killing nineteen escaped slaves.

As the Corporal led his men east to Taos, dashed to pieces on the rocks below the rim of the Rio Grande Gorge were the three lifeless bodies of the only three Indians who knew the secret of the location of four thousand pounds of gold and artifacts the Spanish had murdered over two hundred Cheyenne and Lakota Indians to obtain!

July 16, 1680

Sergeant Solorzano took his remaining eighteen soldiers north to capture the mules loaded with *his* gold. The escaped slaves had a seven day head start. He would have to push his men hard if they were to overtake the slaves who rode north with the king's gold. As Sergeant Solorzano rode at the head of his soldiers, he smiled as he thought about how easy it had been to get rid of a dozen men. He would have a dozen less witnesses to how much gold he recovered. Since the crazy Indians had loaded their pack horses down with gold, his men would be able to ride faster and soon he would get the gold back. He wondered why the crazy Indians had taken the gold. They were really stupid, as they could not spend the gold anywhere. It was just a matter of time and he would recover all the gold. In three or four days, he thought, he would recover the gold when he captured the escaped slaves fleeing Spanish authority.

Since the stupid Indians had loaded the pack mules with the gold, his horses would be traveling lighter and hence faster. They would rapidly overtake the mules loaded with the four thousand pounds of the king's gold. Since his men were traveling light and fast while the Indians' pack horses were loaded down with gold, he would cover two miles for every mile that the loaded pack horses could cover.

For glory and gold, he pushed the remaining soldiers hard. By late evening his men rode into San Cristobal for dinner. His men rode into the Navajo village and helped themselves to the Indians' food. They took what they needed; if the Indians went hungry it was just their tough luck. If the Indians did not like it, they would just have to accept the fact that the Spaniards were their masters and they had better feed them whatever they wanted if they knew what was good for them. His soldiers grabbed the women they wanted for the night. The Indian women had no say in the matter. Two of his horses had pulled up lame from riding over the rocky terrain. So his men just grabbed two of the best horses they saw outside the Navajo lodges. One of the Navajo men objected to losing his horse, but he did not object long after one of his men hit him in the head with his rifle butt. Sometimes you just had to teach the Indians who is boss!

July 17, 1680

After eating breakfast and replacing his two horses at the Navajo village, the Sergeant led his men north. The Sergeant was leading his men north along an ancient Native American trade route known as the Rainbow Trail. He had to get the gold back. That night they camped on the Red River. In the morning he led his men north. By night fall they reached the Costilla River what is now the border of Colorado and New Mexico. They were closing the distance on the mules loaded with gold. He was five days behind, judging by the age of the mule tracks.

As Sergeant Solorzano moved his force north, he hoped he would have a victorious battle against hostile Indians to enhance his reputation as a great leader who led his men to victory in battle. Of course, if he lost a few of his men, he would have fewer men to witness how much gold he recovered. There was also that trivial matter of his having "borrowed" the garrison payroll and losing it in the card game. Any soldier that died would be one less person whose wages he would have to repay. Solorzano thought that a battle with hostiles would be a win-win situation for him.

July 18, 1680

The day began at dawn when Sergeant Solorzano kicked his men who were sleeping on the ground. He wanted his men mounted and riding north. He had never lost an Indian slave he had been chasing in twenty seven years and this Indian was not going to be his first. Of course, never had one of the escaped slaves cover a hundred miles with the king's men in pursuit, either. There was no stopping or rest for his men as they rode forty three miles. After dark they made camp on the Rio Costilla. It had been a very long day but they finally reached the Rio Costilla where they could water their horses.

July 19, 1680

The next morning at dawn his men rode along Ventero Creek. San Pedro Mesa was to their west as they rode north. Throughout the day they followed the heavily-loaded mule tracks along Ventero Creek. That night, Sergeant Solorzano and his men camped along Cuebra Creek. Sergeant Solorzano dispatched four of his men to the east along Cuebra Creek to hunt for elk. His men had not eaten in two days. A delay to feed his men was essential if he was to continue the pursuit of the Indians, mules and the gold. At dusk his men were able to kill an elk feeding in the grassy meadows alongside Cuebra Creek. Butchering an elk, his men finally had all they could eat.

July 20, 1680

The chase had now lasted seven days since Sergeant Solorzano had ridden out of the Presidio in Santa Fe. Sergeant Solorzano figured he could catch up with the Indian and the mules in two or three more days.

He had to get the gold back.

As the day began, far to the north his men could see the huge mountain known as Mount Blanco. It was here he planned to camp that night. While the mountain appeared close in the clear mountain air, it was actually a long day's ride. His men had covered thirty miles that day. At nightfall his men made camp at the base of Mount Blanco along Ute Creek and ate the remainder of the previous day's elk kill

July 21, 1680

At da break the Spanish soldiers were moving north around the western slopes of Mount Blanca. For ten hours his men rode in pursuit of the escaped Indians and the mules loaded with gold. Another thirty miles was covered as they closed in on the pack train of mules. The Sangre de Cristo Mountains were on their right throughout the day. At nightfall they made camp on North Zepata Creek, for water usually determined where they camped for the night, as water was essential for their horses.

July 22, 2007

Sergeant Solorzano was up at dawn. The Sergeant ordered his men mounted and they began another day of pursuit. His men and horses were exhausted, but he would not quit. His men could miss a meal or two; that did not matter. Recovering the gold was all that mattered!

Throughout the day Sergeant Solorzano led his soldiers north along the west side of the rugged mountains. To their west was the flat prairie of the San Louis Valley as far as the eye could see. Sergeant Solorzano hoped to at least catch sight of the mules by nightfall, but the closest he came was the tracks of the mules he followed all day.

After two hours in the saddle his men rode into a sea of sand and sand dunes. For six hours his men rode through the white sands. Progress was slow as the horses' legs sunk down in the sand with every foot they traveled. As they reached the north end of the sand dunes, his men observed a small band of Ute Indians following their progress.

Sergeant Solorzano knew the Utes were no match for his fighting force. His men were armed with the latest weapons, six muzzle-loading rifles, six cross bows, six pikes and a dozen swords. There was no way a small band of Ute's would ever go up against his trained fighting force, armed with modern weapons! Sergeant Solorzano wanted to end his chase of these escaped Indians and recover the gold as soon as possible, so instead of stopping at San Creek on the Northern end of the white sand dunes, he pushed his men for another two hours.

They stopped in the evening alongside a creek with good water and grass to feed the horses. His exhausted men and horses made camp for the night. Most of the men simply drank all the water they could to fill their empty stomachs. Then the men collapsed on the ground to get some sleep.

July 23, 1680

An hour before daybreak, the sole surviving guard whose duty it was to guard the horses raised the alarm, as they heard one of the horses galloping away in the distance. At first, Sergeant Solorzano thought one of his men he had recruited from the jails in Santa Fe had deserted. But the dead soldier was found on the far side of the herd of horses. He died at the hands of a Ute warrior who had come and stolen a horse. Later, when his men referred to that camp they called it "Rio Los Muertos" (Dead Man Creek).

★★★★

Sixty miles to the north Strong Bear, a Lakota with twelve mules, was having problems of his own. In Poncho Pass, the trail he was riding narrowed down to about five feet in width. Suddenly, Strong Bear rounded a curve in the trail following the creek bed when he rode right into a dozen Cheyenne warriors.

The Cheyenne were armed with bows and arrows and war lances. That they wanted to take his mules was obvious from their appraisal of his mules; Strong Bear was also unarmed and bound in chains. Strong Bear knew the Cheyenne warriors had two characteristics which worked in his favor: The Cheyenne always admired bravery, and they had a great sense of humor. When they introduced themselves to each other using sign language, Strong Bear explained that he was leading the Spanish Garrison north to the Wind River Mountain Range in northwestern Wyoming where he would kill them. To get all the soldiers to follow him he told them how he had taken twelve mule loads of the Spaniards' "TEARS OF THE SUN" (Gold). Then he opened up the panniers that were packed on four of the Mules and showed the Cheyenne warriors all the "TEARS OF THE SUN." All the Cheyenne burst out laughing, as Strong Bear pulled the worthless lava rocks out of the panniers and showed them to the men.

They allowed Strong Bear to pass and one Cheyenne warrior handed Strong Bear his battle lance while another removed his quiver of arrows and gave it to Strong Bear along with his prized bow. Strong Bear was grateful for their generosity. He knew that when the Spaniards caught up with him he would need the weapons. In turn, Strong Bear gave the leader of the Cheyenne one mule and the two warriors who had given him a weapon were given two mules apiece. Everyone was happy with the exchange of gifts.

When asked when the Spanish Soldiers would come, Strong Bear told the Cheyenne that they were about two days behind him. The

Cheyenne then promised that they too would give the hated Spaniards who kidnapped and enslaved their people a gift from the Cheyenne Nation. So at Poncho Pass the Cheyenne began making arrows to fill their quivers. They expected company shortly and they wanted to give the Spaniard invaders a welcome they would not forget.

July 24/25 1680

Strong Bear rode north on his seven mules along the Arkansas River. As he did so, he checked the mules and decided now was the time to lighten their load—just a little. Strong Bear did not want the Spaniards to realize that he was only hauling worthless rocks. Strong Bear was risking his life by not dumping the worthless lava rocks, as Wild Buffalo had instructed him to do, after a day or two. The worthless lava rock he had loaded his mules with in Valdez was simply to decoy the Spanish Garrison north to give Wild Buffalo, Red Fox and Fast Runner time to bury the treasure of gold. But by continuing to haul the load of rock, the Spaniards continued to believe he was hauling the gold. Strong Bear knew the Spaniards' greed would cause them to pursue him to the ends of the earth or even to hell itself. Nothing would stop the Spaniards if they believed he had gold! Every day that the soldiers chased him meant that there were fewer men to chase after Wild Buffalo, Red Fox and Fast Runner. Strong Bear was buying his friends as much time as possible.

Yet Strong Bear did not want to risk being recaptured, so now it was time to act. He must reduce the load of the mules gradually so that the mules could travel faster, but he did not want the Spaniards to realize the packs were getting lighter, nor that he was just hauling worthless rock. So as Strong Bear rode alongside the west bank of the Arkansas River, he began reaching into the panniers his mules hauled which were loaded down with lava rocks and grabbing a rock. The rock he then threw out into the Arkansas River, carefully, to keep the pack-weight balanced on each side of the load the mules hauled; one rock after another landed in the river where the Spaniards would never see it. As the load lightened, the mules began to travel faster. Strong Bear wanted to stay ahead of the soldiers who pursued him.

July 26, 1680

The following day at noon, Sergeant Solorzano led his seventeen men into Poncho Pass. The Cheyenne realized the danger the rifles and the cross bows presented them. So they planned to hit the Spaniards once and then fade away into the rugged mountains. On the North side of Poncho Pass where the gorge was very narrow and the Spaniards' horses must move in single-file at a walk, the Cheyenne attacked, sending their arrows into the Spaniards. Sergeant Solorzano, who led his men, took the brunt of the attack. Five arrows slammed into his iron breast plate, but the wooden arrows were deflected by the metal breast plate he wore, so he escaped injury. Two other men wearing the iron breast plates were also fortunate to have the armor save their lives. Few of the soldiers actually had the metal breast plates, and it was these men whom suffered the most under the surprise attack. As his men began to bring their rifles and cross bows into play, the fight began to go in the Spaniards' favor. Immediately the Cheyenne just seemed to disappear in the rocky landscape. As the sergeant checked his men, he found that one horse and three of his men were not as lucky as he was. They did not survive the ambush.

Sergeant Solorzano made camp at the base of Poncho Mountain by Poncho Springs. His men were afraid that they would not return alive from this expedition to recover the gold. Never had Sergeant Solorzano wanted to kill and Indian as badly as he wanted to kill Strong Bear. After he caught the Indian and recovered the gold, he would torture the savage slowly. This stupid savage was making a fool out of me, Sergeant Solorzano thought.

"Nobody makes a fool out of me," he said under his breath.

Sergeant Solorzano felt something was going wrong; he felt that his control of the situation was slipping out of his hands. Four of his soldiers had died due to Indian attacks. This Indian was removing the pack saddles every night so the mules could rest. Then he would put the load on fresh mules each day. Instead of capturing the Indian as he had planned in three to five days, the Indian and the king's gold were still two days ahead of him. No one would ever believe him if he said that an escaped Indian in chains could lead a detachment of the kings soldiers on a chase lasting thirteen days.

July 27, 1680

At daybreak Sergeant Solorzano led his fourteen men in pursuit of the mules of gold. The Rocky Mountains were on the east and west side as he led his men north along a trail on the west bank of the Arkansas River. As they rode north along the grassy valley, his men made good time. Why anyone would want to settle in this God-forsaken place called Colorado was a mystery to him. As soon as he got his four hundred pounds of the king's gold safely hidden near Santa Fe, he would be planning his trip back to Spain. As far as he was concerned, the savage Indians could keep all of this worthless land they called Colorado. The sooner he got out of here, the happier he would be. Madrid, Spain was where he wanted to be right then. That night his men camped at Trout Creek. Sergeant Solorzano was happy as his men had made thirty five miles that day. As his men ate the elk they had killed on the grassy pastures alongside Trout Creek around the camp fire, they were in a better mood. The Sergeant knew that a hot meal and a campfire always picked up a man's spirits.

★★★★

As Sergeant Solorzano and his men were eating elk alongside Trout Creek, Strong Bear was also eating elk meat that he had roasted over a small fire he had build on the North Fork of Lake Creek just to the southwest of Mount Elbert (elevation 14,433 feet). Tomorrow the difficult task of crossing the high mountain pass that in the future would be called Independence Pass, lay ahead. While he had not seen any trace of the Spaniards that were pursuing him after his escape from the mine way high up on the north side of Taos Mountain, he knew they would never stop their pursuit of him. Wild Buffalo, Red Fox, and Fast Runner had taken from the hated Spaniards what they most lusted after; the "Tears of the Sun." The Spaniards would betray their word, honor, integrity, their brothers, and even kill or double-cross their own mothers for the "Tears of the Sun". The Spaniards slaughtered the Native Americans by the thousands to obtain the gold.

July 28, 1680

The dawn arrived with Strong Bear facing east, saying prayers to the Great Spirit that he be up to the task of leading the Spaniards on a trip from which they never returned. People who chained up his people and beat them with whips, slaughtering his people with reckless indifference were an affront to the Great Spirit. If he could send some of the Spaniards home to the Great Spirit, he would be helping all of his people. As he prayed to the Great Spirit for wisdom and bravery to face his enemies so that he could take all the Spaniards to the "happy hunting ground," he suddenly had the answer to his prayers.

Strong Bear took his mules and began climbing up further into the mountains as he approached Independence Pass to the west. He would take his mules over the pass today. Tomorrow he wanted to move the mules down the West side of Independent Pass and leave them where they would not move very far as there would be lots of good grass and water. Then the warrior would have to race back to the top of Independence Pass and reach it about two hours prior to the arrival of the Spaniards. For if he was to reach the top of Independence Pass at the same time or after the Spaniards arrived, he would be riding into the enemy's hands and suffer a horrible death. Strong Bear wanted to arrive early, as he would be have to travel very carefully so as not to leave any tracks as he located a position from which he could ambush his enemies.

So that he did not leave the tracks of his chain dragging in the dirt, he had connected two strips of rawhide from an elk he had killed to the string holding up his breech cloth he wore. The two strips of rawhide held his chain that connected the shackles on his legs an inch or two off the ground. Strong Bear wanted his enemy to realize they would pay a high price to try and recapture him.

July 29, 1680

Sergeant Solorzano pushed his men hard, and tonight he would not let his men rest or make camp until they made the top of Independence Pass, though Sergeant Solorzano would not know the name that this pass through the mountains would be named by the white settlers when they arrived in another two centuries. It is one of life's ironies that one Lakota warrior was fighting for his independence here against an overwhelmingly larger and better-armed force of Spanish soldiers, at Independence Pass.

When the soldiers made camp that night, the tracks they saw on the ground were about one day old. So the soldiers believed the escaped Indian was about one day's travel ahead of them. Never did they suspect that Strong Bear was only three hundred feet away from their campfire watching them. Strong Bear did not look directly at his enemies or they might feel him watching him. Instead, he never looked directly at the camp or his enemies; instead, he would look off to the side and catch their movement in the side or the corners of his eyes. Strong Bear was looking for any men who moved away from the group so that he could catch them by surprise and kill them. About midnight one Spaniard walked about twenty feet out of camp to go to the bathroom. As the man squatted on the ground, relieving himself, Strong Bear was able to move close enough to use his war lance to kill one of his enemies.

As Strong Bear moved by the camp, he also saw one man standing alone guarding the horses. Strong Bear had two types of arrows in the quiver of arrows he had been given by the Cheyenne warrior. When the arrow was placed or notched into the bowstring, some of his arrowheads were in a vertical position. These were made to slide between the ribs of an animal like an elk which had parallel vertical ribs. A man has parallel horizontal ribs, so to most-effectively kill a man, Strong Bear selected two arrows with horizontally-positioned arrowheads to make a rapid kill. Strong Bear silently moved within fifty feet of the soldier, where he could accurately place two arrows into his upper chest so he would not cry out or give warning. Strong Bear rapidly sent two arrows into the sentry. Then Strong Bear slowly and quietly walked over to the dead man. Strong Bear picked up the dead soldier's cross bow and his bolts of arrows which the crossbow fired. Then, with the weapon in hand, Strong Bear slowly and quietly began the mile and a half walk down the western slope of Independence Pass to his mules.

July 30, 1680

At dawn the camp awoke with discovery of two dead bodies! In the last week, six of the eighteen soldiers had been killed in Indian ambushes. Not once had the soldiers even seen the escaped Indian slave they were chasing and already one-third of their companions were dead. The Spaniards began to wonder if this expedition was doomed to failure. For the first time, Sergeant Solorzano had a moment of doubt about recovering the two tons of gold. But he had come this far, and he was simply unwilling to quit now. Sergeant Solorzano simply did not think that an Indian could outsmart him. Never had one of the Indians he chased down with his soldiers ever escaped!

At three in the afternoon the men grew excited. Not only were they only hours behind the Lakota Indian, but they also saw where the mules had been last night. Sergeant Solorzano was excited that for the first time he was just hours behind the mule pack-train of gold.

"I knew I would capture that Indian and recover the gold. Tomorrow," he told his men, "we will capture that escaped slave." He would push his men and their horses as hard as it took to capture the Lakota warrior and his gold.

As his men sat around the campfire that night, Sergeant Solorzano inspired his men with the good news that tomorrow they would capture that escaped slave.

"He cannot be more than two hours ahead of us. Are we going to let an Indian in chains bring dishonor to our king?" he asked his men.

"No!" they all shouted in answer.

Then Sergeant Solorzano told his men, "A 'real eight' goes to the first man who captures this renegade Indian! Tomorrow we ride for the glory of Spain!" he shouted.

The men thought more about how they would like the "real eight" and what it would buy in the cantinas on the plaza by the Palace of the Governors. A "real eight" was two weeks' pay and the thought that one of them would earn it tomorrow would get them all up and moving out early.

★★★★

Strong Bear had just finished concealing the cross bow in a Colorado Blue Spruce. Using strips of elk hide, he had carefully tied the cross bow to the pine tree at a curve in the trail. The site had been selected so that it had a clear field of fire down the narrow horse trail in which his enemies would ride tomorrow. A vine crossed the trail. It was held up by grass and sticks to be about six inches off the ground. When a horse kicked the vine, it would trip a trigger which would then whip a small green spruce with sufficient force to trigger the cross bow. Strong Bear had test-fired the cross bow twice, so he was sure it would work when put to the test. Now the first Spaniard riding a horse down the trail would put his trap to the test.

July 31, 1680

Sergeant Solorzano kicked his remaining dozen soldiers awake at approximately 4:30 am. The sun would not come up for another hour and a half, so all was pitch black outside, but Sergeant Solorzano wanted to catch the escaped slave by surprise still asleep in his camp at dawn. The men saddled their horses and mounted them. The Spanish soldiers moved out in the dark. Two men moved out ahead of the others, as each of them wanted to capture the Indian and get the reward. Today each of them wanted to get a "real eight;" yes, this was going to be easy money.

The soldiers riding point never saw the vine his horse tripped as the trigger to the crossbow was pulled and the crossbow bolt flew by him, missing him by inches. The second soldier was wearing a metal breast plate designed to withstand any arrow with a stone arrowhead. Indeed, just days earlier, it enabled him to survive the ambush by the Cheyenne, when the arrow aimed for his chest bounced harmlessly off his protective metal breast plate. But this crossbow bolt was traveling with much greater energy, and it had an iron point on it which easily punched a hole through his protective armor. A loud scream escaped his lips as he was knocked off his horse and onto the ground. The soldier had taken his last ride. The long-range crossbow which the Spanish had often used to kill the Indians was used against them for the first time on the west slope of Independence Pass by a Lakota warrior trying to regain his freedom.

★★★★

Strong Bear was awoken by a scream he heard in the distance. Quickly, he saddled the mules and rode out twenty minutes later. Strong Bear wanted to keep his lead on the soldiers who were pursuing him. He would not try to lose them, as he wanted to lure the Spaniards towards the Wind River Mountains in northwestern Wyoming where his tribal members could help him. It was essential to keep the panniers on the mules loaded with rock so their greed would make the Spaniards pursue him to get his "Tears of the Sun." Strong Bear wanted his enemies to pay a high price as he and his companions had when they had been tricked into slavery with the opium laced whiskey and rum.

★★★★

Sergeant Solorzano and his men rode into the empty Lakota's camp an hour later. They knew it was his camp by the cropped grass and the mule tracks. It looked like the Indian had just left his camp an hour earlier. If they had not been ambushed they would have the Indian within sight now.

The soldiers had a sinking feeling as they viewed the empty camp. They had ridden out of their garrison in Santa Fe eighteen days ago. Not once had they even caught sight of the Indian, nor the mules they were pursuing. Counting the Sergeant, there were only twelve men left. Each man knew that if they encountered a large war party of

Indians they might not make it back to Santa Fe alive. Never had they lost six of his majesty's soldiers chasing a single Indian before.

★★★★

Strong Bear saw the Spanish soldiers pursuing him. Around noon he stopped and watered his mules along Roaring Fork. He stopped and switched his loaded panniers to a fresh set of mules. When he rode out he was on a fresh mule, too. The mules which had carried his pack loads on the panniers and the mule he rode this morning were exchanged for fresh animals which had been traveling with light loads. He wanted to rotate all his mules, giving them a rest in case he needed a burst of speed to outride the men chasing him.

Nine days and 280 miles later, the Sergeant Solorzano was still following those mules, and not once had they caught sight of them or the Indian. The chase had not been going as the Sergeant had planned. He had begun the pursuit of twelve mules at Valdez. Now nine days later he was chasing seven mules and these mules' loads seemed to have gotten lighter every day. What was even worse is the escaped slave was changing the mules he rode regularly every couple of hours so the mules did not get as tired. Sergeant Solorzano and his men were exhausted and their horses were exhausted from the long pursuit. Never had an escaped slave traveled so far and so fast. As his men descended the mountain slopes of Independence Pass along the Roaring Fork, his men swore as they saw the Indian warrior with the pack mules off in the distance below them.

As nightfall descended upon Mother Earth, Strong Bear made camp along the Roaring Fork at Woody Creek. Three miles behind him on Owl Creek, Sergeant Solorzano ordered his dozen men to make camp. No one had earned the "real eight" and one more man had died today. The men wondered if they would be next. Would they even make it back to Santa Fe alive? As the men lay down to sleep they listened to the occasional hoot of the owls in the night. They hoped the hoots were coming from owls and not Indians hidden in the woods.

August 1, 1680

As daybreak arrived, the Lakota warrior broke camp and quickly moved his mules towards the north west along the Roaring Fork. At the same time, three miles to the southeast, the Spaniards also broke camp. They would ride hard, making thirty-three miles, camping near where Carbondale would later be built.

Up ahead where Cattle Creek joins the Roaring Fork, Strong Bear rode into a party of nine Northern Cheyenne and Lakota. Some of the Northern Cheyenne and Lakota were personal friends of Strong Bear. He told his companions how they had been tricked by the Spaniards and given whiskey and when they awoke they were all in chains. He told how they were treated in the mines and he told them of their loved ones who had died working in the Spaniards' mines. The warriors wanted to attack the Spaniards now, but Strong Bear showed them his chains and insisted he was entitled to justice. To that end he wanted to lure the Spaniards into the Wind River Mountains where the Spaniards had originally tricked and enslaved his companions. Of course Strong Bear had no objection to them capturing one or two Spaniards to torture and frighten the men pursuing them. Never could his people get even for the many Lakota and Cheyenne who had been enslaved by the cruel Spaniards and who had died in their mines.

Three of the warriors left the camp to observe the Spaniards' camp. If they should have the opportunity, they wanted to capture one of the Spaniards alive. They wanted to pay the Spaniards back for killing their friends.

August 2, 1680

At daybreak Strong Bear rode to the Northwest. With Strong Bear were six of his friends who accompanied him to the Wind River Mountains. Four miles behind them, the Spanish soldiers from Santa Fe pursued them. Unknown to the soldiers, behind them were another three Indians observing their enemies and hoping to catch a straggler.

Sergeant Solorzano was in a bad mood today. He could read sign and he knew that instead of one Indian, he was now pursuing seven. It was not his concern that seven Indians could out- fight his men, for he knew that any Spaniard was worth three Indians. It was just that he had never expected such bad luck--and he had been having a run of bad luck lately; six of his men had died. He would not have minded the loss of his men, as it was six fewer men to repay whose wages he'd lost gambling. The trouble was he was so far away from Santa Fe that should he need assistance there would be none. Sergeant Solorzano was on his own if he ran into trouble.

The soldiers from the Santa Fe did not like what they saw, either. They had been chasing one Indian. Now there were seven Indians they were chasing, and the odds which were in their favor might go against them, should them ride into another ambush or more Indians join the group they were pursuing. They just might be lucky to get out of this wilderness alive. Just in case there was another ambush ahead, the men began straggling further and further behind the Sergeant. Let the Sergeant located the ambush first, each of his men thought; so each man found one excuse after another to lag further behind. They had to check the tightness of their saddle cinch, or there was a rock in the horse's hoof they pretended to remove; any excuse to avoid the ambush they feared lay ahead. That night, when they made camp one Spaniard was missing. No one saw him leave or ride off, he was just gone. No one knew if he deserted or was killed by Indians. That night, the soldiers camped along the Colorado River at Elk Creek. When they went hunting for elk for their dinner, another Spaniard disappeared.

August 3, 1680

After two hours of pursuing the seven Indians, the Spaniards came upon the camp where the Indians had spent the night. There they found the missing Spaniard from last evening's elk hunt. He had been captured by the Indians and killed in their camp. The Spaniards were angry the Indians did not even give him a catholic burial; they were just savages and only good dead or as slaves. Yet the Spaniards did not have time to give their companion a Catholic burial either, as they wanted to catch the Indians they were chasing so they could torture and kill them. The soldiers rode north along Government Creek swearing vengeance.

In the late afternoon the soldiers observed that they were now chasing a dozen Indians, for Strong Bear had been joined by another five Northern Cheyenne warriors. The soldiers still failed to see the three warriors who were following them. The balance of power had changed on Sheep Creek as the ten soldiers were now chasing fifteen warriors!

August 4, 1680

The Spaniards' pursuit of the Indian warriors continued north along Sheep Creek. Throughout the day the Spaniards observed the Indians up ahead in the distance as little black dots. The Indians did not appear to make any effort to escape; nor did they allow the Spaniards to close upon them. The soldiers had the feeling the Indians were waiting for something.

August 5, 1680

The Lakota warriors waited at Devil's Hole Gulch while Strong Bear walked to a location overlooking the trail. He selected one arrow, which he fired into the men pursuing him. Then Strong Bear mounted his horse and accompanied the warriors as they continued riding north towards the Wind River Mountains of Wyoming.

That day around noon the Spaniards chased the Indians into Devil's Hole Gulch. It was an ideal spot for an ambush. The ambush was expected; the type of ambush was completely unexpected. A single arrow slammed into one soldier, knocking him off his horse and onto the ground, dead. No one saw where the arrow came from; nor who had shot the arrow with deadly effect. Immediately, the soldiers drew their weapons and took cover behind trees and boulders, expecting a full assault by the hostile Indians. But they saw no one, and there was only silence. It was scary--death had come out of nowhere. No one saw where the arrow had come from. There was just silence and fear. Each soldier though he might die next. Forty five minutes later, the men remounted their horses and continued on in pursuit of Strong Bear. The dead soldier was left where he lay. The nine soldiers mounted their horses and with weapons in hand, carefully rode north.

August 6, 1680

The sergeant led his men due north and at dusk they camped on the Yampa River in northern Colorado. They could clearly see where the Indians they pursued had crossed the Yampa River only an hour ahead of them. Based on the mule tracks, Sergeant Solorzano was positive his gold was only an hour ahead of them. All the soldiers saw was that they were getting further and further from Santa Fe and their home. If they got into a battle with the Indians--even if they won the battle--it was unlikely that one or two survivors would ever make it back through hundreds of miles of wilderness.

August 7, 1680

All day long the soldiers followed the Indians north. The land had flattened out and had become flat prairie with grass and rolling hills as far as the eye could see. The Indians were never seen, but the soldiers knew that they were not far ahead as they followed their hour-old trail. At nightfall the soldiers camped on Spring Creek. The men were happy to have water for their horses. A man on foot out here simply did not have any chance at all of surviving.

August 8, 1680

The Spaniards rode north along the Big Hole Gulch throughout the day. By nightfall all the men wanted to make camp. Sergeant Solorzano would not make camp, as he wanted to stage a surprise attack on the Indians he pursued. On he rode throughout the night, until at nine that evening the exhausted sergeant ordered his weary men to make camp. The men could go no further. The soldiers made camp on the south banks of the Little Snake River.

August 9, 1680

Dawn found Sergeant Solorzano fording the Little Snake River and they pursued the Indians northward. By seven am the soldiers had crossed the imaginary line which separates the state of Colorado from Wyoming. Sergeant Solorzano had pursued the Lakota warrior and his gold through over five hundred miles of wilderness. He would not stop until he recovered all his gold, and killed these Indians that he was chasing for causing him so much trouble.

August 10, 1680

Sergeant Solorzano was completely unaware that five- to six hundred miles to the south, the battle for Pueblo Indian Independence had just erupted. The Pueblo Indians were tired of being forced to work in the mines, of having their best land seized by the Spaniards, and being forced to work as slaves for the Spaniards. They wanted to be able to worship their own religion and not be tortured or murdered for their religious beliefs and practices. Pope began the freedom fight in Taos, and there the Indians began throwing off the chains of their Spanish oppressors. Pueblo after pueblo kicked out the Spaniards and they were forced to flee south to El Paso.

Up in Wyoming the Spanish soldiers pursued the Lakota and Cheyenne towards South Pass on the east side of the Continental Divide. Three and a half days later, Sergeant Solorzano and his men entered the Wind River Range. They saw in front of them Strong Bear and beside him stood the pack mules with the loaded packs. As the Spaniards watched in disbelief, the Indian's knife slit the packs the mules carried and out tumbled lava rocks! There was no gold!

Enraged that he had been made a fool of, Sergeant Solorzano ordered his men to charge, and the nine soldiers chased after Strong Bear into a narrow canyon. As they pursued Strong Bear, the Spaniards rode into a trap the Lakota and Cheyenne warriors had set. The ambush the Spaniards rode into resulted in all their deaths. Strong Bear died fighting his enemies who had lead to the location where he and his people had been originally enslaved by Spanish slave traders. Strong Bear died in the Wind River Mountains of Wyoming fighting for his freedom.

★★★★

Moments after his death, Strong Bear's spirit looked down upon his lifeless body. Then Strong Bear faced east and said a prayer to the Great Spirit. Then he remembered his friends Wild Buffalo, Red Fox, and Fast Runner who he had agreed to decoy the soldiers north so that they would have time to hide the gold the Spaniards forced them to mine high up on Taos Mountain. Instantly Strong Bear's spirit flew down to the Taos Gorge to find his friends.

★★★★

It was here, 324 years later, that the spirits of Strong Bear, Red Fox, and Fast Runner watched the three women in the canyon below them. Strong Bear laughed aloud; he thought what a funny sense of humor the *Spirit That Moves Through All Things* has. Girls! Who would have sent them women? No one but the Great Spirit could have such a funny sense of humor.

★★★★★

As Dancing Wind slept fitfully and tossed and turned in her sleeping bag, into her dreams came Strong Bear, Red Fox, and Fast Runner. They showed her their life of freedom they lived on the Great Plains and then how they were tricked by the Spaniards, enslaved, and forced to mine gold on Taos Mountain. They showed her the beatings with the whip as they were lashed to a tree and beaten for praying to the Great Spirit and how the people died in the mine cave-ins and malnutrition. They showed Dancing Wind their escape and how Strong Bear lured the Spanish garrison up into the Wind River Mountains where they were able to fight at close range and kill the Spaniards. They showed her how Red Fox, Fast Runner, and Wild Buffalo died and how they had made a vow to GOD to use the gold they had buried centuries ago for the benefit of mankind in a healing center where people of all races could come to heal their bodies and spirits.

What Strong Bear, Red Fox, and Fast Runner told Dancing Wind was they wanted her to go down to the river where they had buried two of the Indians who had been murdered by the cruel Spaniards. The three teenage girls were told to remove the shackles which bound their legs and then take their two brothers *Home*. Their second task would be to remove the three small barrels of gold and use it to build a healing center.

Dancing Wind, Molly, and Sarah accompanied the warriors' spirits to the site where their two brothers were buried alongside the Rio Grande River over three centuries ago. The Spirits had no ability to remove the chains from their brother's legs, nor could they lift the barrels they had buried in 1680. Dancing Wind scanned the site with a metal detector and nothing was there. Although she used a Pulse Induction Metal Detector that could detect down to a depth of 5 meters, she could find no trace of metal!

The burial site down by the river had been repeatedly flooded over the centuries. There was no longer any trace of the chains the Indians were bound with. There was no trace of the barrels, or of the gold! Over the centuries they had returned to the Mother Earth wince they had come from centuries ago.

Dancing Wind turned to her Guardian Angel beside her and asked her Angel why the Indian warriors saw the gold and the Indians in chains yet she detected nothing. Dancing Wind's Guardian Angel lovingly explained to Dancing Wind, Molly, Sarah, Strong Bear, Red Fox and Fast Runner that the Indians were correct that this was the exact spot that they had buried the gold and their brothers in 1680, yet this site had been repeatedly flooded over the centuries and what had been buried here beside the Rio Grande had been gone for a long time. Now only a memory or spirit imprint remained.

Dancing Wind told Strong Bear, Red Fox, and Fast Runner that it was now time for them to return *Home*.

"Why don't you accompany Molly and Sarah to the top of the east side of the gorge cliffs and tonight we will make a sacred circle and you can sit down and drum with us?" Dancing Wind suggested to the Spirits, "Then tomorrow as we drum at daybreak, we will call in two Angels to accompany you on your journey to the Great Spirit."

So up the old Indian trail, and what would then become part of the Old Spanish Trail, the three teenage girls climbed. Beside them they were accompanied by three Spirit warriors. Alongside the six individuals were also six Angels, their Guardian Angels (Spirit Guides). They all wanted a successful outcome with the coming of daybreak.

Above the Stage Coach Hot Springs, the teenagers walked along the gorge rim until they found a suitable location they all liked. There they made a circle and the three teenagers and the three warriors sat inside it. Dancing Wind looked at Strong Bear and indicated to him that he should set the pace or beat of the drum. Slowly Dancing Wind, Molly, Sarah, Strong Bear, Fast Runner, and Red Fox began drumming. As darkness descended upon the cliffs and the Rio Grande, the sound of drumming could be heard through the hills. In the morning the spirits would be going *home*.

★★★★

At dawn the next morning the three teenagers again began drumming. They drummed very slowly. They had lit incense burning around their sacred circle, and because they were helping Cheyenne and Lakota warrior's spirits go home, they also lit and smudged themselves with sage and sweet grass. Dancing Wind put down her drum and asked the three warriors to accompany her as she moved around the circle to the drumming. Dancing Wind prayed as she moved to the drum beat. She prayed that GOD would send his Angels to accompany the warriors home. Over time, the drums beat faster and faster as the drummers picked up speed.

Suddenly two Angels of the LORD appeared and between them was a tunnel of golden light. As the warriors danced around the circle to the beat of the drum, each in turn came to be beside the golden door. Looking inside they saw many of their loved ones calling out their names and beckoning them in a loving manner to come on, as they waved them inside. The warriors instantly recognized their loved ones and friends. Into the tunnel of light they flew between the two Angels who guarded the gates to heaven itself. Instantly, all three spirit warriors, Chose to return *home*. With the disappearance of the three warriors' spirits, the two Angels also entered the door of light and instantly the door and the Angels were gone.

Sarah and Molly stopped drumming and the silence engulfed the sacred circle. Then Dancing Wind and Molly independently checked with their own Guardian Angel to be sure that everyone who chosen to do so had gone *home*. Their Angels told them both that the warriors were now *home*.

★★★★★

During the drumming, Sarah did not know the speed or rhythm to drum, so she just watched Molly and followed her lead. Sarah had not seen the Angels, she had not seen the Spirit Warriors, but she had felt her entire body tingling and shaking as the energy built up and the Angels appeared. Because of the high energy, Sarah's own Guardian Angel was utilizing the effort on Sarah's behalf combined with all her effort to help her establish a connection with her charge. Sarah's Guardian Angel was doing her best to open a channel of communication between herself and Sarah. Gifts of the spirit do not come instantly. It takes effort as well as need, and a demonstration that you use your gifts properly. The effort in a pure and loving manner to help others in need would help open Sarah to establish and build her relationship with her Guardian Angel.

★★★★

Two weeks later the three teenagers went to see the Lakota medicine man, Dan. They began by greeting each other with handshakes which developed into warm hugs. They told Dan about their canoe trip from southern Colorado down south to the Elephant Butte Dam along the Rio Grande and their adventures with Strong Bear, Red Fox, and Fast Runner. They told Dan how Strong Bear had died in the Wind River Range of Wyoming, yet his spirit returned to the Rio Grande Gorge to locate his dear friends Wild Buffalo, Red Fox, and Fast runner who had died trying to regain their freedom.

So the old Indian asked them if they were able to take Strong Bear, Red Fox, and Fast Runner *home*. With smiles on their faces the three women proudly told them they were able to take them all home. Then their smiles faded as Dan asked about Wild Flower.

"Did you take Wild Flower and her baby home?"

Molly said "Well, we assumed that she might have gone home, too. Certainly, if she was there, the Angels would have taken her, as well."

Dan mildly admonished the three women. "Never assume; be certain. Don't just assume it is taken care of, or guess that it was done. Do not repel off a cliff assuming that the end of your repelling line is properly secured. The mistake of assuming could cost you or someone dear to you their life. Do not assume the batteries in your walkie talkies or your Global Positioning System (GPS) are good unless you just replaced them and are carrying a spare set. Do not assume some one else has the water as you travel in the desert, unless you plan to completely do without water! Do not assume; it can cost you your life.

Now ask your Guardian Angel if Wild Flower and the baby's spirits went *home.*"

The three teenagers then turned to their respective Guardian Angels and asked them if the two spirits had gone home. They sheepishly looked at their feet as they learned the answer. They had failed to take *home* two of the spirits there who needed their help.

Sarah then told Dan, "It is not our fault she did not go home. We all asked our Guardian Angels if all the Spirits who wanted to go home had gone home and they told us they had."

Dan told Sarah "The Angels had spoken truthfully. Only the three Indian spirits were ready to return home. It is not about blaming you for making a mistake. It is simply about doing your spirit work to the best of your ability and not assuming anything. Try and get the facts. When you work in the Spirit realm and with the Angels, you want all the facts you can get, to try and avoid making mistakes. Now ask your Angels why Wild Flower was not ready to go *home.*"

Moments later, Molly and Dancing Wind replied "It's the Baby"

"She still cries and mourns the baby."

Dan asked where the baby was now. Dancing Wind replied that the baby's spirit is not at the site where she had been murdered, but beside his mother, watching over and helping her. Dan told them that Wild Flower was so distraught or upset over the murder of her child that she regularly went to the site where both of them had been murdered. She did not accept or realize the fact that her child's spirit was beside her and had been watching over his mother for centuries.

So Dancing Wind asked, "What are we to do?"

Dan told them that first they need to find the exact spot the baby was buried at in 1680. Then they will need to be at that exact spot as they call in both the mother and her child as well.

Sarah asked Dan, "Do you realize you will have to locate a spot about two feet square in an area encompassing over ten square miles of terrain? There will be nothing to guide us to the spot the baby died and was buried approximately 325 years ago!"

"Well," Dan replied, "it needs to be done so let's go do it! I will give you a hand on tracking this trail." Dan knew that the Angels were aware his purpose and desire was pure, so they would help him all they could.

So the three teenagers followed the old Indian south along the Rio Grande Gorge. For an old Indian he sure walked fast. They knew if they did not hurry along that they would soon lose sight of the Indian. As morning turned to noon they saw numerous treasure signs and markers, but Spanish Treasure was not what they were hunting. So the four trackers walked on past the treasure signs like giant pack horses and turtles leading the way to treasure; they were trying to track a far harder trail to follow, to where the little child lay buried centuries ago. The day turned hot and they drank from their water bottles as the frozen water melted. At 1:00 pm they began the descent of east side of the gorge. For four hours the three teenagers carefully followed Dan down the cliff face. A single misstep and the fall might be fatal. A hundred feet above the river, on the south side of the Indian trail, Dan told the three teenagers to talk to their Guardian Angels and locate the ancient burial site.

When Molly and Sarah talked to their Guardian Angel silently in their minds, Dan stopped them and admonished them to talk out loud. It is easier for me as well as your Guardian Angel to understand your questions or what you are thinking instead of both of us trying to struggle with reading your thoughts. Asking their Guardian Angel questions, they asked of the baby burial site was down by the river.

The Angels told them: "*No.*"

They asked about the north slope along the cliffs along the north side of the trail and were again told "*No.*"

They asked about the Sandy Wash curving slightly to the northwest leading into the Rio Grande and were again told "*No.*"

They asked about the smaller area curving to the southwest and were told "*No.*"

They asked about the higher ground between the drainage going to the northwest and the southeast and both received the same answer "*No.*"

The only place they could further guess was the way the shadow Indian with the single large feather curved around a rock face along to the south, on the east side of the river and just to the south of the south drainage area. Here Sarah got no answer at all and Molly got a half-way yes. Molly knew it was not exactly right or correct but she did not know what else to say or ask the Angel beside her.

Dan told them that the site was not really correct; it was another 15 meters east and higher up on the sloping cliff face. The burial site was beside the stone man laying flat on the ground. Specifically, just about a meter or two to the north of the stone man.

Dancing Wind had not answered the questions, as she wanted to give Molly and Sarah the opportunity to track the ancient trail without her answer influencing their answer. Dancing Wind knew the baby's location simply by looking at her Guardian Angel's eyes when Dan had asked the question. Dancing Wind saw where the Angel had glanced. All four of the trackers then moved over to the burial site.

Removing their backpacks, they began to set up for the work that was to come at twilight.

Food and water was set out for Wild Flower and her child to take with them on their journey *home*. Incense was set out upright in a crack in the black lava rock so that it would remain upright yet not be a fire danger when lit. Drums were removed from their packs and set out along with sage and sweet grass to be lit and used during the ceremony. The four dear friends then relaxed and talked awhile. The discussions bounced around to various questions that they had from the weather front moving in from the west to how many spirits were present around them and how many were male, female and how many children's spirits were present. Dan was always pushing his students to think and extend and develop their senses.

As sunset arrived, the approaching night began engulfing the Rio Grande Gorge. Birds' black forms could be seen flying before settling into their nests for the night. An owl could be heard hooting in the distance. Lightning and Thunder Spirits could be seen and heard in the distance. The Rain Spirits spoke of the approaching storm. Gusts from the Wind Spirits could be felt by all. The time had come.

Dancing Wind began praying as Dan lit the incense and the smell of sage and burning sweet grass filled their small circle. Molly and Sarah began drumming slowly. Soon the prayers of Dan and Dancing Wind could be heard reaching up to the heavens above. Many spirits who had come from heaven itself came to help to ensure everything went smoothly

Dan and Dancing Wind prayed to GOD to send his Angels to help take the spirits *home*, they prayed that everything would have a positive outcome for the highest good. Then they prayed for Wild Flower and her baby. Wild Flower was always a very loving spirit, trying to help whomever she could. Even though she always returned to pray for her child at the site she and her child had been murdered, whenever she encountered spirits needing love, guidance or her help throughout a vast region, she endeavored to help them. So it was that she had brought three spirits along with her who she wanted to also help go *home*.

As Dan and Dancing Wind prayed Molly and Sarah began drumming faster and faster, speeding up the rhythm. Suddenly the medicine man shouted out

"Stop! You are drumming too fast. You are spooking the other spirits we have come to help. Slow down! Now stop for a few minutes while the spirits whom have come in from heaven have time to calm the three spirits down so we can safely help them go *home*."

A "Being of Light," who traveled from France, suddenly appeared and surrounded the spirits with her unconditional love.

Molly and Sarah would try not to make that mistake again. Slowly they began drumming. Then Dan called in Wild Flower beside him. She was so nervous that Dan had to repeatedly tell her to calm down and stay at his side. Then Dan lifted up the baby's spirit energy from where he had been buried And the medicine man held the Spirit in his outstretched arms towards the heavens asking for GOD's blessings and love. Then he had Wild Flower move around in front of him and he lowered his arms and placed the baby's essence into his mother's arms. Tears rolled down Wild Flower's face as she held her child. After a few minutes, Dan asked Wild Flower if she would like to see the son her baby has grown up to be. When she nodded yes, then the spirit of her son appeared as the man (spirit) he had become. He hugged his mother in both arms as tears of love and happiness rolled down their faces.

Her son had actually been watching over his mother, Wild Flower, for centuries. Yet because of Wild Flower's grief over the loss of her child, she was unable to realize the spirit beside her and watching over her was her son. Once both spirits were in each other's arms they were both ready to return to heaven whence all spirits of GOD originate.

The drumming slowly picked up speed and then with the crash of lightning and thunder accompanied by gust of wind, two Angels of the Lord appeared. Between them was a door of golden light into which walked Wild Flower and her son. After they entered the tunnel of light taking them to heaven, the three remaining spirits, who Wild Flower had brought to this site, slowly approached the door. Looking inside the tunnel of golden light, they saw their loved ones they had not seen for centuries calling out their names and welcoming them home again. And instantly the three spirits chose to return *home* into the arms of their loved ones. Instantly they traveled between the two Angels and traveled into the tunnel of light taking them to heaven.

With a roar the storm was upon the four trackers. Sheets of rain poured down upon them. Gusts of wind shook them and quickly the rocky slopes above were too dangerous to climb in the night, as the soil turned to slippery mud and night descended upon them. Beside a stone man, and twenty feet above the shadow warrior with one feather in his hair, the teacher and his two students huddled together for warmth as the hard-driving rain soaked them to the bone. In later years, if you had asked any one of them: "Would they ever do it again?" Their answer would come instantly and without hesitation:

"Of course."

Would you?

God so loves the Children
That he loves to talk with them
That he loves to play with them
That he loves to laugh with them
That he sends Angels to watch over them

Grandfather Mike's Gift

Cathy loved her grandfather and she always looked forward to the time they spent together. Sometimes he would read to her, sometimes he would take her for an ice cream. Her mommy and daddy had to work during the day to pay the bills so she would spend her days with her grandfather, Mike.

Cathy knew her grandfather loved her, as he purchased her tennis shoes that had lights in the shoes. Her mommy told her she would have to make do with her old shoes which had holes in the shoes, but when Cathy asked Mike if she could have new tennis shoes with lights like the other kids in school her grandfather told her of course she could and let her chose the white tennis shoes. Cathy knew she was a big girl now, as she could tie her shoe laces. Her grandfather had taught her how. She had a smart grandfather who could answer all her questions. Even her daddy told her to go ask her grandfather when she had questions.

★★★★

Mike loved spending his free time watching and playing with his granddaughter. His daughter and her husband both made minimum wage so they could not afford a baby sitter to take care of their daughter, Cathy. Mike was living alone since his wife died in an auto accident so he enjoyed spending time with his granddaughter. She was the light in his life now that he was alone. Today he was taking Cathy to a book store and he would let her chose a book. Then they would spend the afternoon together, reading the book or playing with a ball out in the yard until her parents got home for dinner.

★★★★

After Mary fixed dinner, Mike took Cathy out for a walk. Mike knew that sometimes married couples needed a little time alone. Occasionally Mike would take Cathy for a short walk in the dark and together they would explore the night. Nights with a full moon were best, as it made it easier to see. They would see the owls out hunting mice. Sometimes they looked at the stars and Mike would show his granddaughter the different star formations. Soon Cathy could easily find the Big Dipper, the Little Dipper, the North Star, and the first star one sees in the night sky, Venus. Sometimes she and Grandfather Mike chased the fire flies at night. In the winter Mike showed her how to follow the rabbit tracks in the snow. Several times they saw a rabbit on the snow running away from them.

During the summer they would take walks during the day while her parents were working. They would see red birds, and black birds and once they even saw five quail. They would see rabbits, squirrels, and tiny brown chipmunks. Mike would also talk about the trees and plants. One day her grandfather showed her how to pick mint plants and they took the plants home and made mint tea. Cathy knew no one in the whole world was as smart as her grandfather. She had the best grandfather in the world.

★★★★

When summer came Mike decided he wanted to teach his granddaughter how to paddle a canoe, swim and catch fish. Mike took his daughter to Faucetts Marine Supply in Annapolis where he got her a flotation vest to protect his daughter around the water. Mike always made Cathy wear her life vest once they got near the water and he would continue to do so until she learned how to swim. He got a life vest for himself too, but he did not always wear his. Mike owned a ten foot aluminum John boat which he used to take his granddaughter out boating, and purchased two fishing rods so Cathy cold fish with him. Mike got a new dip net for crabbing too. Then Mike purchased a canteen to hold water. When Cathy saw Mike had a canteen she told him she wanted a one, so he purchased his granddaughter a smaller one for herself. After shopping, Mike took Cathy out for a Happy Meal at Mc Donald's. Her grandfather always thought that Cathy was more interested in the toys than the food.

★★★★

Often, Mike would take Cathy motor boating by Chincoteague Island and Assateague Island National Seashore. This is a long barrier island along the Atlantic Ocean in the states of Virginia and Maryland. Here they would fish and take walks on the island. Cathy liked watching the wild Spanish horses that lived on the island.

Sometimes they would catch fish which Mike would then clean with his knife and place in the ice chest to keep them fresh until they returned home to cook them. Other times they dug clams to take home and cook, or they picked raspberries. Mike always tried to show Cathy something new as she loved learning. Mike would teacher her the names of the birds and often they saw seagulls and ducks.

Since Cathy did not know how to swim, Mike always insisted that she wear a life vest he had purchased. Cathy always also carried her canteen; she was wearing it with a strap around her neck as she wanted to be like her Grandfather Mike. As Cathy swam in the water Mike became concerned that she was getting a little bit far away from him. So Mike called to Cathy to swim towards him. Cathy did not seem to be making any progress-- the outgoing tide seemed to be carrying Cathy further away.

Mike jumped into the water and swam towards her. He was rapidly closing the distance when he felt pains radiating across his chest and down his left arm. Suddenly he could not get enough air. Mike was having a heart attack. He slipped beneath the water as he died.

Cathy kicked her feet trying to get to shore as the current carried her out towards the open ocean, but she suddenly lost sight of her Grandfather Mike and could not see him anymore. She saw some land not too far away and she kicked with all her might to reach the land. Beside Cathy was her Guardian Angel showing her the land and telling her to kick hard. The Guardian Angel grabbed Cathy's life vest and pulled as hard as she could to shore. As the

Guardian Angel pulled on the life vest, she also prayed to GOD for help. "GOD please send me help now!" Suddenly, as Cathy kicked towards the shore and her Guardian Angel pulled upon her life vest, two Angels of the LORD appeared and they tugged on the life vest too. As the three angels tried their best to pull the little girl towards shore, four more Angels appeared and they grabbed the life vest and they pulled too. The shoreline which Cathy almost drifted away from was suddenly within reach. She grabbed hold of a log, which was jutting out into the water. With a mighty heave the Angels pulled her to shore and the extra Angels disappeared. Cathy was laying half in and half out of the seawater, then she looked around. She failed to see her guardian Angel sitting on the shore line beside her. Her guardian Angel was exhausted and laying on her back on the sand. As the Angel recovered, she got on her knees and thanked GOD for the help.

Then Cathy got out of the water and crawled up on the bank. Cathy could not see their motor boat or her grandfather Mike, she was all alone. Cathy started walking north looking for her grandfather Mike. Beside her walked her Guardian Angel, watching over her charge. The Angel began praying to GOD as she walked north following Cathy.

An hour later, Cathy saw a pretty rabbit. She followed the brown and white cotton tail for an hour when she lost sight of it. All around her she saw raspberries, red raspberries. For the next two hours Cathy ate raspberries and then she turned towards the sound of the waves crashing on the beach. Cathy walked towards the beach and then turned north. When she was thirsty she drank from her canteen.

As evening came, she walked back from the firm wet sand to the softer sand in a hollow out of the wind. She slept for six hours and when she awoke she looked at the stars. Finding the North Star, she returned to the beach and followed it.

★★★★

When Grandfather Mike and their daughter did not return from the boating trip, Cathy's parents John and Sarah called the police. They were afraid that Grandfather Mike might have been involved in a traffic accident. There were so many crazy drivers on the road nowadays. The police took a report and checked with the U. S. Park Service at both Assateague and Chincoteague Islands. The pickup truck was there by the boat ramp.

Grandfather Mike and Cathy had not come back from their boating trip. At first light a search would start. By midmorning the search party had found Grandfather Mike's boat. The searchers did not realize the wind and the tide had moved the boat and Grandfather Mikes body many miles along the shore line. The family was told the sad news that the search party had found Grandfather Mike the following day.. It appeared he had drowned. There was no sign of their daughter Cathy.

Sarah and John were told that a search would resume in the morning. The parents were not told by the searchers that there was only a remote chance of finding the daughter. For two more days the search parties searched Assateague Island. No trace of Cathy was found. Sarah and John prayed that their daughter would be found, for Sarah had unceasing faith in GOD. Did not God's son Jesus say: "Ask and it will be given what you ask for. Seek, and you will find. Knock and the door will be opened. For everyone who asks, receives. Anyone who seeks, finds. If only you will knock, the door will open," – Matthew: Chapter 7 verse 7-8.

After a fourth day of searching the search was called off. The police and U. S. Park Service would continue to keep an eye out for Cathy but they thought their mission had changed from a rescue mission to a recovery mission. They held little hope of ever finding the little girl if no trace of her was found in four days. Throughout the day and night Sarah prayed for her daughter because she felt in her heart that her daughter was still alive.

★★★★

As Cathy walked north, she stopped and ate the red flower fruit buds of the Prickly Pear Cactus and drank water from her canteen. Later that day, she saw that brown rabbit again. Again, the rabbit led her to some raspberries. For several hours she ate raspberries. On the night of the second day she had drunk the last of the water in her canteen. She slept in a hollow of dry sand seventy feet back from the beach. She awoke about three in the morning when the wind shifted. She saw the North Star when she looked at the stars, so she continued to walk north. She missed her grandfather. She wished her mommy would come and get her.

On the morning of the third day, Cathy saw a large white owl land near her. She ran after the owl but the owl always seemed to stay twenty or thirty feet ahead of her. When she was tired and could go no further, so she sat down to rest in the sand. As she rested she noticed the pretty white owl on top of the hill in front of her.

Cathy got a smile on her face. She had an idea. She would sneak up on the owl and catch it. Crawling towards it, she saw the owl go behind the hill. Quietly she crawled towards the bird.

As she crawled over the little sandy hill, she saw that below her was a small pool of water about four feet long, two feet wide, and six inches deep. The girl forgot about the owl. Cathy wanted the water. She stuck her face in the water and drank and drank. Then she filled her canteen full of water. Only then did Cathy wonder where the owl had gone.

On the fourth day Cathy continued walking north along Chincoteague Island. It was fall and the day time temperatures were in the seventies. At night she was cold as the temperatures dropped to the fifties, but her life vest helped keep her warm. Cathy prayed to God to send her mommy and daddy to find her. Cathy prayed to God for her grandfather Mike to come find her. Her grandfather must have gotten lost. It was not like him to leave her like this. Cathy did not know what happed to her grandfather.

Cathy was hungry as she walked north. She wished mommy would come and fix her a sandwich and give her a glass of milk. She knew her mommy and daddy must be at work as it was day time. Her parents only come home to see her after work. She was hungry. She missed her warm bed. Her legs were tired. She wished Grandfather Mike was here to carry her.

Suddenly her thoughts were interrupted by the sound of dozens of gray and white Seagulls. Looking around, she saw many Seagulls circling to her right. Cathy went over to see the Seagulls and see what they were doing. As the Seagulls fought overhead, she suddenly realized that they were fighting over a soft shell clam. Walking along the muddy stretch of shore line at low tide she remembered her grandfather Mike had showed her how to find soft shell clams. They made a hole in the sand just above them. She looked around and found a stick on the mud flat. After taking the stick, she dug down to the clam. Then she pulled the clam out of his broken shell and ate the it. Those birds were sure smart. They knew where clams were. Cathy was soon covered in the black mud of the clam bed, and when she could eat no more she noticed the tide was coming in and the clam bed was being covered by water. Cathy returned to the sandy beach on the east side of Chincoteague Island and walked north. The swamps with the clams can be found on the west side of the island. The Atlantic Ocean was on her east side. The sandy beach leading north was ahead of her.

★★★★

Seven days later, just south of the Ocean City inlet, an old fisherman in a skiff was trying to catch flounder. Henry looked up from his fishing and glanced around as his dog barked at a strange black object moved towards him from Chincoteague Island. For a few minutes he stared as the little object moved towards him. Henry was a senior who did not like to wear his glasses so he squinted to see more clearly. There was a possibility that it was a dog, he thought. Henry returned to his fishing. Very slowly the black speck in the distance was getting larger. His dog kept barking at the black object to the south of his boat. For some reason unknown to Henry, his eyes kept returning to the black object, which was slowly moving closer and closer. Henry wished he had his glasses but he had left them in his pickup truck where they would not get broken. Henry just kept looking as the speck got larger and larger. Putting one hand over his forehead to block the sun from his eyes, he looked at the black object moving up the beach towards him.

Suddenly Henry said: "Oh my God!" For Henry saw a little girl all by herself walking towards him. She was wearing a life vest and was covered in black mud. He pulled up his anchor line and quickly rowed his skiff towards the South shore. Henry ran towards Cathy and grabbed her up in his arms. That she covered him in black mud did not matter in the least. He carried her to his skiff and there Cathy asked for water. She drank the entire bottle of water without stopping. As Cathy drank the water Henry gave her, Cathy's guardian Angel thought back to an old saying in the Bible and smiled as she recalled the words, "And if as my representatives, you even give a cup of cold water to a little child, you surely will be rewarded."(Matthew: Chapter 10 verse 42.) Henry did not know the number for the police. He simply dialed 911 on his cell phone. Before he got his skiff back to the boat ramp, the police car was already waiting there to pick Cathy up and take her home to her parents.

★★★★

The Angels in our lives may come in many forms. They may be the person who gives you a helping hand changing a flat tire as we are stuck on the side of the road. The Angel may be the person who suggests to you that you write stories, suggest a life changing job or to apply for a job in a different field of work, in which you will really excel. Angels' acts can be found in individuals taking the time to teach you a new way of thinking about the world around you. Certainly Cathy's grandfather Mike, in taking the time and making the effort to teach her about nature and her environment, embodied the actions that Angels really do take. I would hope if you have the opportunity to teach a child or grandchild you do so. For the actions you take in helping another are sure to put a smile on your Guardian Angel's face. Do not wait to go to heaven, but through your actions bring heaven into the here and now. It is by the small actions of love and grace and helping one another that thousands of you working together will create heaven on earth.

There was a man who lived in Galilee who said as you treat the least of my children that is how you treat me. So when you take the time to teach a child what you know or love, are you not helping the least or smallest ones in the world around you and literally helping the Angels in their work? So what are you waiting for, an Angel to accompany you? The Angel is right by your side now!

Some people think Angels are Male
Some people think that Angels are Female
Some people think Angels are Tall
Some people think Angels are Small
To the Angels it does not matter at all
For Unconditional Love (for GOD)
And all GODS creation
Is the Path for us all!

Our Neighbors

Many years ago Dancing Wind and Molly O'Brian were prospecting on a mesa south of Abiquiu. As the sun set in the western sky, both trackers were headed home to Dancing Wind's old brown trailer in Abiquiu. It had been a long day of tracking the ancient trails and they were ready to return home. As their vehicle bounced along the potholes of the old dirt road, their thoughts consisted of looking forward to a hot shower to wash off the dust, as well as eating a hot meal before they called it a day.

The sun had set and stars were now appearing in the sky when Molly noticed an aircraft to the west of the dirt road they were traveling on. The aircraft was about four hundred yards away, and was just sitting there in the sky about four hundred feet above the ground. The aircraft was not moving and one could even see numerous individual lights on the aircraft. This was certainly most unusual.

Molly pulled the jeep over to the side of the dirt road, and even before she said anything to Dancing Wind her eyes, too, were focused on the aircraft just moving slowly in the sky. Soon the aircraft was joined by another aircraft, then another. The aircraft seemed to be moving very slowly across the ground. The approximate speed of this aircraft was about the speed of a person walking. Sometimes the saucer-shaped aircraft moved closer--to about three hundred yards away from the teenagers. Other times the aircraft slowly moved back and forth from three to six hundred yards away.

Within minutes, the girls had reached into their backpacks and pulled out their binoculars. When they looked at the aircrafts they thought they looked like two saucer plates placed together with the curved portion being located in the center of the top and bottom of the aircraft. Then there were lights around the middle, or wider, portion of the aircraft.

After watching several aircraft for about fifteen minutes, the teenagers carefully opened the doors of the jeep and when the interior lights of the vehicle turned on they carefully turned all the lights off. What Molly and Dancing Wind were doing was making their car completely dark. Their reason for insuring that even the interior or the door lights did not come on is so that they could remove their night vision equipment from the vehicle. Night vision equipment can easily be damaged by light as it magnifies the starlight and the moon light 50,000 to 100,000 times so images can be seen much more clearly in the dark of night.

The teenagers removed their night vision devices from the black duffel bag and removed the lens covers and turned them on. With the devices on, they again examined the air crafts to their west. Two changes were immediately apparent with the aircrafts. The smaller of the two changes was that there seemed to be a form of light or energy around the aircraft. Like a greenish fuzzy glow around the aircraft. But the most significant change was an energy beam of light radiated down towards the ground from the center of the aircraft. This downward-focused energy was not a tight beam of light but appeared more like the hot gasses coming off a rocket being launched into space. This downward-focused energy was not visible without the use of the night vision.

For two hours the girls watched the numerous aircrafts three-hundred to six-hundred yards to the west of them. Sometimes the number of aircrafts climbed to six. Other times there were just two aircrafts hovering above the ground to the west of them. Many times the teenagers had seen helicopters and these aircraft were definitely not helicopters.

Although the aircraft continued to slowly fly over the mountains to the west of the mesa, the teenagers finally, decided to call it a night and went home for a shower, a meal and to sleep.

★★★★ Five Years Later★★★★

Molly O'Brian and Dancing Wind had crossed the border into Mexico and were engaged in a search for the Apache stronghold of Nana Cochise. As they camped one night on a forty acre plateau well south of the United States border, they sat around their campfire and discussed their strategy for their next few days of searching. Their eyes were drawn to an aircraft doing unusual maneuvers in the sky. Walking over to their tent, they removed their binoculars to observe the aircraft. Over the next twenty minutes the aircraft slowly approached them, stopping and hovering about two hundred yards to the south of them. Removing a pair of night vision binoculars from its protective case, they examined the aircraft moving slowly through the evening sky. The aircraft seemed similar to the aircraft they had first seen five years earlier in the mountains south of Abiquiu.

This time the aircraft seemed to land on the southern end of the mesa which they were camped upon. Molly looked and Dancing Wind and Dancing Wind looked at Molly. While neither had said a word, they both had mentally asked each other the same two questions: Did you see what I just saw? Do you want to investigate?

★★★★

Dancing Wind and Molly slowly moved south, cautiously walking closer to their visitors. Suddenly Dancing Wind smiled and Molly's jaw fell in surprise. For their visitors were sitting around a campfire—just like they often did. Slowly moving forward while remaining aware of their surroundings, Dancing Wind and Molly slowly advanced towards their *neighbors* sitting around a burning campfire. Sometimes they only moved twenty yards closer towards the campfire; sometimes they only advanced ten yards before they would stop and study the individuals around the campfire.

Molly and Dancing Wind slowly advanced upon the campfire. Their senses were alert to any possible danger, yet they detected none. They moved around the camp and were cautiously moving closer when suddenly they froze in place. One of the individuals by the campfire slowly stood up and looked directly at them as they stood hidden by the surrounding darkness of night.

As they looked at the individual who was looking at them, they knew it was impossible for the individual by the campfire to see them as they were still fifty yards away, concealed by the night. Then, slowly, the individual raised their right hand and waved at the teenagers to come on over and join them at their campfire.

Dancing Wind and Molly O'Brian were astonished; normally no one could detect their presence at night when they were quietly approaching or moving past a camp. Then they smiled at the thought that they had not only been sensed by the individuals sitting around the campfire, but invited to join them. Yet even with the invitation, it took Dancing Wind and Molly forty-five minutes to advance the fifty yards, as they were both very apprehensive and nervous at this meeting with their *neighbors*.

At ten yards, or thirty feet, Dancing Wind stopped and observed their four neighbors. Two of them were sitting on stones and another two were sitting together like a couple will often be found sitting together. They had carefully left open one third of the circle for the arrival of Dancing Wind and Molly. There was a log for them to sit upon and watch the fire with them.

Very cautiously and carefully, Dancing Wind and Molly approach the campfire and they constantly scanned the actions of their friends for movement or hostile action. As careful as they were, and Dancing Wind and Molly were being very careful, they observed no hostile intent or action. Curiosity and open friendly intent was all they detected in the thoughts and actions of their neighbors.

As Dancing Wind and Molly glanced at the log placed by the fire for them to sit on, they were surprised to see their Guardian Angels walking over to the log and sitting down. So both teenagers followed their Guardian Angels' examples.

Occasionally one of their *neighbors* slowly moved to add wood to the fire. The slow movements were intentional so as to not frighten Molly or Dancing Wind. As they sat around the campfire, it was like each was scanning the thoughts of the other and was trying their best not to frighten one another. The *neighbors* reminded Dancing Wind of the stories she had heard of the *neighbors* dancing with the Hopi Indians during their celebrations in the fall season. Molly observed their hands had no fingers. Their hands were shaped like the palm of our hand. Yet there palms were flexible so they could easily pick up a stick or move the pan they had on the coals of the fire.

In the firelight they saw the *neighbors* use a stick to remove a pan from the reddish gray coals of the fire. When the lid was removed small biscuits of golden brown bread was removed from the pan and shared by everyone. The breaking of the hot golden brown bread was a simple act of friendship.

Sometimes the *neighbors* added a little wood to the campfire. Sometimes Dancing Wind or Molly added wood to the fire. Each was adjusting to the presence of the other. Both groups (species) were slowly getting over their fear of the unknown, adjusting to each other's presence, for should you encounter our *neighbors,* you too will need some time to adjust as Dancing Wind and Molly did.

As the night grew late and Dancing Wind and Molly felt themselves nodding off to sleep; so they thought good night. Each girl picked up a thick burning branch to light the way back to their camp. The teenagers then slowly walked back to their camp using the burning branches to light their way. When they were fifty yards away from our *neighbors'* camp, they stopped and both turned to wave. At the campfire they saw the four neighbors stand up and wave back at them.

★★★★

The military response to visits by our *neighbors* is like the early naturalists who, upon seeing an unusual bird or animal, responded by killing it with a weapon and then mounting the trophy on the wall. That is how the early naturalists then studied the object of their attention. It is possible in Washington, DC to go and look at an extinct Carrier Pigeon a naturalist killed to study the bird. Since the founding of the 13

Colonies centuries ago, this approach has had little change. Of course our modern weapons are much more destructive.

If we as a people choose to kill / capture / attack / our *neighbors* on sight we are throwing away a wonderful opportunity to engage in an exchange of ideas, knowledge and advance beyond a cave man mentality. When we allow our "government of the people and by the people" to engage our *neighbors* in a hostile manner you never will give our *neighbors* the opportunity to know and learn from us and for us to get to know and learn from them.

Individuals often react with fright or raw emotion to circumstance and events they do not understand. Lack of tolerance for other races, religions and species often causes narrow minded individuals to lash out in violence. Fear is a natural response, but we as a people need to show tolerance, respect and acceptance for *everyone*.

We as a people need to advance beyond discriminating against individuals because of their race, sex, religion or color. For Protestants and Catholics to battle and fight each other (Ireland) or a Sunni to murder a Shiite (Iraqi) must cause their Guardian Angels to throw up their arms in despair, as clearly both are so immature they are simply unable to understand the most basic of concepts that Jesus and Mohammed were teaching.

Many regions of the Middle East have not accepted the concept of equal rights for women. Certainly women are entitled to the same rights as their husbands it unfortunately took hundreds of years for us to get to that point in the United States. Many areas of the Middle East and Asia have an abundant opportunity for the men to grow up! When anyone tortures and murders a woman because she is not wearing a scarf (burka) it is not she who committed any offense before GOD but the stupid ignorant man who kills her. When you do not allow women into a life boat (Madagascar / East Africa) or even hold on to the sides of a life boat, without smashing their hands with the wooden oar's so that they too might live; it is not the women who drowned whom will be explaining their actions (to GOD), but the men (Muslims) in the life boat whom refused to help the women in any manner.

When a Palestine cannot live in peace with a Jew clearly someone(s) failing to show religious tolerance. When Jews seize Palestine lands and bull dozer down a home without providing just compensation to the home owner they are certainly not establishing a lasting friendship or rapport with their neighbors.

I do not know the solutions for these problems. Possibly the Angels do. But if we are to grow up, we need to listen to the advice and counsel of the Angels for if we as a people, we as religions, we as countries, we as the people, are to live and work in harmony, we need to get past hurting one another and reach out to one another with a helping hand. Possibly then we will then be ready to reach out in a loving manner to our neighbors whom come and visit from distant stars.

It cannot be a one way street where they help us without our making the effort to help them. Nor can it be a one way street where we help them all the time without their helping us. It will not work if we greet our *neighbors* with an armed assault team intent upon destroying them. Nor is the correct approach to get upon our knees and worship them as God's. What I am advocating as greeting them / interacting with them, in a slow manner using caution but without self serving or hostile intent.

★★★★

That our *neighbors had carefully arranged a peaceful setting for the meeting that evening was obvious to Dancing Wind!* This second meeting was the beginning of the opening of a dialogue. For it is in friendship with our *neighbors* that we can begin to explore common ground and interest.

It is within the realm of possibility that hundreds of my readers will also have these fire side visits; should they choose that path! It is possible that major advances on the cutting edge in science, space explorations, physics, chemistry, medicine, healing, geology, humanities, history, ecology, energy and cleaning up our environment of pollution will have its foundation in conversations around a campfire.

Imagine the possibilities if a doctor working on the cures for cancer could speak with a specialist that understood the causes and cures for cancer centuries before us! Imagine the solutions for environmental cleanup from cyanide leach dumps of abandoned mines in the western US; ecologists and environmental engineers could openly discuss the solutions with knowledgeable specialists who possessed the knowledge and were willing to share their understanding! It will be / no it must be / a free exchange of knowledge and it must benefit both our *neighbors* as well as ourselves. I am sure there are actions we can take to help our neighbors, just as there are actions they can take to help us. *So I have thrown out to you the reader the invitation that was extended to Dancing Wind and Molly O' Brian; one of friendship and mutual help---it is a concept as basic as fire—as basic as being friends with our neighbors.*

GOD knows what's in your Heart
GOD knows what's Right
There are times when GOD says: "Enough!"
And allows his Angels to set things Right

Flight Of The Angels

9/11 was a day few Americans will ever forget. Most Americans can tell you what they were doing when nineteen Moslem terrorists--eighteen from Saudi Arabia and one from Pakistan--hijacked four American passenger jets full of innocent men, women and children. The nineteen terrorists killed the pilots and took over the passenger jets, which they then flew into each of the twin towers of the World Trade Center in New York City. The terrorists slaughtered all the passengers on the jets and very nearly every person in the two skyscrapers. Then hijackers flew a third passenger jet into the five-sided Pentagon building, at Washington, DC. The fourth jet, possibly intended for the Capital Building in Washington, D.C. was deliberately crashed into a field in Pennsylvania when the passengers on the jet tried to regain control of the jet from the hijackers. On 9/11 the nineteen terrorists killed 2,775 people!

★★★★

She began tracking her trail on the eastern slope of the Rocky Mountains. These rugged mountains run north and south cross the heart of the land of the free. Dancing Wind began tracking the trail on a mountain named for the Cheyenne (this is the mountain with all the antennas visible on the top of the mountain), located west of Colorado Springs. Locals call these mountains the Front Range. She was moving through the reddish brown bark of the tall majestic Ponderosa Pine at the base of the mountain. As the trail she was tracking wound up the side of the rugged mountains, the Ponderosa Pine gave way to the darker gray bark of the smaller Colorado Blue Spruce trees. Small scrub oak grew along the trails and clearings. As she tracked to the west, she came to a beautiful canyon with numerous waterfalls. Here the water spirits played in the streams and waterfalls. Dancing Wind's Chesapeake Bay Retriever, Maggie, played in the streams with the water spirits and then ran over to Dancing Wind, where she shook off her thick red hair and splattered Dancing Wind with the cold water.

As she tracked the trail beside her Guardian Angel through the mountains, she encountered beautiful brownish gray 500 to 1,000 pound Elk in the higher elevations. She smiled when she saw small groups of Elk, wished them well, and continued tracking the trail in a westerly direction. She encountered reddish brown foxes and many small brown chipmunks with a white strip down the center of their back and tail. Dancing Wind had to keep Maggie close to her as she became excited seeing the little brown chipmunks and wanted to chase after them. This Dancing Wind would not allow.

As the teenage girl tracked the trail over the weeks, the trail moved to the west and a little north. She stopped at Woodland Park for a hot meal before crossing the Continental Divide as she continued tracking the trail west. To the north of Lake George she crossed the South Platt River as she moved through the Pike National Forest. It took several days to cross the mountains by Wilkerson Pass.

As Dancing Wind moved west she came out of the mountains into a vast, gently rolling grassland. Here the walking was much easier. Occasionally she would stop and watch the Hawks hunting mice in the grass. Sometimes the horses she encountered would keep an eye on the teenage girl with the red dog to ensure they were not up to any mischief. When she encountered grazing elk, they too would keep an eye on the teenage girl with the dog, but since she did not carry a rifle and did not approach the elk, they continued grazing on the grassy meadows. As she crossed a second fork of the South Platte River, Maggie and Dancing Wind spotted a flock of ducks feeding along the river banks. When Maggie saw the ducks she barked excitedly and the flock of ducks quickly took flight. South of the old placer gold mining town of Fairplay, she moved into the mountains, crossing them at Weston Pass. Then she and Maggie crossed the Arkansas River and highway 24, which is the north / south highway. Then they again started climbing in elevation as they moved into the mountains to the west of the highway.

As Dancing Wind tracked the trail over many weeks, the trail she followed with her Angel moved to the west. She crossed mountains, valleys, grass lands and rivers as she tracked the trail with her Guardian Angel and her dog Maggie. Often, her path was blocked by snow drifts as the trail she tracked climbed higher into the Aspen and Blue Spruce trees at ten and eleven thousand feet. In her backpack she carried a map, matches, magnesium fire starter, first aid kit, global positioning system (GPS), spare batteries for the GPS, water, two sandwiches, a couple pieces of fruit and her Glock 9mm with a spare magazine holding 10 extra bullets. Sometimes a teenage girl in the wilderness needs a little extra protection, which a Glock provides!

As Dancing Wind tracked the trails, she was accompanied by an Angel. Sometimes they talked as they walked. Sometimes the Angel walked ahead and looked for a path that Dancing Wind could follow. Sometimes when the going got rough, the Angel would take out a spool of golden thread and lay it on the ground for Dancing Wind to follow. Sometimes the Angel would have Dancing Wind focus on an Eagle or Falcon in flight and shortly thereafter she would get to see the terrain from the prospective of the bird in flight looking down at the ground from above. This helped Dancing Wind see the terrain from above so she could pick the easiest path to travel.

Actually, the Angel was simply showing Dancing Wind different ways of following a trail. When they stopped tracking at the end of the day they would remember where they had stopped so that come the next weekend they could continue following the trail, beginning where they had left off. This was the longest trail she had ever tracked and it was running into months as she and her Guardian Angel tracked the trail further and further west.

Angels know as one tracks a trail one begins to learn about the individuals one is following. If one isfollowing or tracking outlaws, one will learn where they camp, probably pick up on the number of outlaws you are following, and it is even possible to pick up on the manner of how they do robberies and even their method of killing the individuals they rob and murder. If one were tracking a century old trail of a man of dignity and honor like the Spaniard Arturio, before long, his dignity, honor, and loyalty would become apparent to the tracker. Certainly, as Dancing Wind had tracked Arturio's trail through the mountains of northern New Mexico, she could easily recognize the campsites as well as the character of the man she tracked, even though Arturio had been murdered by a band of assassins over a century before she was born! And so it was as she followed this trail to the west that she noticed some discrepancies to the trails she normally selected to track. As her Guardian Angel knew, Dancing Wind would not have normally selected a trail less than a century old to follow. This trail was less than a dozen years old; but as she was clearly on the right trail she continued westward, trusting her Angel's guidance.

Dancing Wind liked to make an early start and she often dragged herself out the door at four in the morning when the night air was still freezing and it was hours before dawn's sunrise. Long before sunrise she was out on the highway, driving to the last point of the trail she had tracked. She would find a location to safely park her Jeep and put on her backpack and continue following her trail as the sun rose to begin a new day. Often she tracked until dark. It was not unusual for Dancing Wind to return completely exhausted from her day's adventure at ten or eleven at night. When you love what they do, your day passes very quickly, for literally time flies.

This was the most unusual trail that Dancing Wind had ever tracked. Dan was a wise old Lakota medicine man who had spent years teaching Dancing Wind the basic fundamentals of how to track both animals and man. Dan repeatedly told Dancing Wind that " *There is no trail you will track that you were not supposed to track"* Certainly, her tracking teacher never envisioned her tracking a trail into a high-risk situation or her teacher would have accompanied her to ensure her safety. Yet make no mistake: *When your Angel guides you on a trail, the Angel intends to help you with a lesson you need to learn or for the highest good to occur.*

As she moved through the Twin Lakes area, her trail led into a beautiful little mountain valley with tall, lush, green grass. It was surrounded by green forested mountains that were covered in the tall blue green Colorado Blue Spruce and Aspens which were just beginning to develop the small green leaves. Dancing Wind and Maggie descended down into the beautiful lush green valley following the trail she had tracked over the past three months.

At last, Dancing Wind realized that the trail she had tracked for months would end in the mountain valley below. She descended the steep mountain slopes. The barbed wire fence she encountered was simply crawled under in the ravine, where rain water had eroded a large hole under the fence. The further she descended into the valley, though, the more cautious she became. She could not put her finger on anything out of place but she leashed her dog and held her in close. She began speaking in whispers to her dog instead of her normal tone of voice. The closer she got to the end of the trail, the more cautious she became. Instead of just her normal upright walking, she bent her knees and waist to keep her body close to the ground. No longer would she walk out in the open. Her path, though longer, kept her in the forest. She became careful not to skyline herself. She often scanned the surroundings and she carefully looked for the dry washes and low ground to move through. When she stopped to scan the terrain about her, she always stayed close to a small spruce tree which would hide her from the view of any watching eyes. Dancing Wind removed her Glock from the back pack and belted it around her waist.

Dancing Wind took photos and GPS readings on two sites, for she was astonished at what she had found. There were jagged red and black auroras emanated upward from the ground in two locations. The heavy-duty improved road ran to each location, from which the red and black lines streamed up from the ground. These jagged red and black lines, through much smaller, came out on the ground along a two thousand, five hundred foot straight stretch of flat, heavy-duty, improved road in the center of the valley well clear of the trees. Black and red lines also streamed out menacingly from the old farm house. Clearly this was not a place Dancing Wind wanted to be! She knew the tracks did not lie and she realized the peaceful valley up in the high mountains was an illusion both GOD's Angels and now she, too, saw through, for the trail she had tracked with the Angels led into the al-Qaida complex, literally a Terrorist's supply base, operational center, and arsenal!

The Wind Spirits and the Rain Spirits came and told the young tracker that she must leave now! Repeatedly they told her she must move quickly up the mountain slopes to her vehicle and leave the mountains quickly. She pressed hard to return to her vehicle through the thin mountain air. She had a very hard time climbing the rugged mountain slopes. Dancing Wind was so tired that if an Angel hit her with a feather she would have been knocked to the ground. She was just so completely exhausted in the thin mountain air. Many times, she asked the Angels the best path to travel as she exhaustedly climbed the mountain with all the speed she could manage. She never stopped her climb, except to drink water or ask the Angels for direction. Many times the Wind Spirits and Rain Spirits came down beside her to encourage her and to implore her to move faster.

At last, her Jeep was reached where she had hidden it: out of sight in a grove of Spruce and Aspen trees. She did not go straight to her Jeep, but carefully circled the grove of trees, checking for signs or tracks that any intruders had approached her Jeep. When she was satisfied it was safe to enter her vehicle, she did so quickly and then she drove out of the rugged mountains as fast as possible.

She must give a warning! But who would believe her? Dancing Wind knew that neither the Alcohol Tobacco and Firearms nor the Federal Bureau of Investigation (FBI) had any competent men that she had personally encountered. The F.B.I. supervisors had blocked the F.B.I. agent who had tried to get a court order to examine the lap top computer of one of the 9/11 al-Qaida terrorists prior to the attack on the World Trade Center. When the dust settled and the buildings were completely destroyed by the terrorists attack, the F.B.I. supervisors who had blocked the competent agent from getting the search warrant were promoted and got pay raises. The F.B.I. agent who had done her best and failed to prevent the attack was *not* promoted over her incompetent supervisors. There was just utterly no chance that all that they would believe the stories of a teenage girl that the peaceful and serene mountain valley was an illusion. She could think of no one to tell except another more experienced tracker. As soon as Dancing Wind got home, she placed a phone call to Fort Benning, Georgia.

★★★★

The terrorists had positioned their weapons armories and support base in the remote valley in the Rocky Mountains of America's heart land. Oh, how stupid were the Americans; even after 9/11 they were so gullible. They would never suspect the next major terrorists attack would originate in their own back yard! The foolish Americans would never think to look for the largest terrorist operation in United States history in America's Rocky Mountains! These terrorists, supplied with unlimited funds, had been able to buy the state of the art weapons systems only available on the world-wide black market. Since they had access to many millions of dollars to purchase the very best, it should be no surprise that they had weapon systems capable of engaging multiple advanced jet fighters as well as armored vehicles on the ground, or destroying passenger jets and even trains transporting passengers and cargo across the country. Within two hours of launching a surprise attack upon the target or targets of their choice, they could be hitting and destroying multiple sites throughout the United States. Within the first twenty four hours they could easily destroy forty trains, passenger planes, buildings, factories, oil and gas refineries, power plants, hydroelectric power plants, dams and any fighter planes sent to try and stop them. If the Americans thought 9/11 was unforgettable, this planned attack would cause fear and panic previously unknown to their sheltered culture!

★★★★

The Lieutenant Colonel took the call during the officer's staff meeting he was attending. He had never expected that his niece would ever use the number he had given her two years previous. This call from her came from out of the blue; it was a complete surprise. On a note pad he wrote down six words: Terrorists, Command and Control, Armories (which he circled) and Runway, followed by the notation 'N' and a six-digit number. Following this, he had another notation: 'W' and a seven-digit number. The note stayed in plain view of everyone on the table, but the meeting continued where the men had left off before being interrupted.

When the meeting was completed, the Lieutenant Colonel asked a Sergeant Major who specialized in Satellite Interpretation to look at this site, off the record, and to let him know if this was reasonable or probable. Then the Lieutenant Colonel handed the Sergeant Major the note he wrote. Glancing down at the note, the Sergeant Major's biggest surprise was not what he was asked to look for-- that did not surprise him at all--but *where he was asked to look astonished him.*

So the Sergeant Major went to the Satellite Reconnaissance Center and brought up ten images of the site in the Colorado Rocky Mountains. He often used his skill in the interpretation of satellite data to find command and control centers, armories and run ways for aircraft to take off and land. He could tell you more about the military capability of many European and Middle Eastern countries than the president of the particular country was aware of. The Sergeant Major made it his duty to know what was going on militarily where American Forces might possibly be sent into combat.

First, he viewed the satellites images in color looking for structures which could be used for command and control. He studied the images for possible aircraft runways, then he looked for possible armories, vehicles present and their location to the terrain, firing ranges, defensive positions or emplacements, and possible air defenses. Finally, he examined the site for incongruities—something out of place, things which did not belong. He looked for what simply did not fit. Often it was his hunches which provided him with the manner or ideas on how he investigated a site.

What he had before him was simply a typical rural farm house. The farm had not been maintained, and certainly generated no money from crops, as there was no evidence of agriculture activity. This was typical of many farms or ranches throughout the United States. They were no longer profitable so they were sold to bankers, stockbrokers, attorneys and doctors. People with money or developers often bought up tracks of land like this and developed them into tracks of housing or vacation home sites. Certainly the only two incongruities he observed was the hundred foot high short wave antenna and the well- maintained driveway, since the old farm house was in general disrepair. Clearly, the owners put a high priority on maintaining the road or driveway to the house and throughout the property. This driveway had clearly been highly maintained and had a 2,500 foot straight, perfectly flat run. In addition, the trees were hundreds of feet back from the driveway. At both ends of the straight run of the driveway were long clear meadows. The Sergeant Major knew there were a number of aircraft which could easily take off and land from this old farm or ranch. Yet the Sergeant Major did not need to guess what type of aircraft were using the runway, as he immediately saw four Russian SM-92 Finist aircraft.

The next satellite photo the Sergeant Major examined was in infrared of the same ranch. The same improved driveway appeared, as well as the same old farm house. But what also appeared were two large and two small squares on each end of his runway where nothing was visible to the human eye. These large squares appeared eight feet wide and forty feet long and were exactly two thousand five hundred feet apart and were fifty feet back from the driveway or runway. Thirty

272 | Flight of the Angels

feet away from the large squares were two smaller eight by twelve foot rectangles. Beside these structures, the infrared satellite photos showed him that even though the area was covered in grass, that heavy traffic had occurred in the past between the runway and the underground structures. The Sergeant Major was convinced there were two large and two small, concealed, underground structures at both ends of the runways. In addition, it appeared that aircraft had been taxing up to the location of the underground structures. The Sergeant Major was experienced enough to easily distinguish between the tracks of trucks and aircraft. Aircraft were using both ends of his runway…and there were four SM-92 Finist high wing aircraft parked at one end of the runway! The hair on the back of the Sergeant Major's neck rose up.

The Finist aircraft might be mistaken for a Cessna from a distance; but unlike the Cessna the Finist could be ordered from the factory equipped with two machine guns, with rocket launchers installed on the wind pylons and with the capability designed into the aircraft of conducting bombing runs.

The Finist is a high performance Short Take Off & Landing (STOL) aircraft. Their military capability included attack functions as well as inserting Special Forces teams into remote or mountainous terrain. But what disturbed the Sergeant Major even more were some circular halos he could distinguish in the wind blown grass. He had seen those before! Well, he would ask TARSP about those as soon as he got the authorization papers signed.

Next came examinations of the site in false color composite. This was followed by the examinations for gravitational anomalies. While the U.S. Navy often used this analysis to locate enemy subs because of their mass he could use this data to help in his interpretation of exactly what was located at the site and if the density exceeded the back ground mass of the native soil and rock.

The Sergeant Major then conducted examinations for metals. A hydrocarbon exam followed; as he suspected, the smaller squares located at the opposite ends of the runways screamed out when checked for hydrocarbons. The smaller squares were fuel dumps! Then a Ground Penetrating Radar analysis followed. From this he could tell that all four structures were encased in steel.

Examinations followed for radioactivity; for if there were a nuclear weapon on the site, he absolutely wanted to know about it so he could properly assess the risk this site posed to the national security of the United States. Next he began a series of thermal imaging scans. These would tell him if the above-ground structures as well as the underground structures were emitting heat. Thermal imaging scans would also show him every source emitting heat from a vehicle or aircraft as well, as the number of individuals in the structures and their location. The thermal analysis went into such depth that it would include the number of individuals outside in the surrounding forest as well as those inside the structures who might be sleeping or even taking a shower. The examination progressed throughout the day.

Looking up at the wall clock and seeing the time, the Sergeant Major stopped his work, as he needed to catch the Lieutenant Colonel before he left for the day.

The Sergeant Major entered the Lieutenant Colonel's office and said to the Colonel, "I need your John Hancock on four documents. If you want I can keep this off the books for now; but awfully quick this site and the actions we must take to protect the national security of the United States will come to a head. We might as well take care of the paperwork and the authorizations I require to properly analyze this site now.

"The first document is your assignment of the priority and code name of the target. The second is your authorization for me to allocate the manpower I feel is appropriate to this site of yours. The third is your acknowledgement that I am going to need three to five hours of computer time on this site from the satellite reconnaissance archives. The last is your authorization to assign this site on to the Tactical Analysis Reconnaissance Satellite Program and I will insert it into five lap top computers so a window will pop up when any live time activity occurs at the site. Naturally none of the computers will leave the Command and Control Center."

★★★★

The Tactical Analysis Reconnaissance Satellite Program (TARSP) was a product of the computer age. The TARSP allowed any one with the proper access codes to utilize all the satellite intelligence available to make informed decisions about anything you can conceive of. A United States fast-attack submarine could get instant live-time intelligence on the location, size, speed, compass course, and weapons armaments of every ship within a thousand miles of his position. If, at Cheyenne Mountain, the defense department wanted to know the position of every MIG 31fighter Strategic Bomber, or SU-24 Fencer in the Soviet Union the TARSP allowed the instantaneous transfer of data to the proper military authorities. Should the United States Strategic Air Command (SAC) want to know the speed, direction, and offensive capability of a Russian MIG 31, the officers at the SAC could obtain this from TARSP. Yet over the years this program had been constantly upgraded, resulting in improvements unimaginable by most people. For example, a TARSP can immediately give SAC the number and location of missile silos in the Soviet Union which have their missile silo doors sealed,, or if the doors are being opened to fire a missile. As the Silo doors open, this data is available to be instantly seen through a pop up window on the computer screen due to TARSP.

The complete tactical value in a crisis or war is beyond most individuals' imaginations, as TARSP can give live-time movement of any recognized weapon system. It does not concern us seriously if the Russians or the Ukrainian Army has a hundred tanks parked in a military base, but should dozens of tanks or hundreds of soldiers start moving then this would concern us enough to examine what they are doing. Should a nuclear warship leave port, TARSP can track the ship--and if the ship should use its onboard weapon systems, we can identify the weapon system deployed, as well as its intended target. TARSP can even identify when a nation's navy, air force, or army have prepositioned their military forces to engage in overt hostile actions.

When Iran loaded the cargo ship *Karine-A* with eighty crates of weapons at Qeshm Island (2002) and sailed for the Suez Canal on its way to deliver its cargo to the Palestine Liberation Organization in Gaza, TARSP notified the Pentagon what was occurring. The fifty tons of advanced weaponry could have easily changed the balance of power in the region. It was TARSP which told the United States Defense Department about the shipment of weapons. The president of the United States in turn notified Israel, which intercepted the ship load of weapons. The net result because of TARSP was that the fifty tons of advanced weapons Iran gave to the Palestine Liberation Organization (PLO) to attack Israel were instead delivered as a gift to Israel.

When, in 2006, Iran fired off dozens of their Shahab missiles to demonstrate their military might to the world, their actions strengthened the United States offensive capability by allowing us to update the TARSP data on all their missile systems. TARSP data includes the range, speed, payload it can carry, as well as types of payload, electromagnetic emissions sent to, or emitted from, the specific missile, as well as the precursors observed prior to the missile launch and types of guidance systems and their electromagnetic emissions.

TARSP can also tell you if a dozen men walking through the hills of Afghanistan are carrying rifles or they are unarmed. If you are a naval officer on a U.S. warship and you want to know the location of the closest French Warships or Iranian Warships and their offensive weapons, you simply type in your question and ask TARSP. If you want to be instantly notified when a specific Iranian warship leaves port or when any Iranian ship is leaving port, simply tell TARSP what you want and you will be instantly notified! So when the Sergeant Major was getting permission to utilize TARSP to analyze a site in the Colorado Rocky Mountains, he was very serious about bringing extremely intense scrutiny and analysis of the site.

★★★★

Georgia is the home of some of the most highly trained and experienced combat soldiers in the world. One of these highly trained and experienced combat units in the United States are the Army Rangers. These Rangers have fought in the Vietnam War to the Iraqi war, and even today; many experts say they are literally among the "Best of the Best" of the men and women the United States has to protect our country against terrorists. Several times a year these men are deployed to protect American interest, save American lives, or deployed against terrorists.

In addition to the Special Forces units, there is also the Army 160th Special Operations Aircraft (AOS), found at Fort Benning. The AOS are not just a regular group of pilots / fliers, but some of the most highly experienced combat pilots in the world. They specialize in supporting the United States Special Forces, getting them into and out of the combat hot spots throughout the world. Should the President of the United States authorize an assault against terrorists; the pilots of the 160th Army Special Operations will very likely be taking our

Special Forces into combat, supporting them on the ground with combat supplies, fire support, or extracting them when the mission is completed.

★★★★

Meanwhile, at Fort Benning, Georgia a group of young men sat at a conference table listening to the instructions outlined by their Operational Commanding Officer. They were working on scheduling on their lap top computers, time tables, resources at their disposal, allocation of their resources (assets) to the situation at hand. Some of the problems they were working through were the effect of the elevation on the helicopter payload, electrical, or phone lines which could entangle the helicopters rotors.

They considered the maximum elevation that a fully-armed Black Hawk helicopters could hover / lift off the ground. The flight time that the helicopters could remain to provide air support before their fuel ran low. The degree of moonlight, and how it would affect their operation. For literally the blacker the night, the bigger tactical advantage they held during an assault. For these men wanted the element of surprise. They were not going there to fight fair; they were going there to win the battle.

They also wanted the maximum number of al-Qaida in the camp. They had to figure the flight time to refuel and rearm the helicopters should the battle turn against them. They needed to have a combat surgeon available or on call to treat any wounded men. They needed to estimate the best defender fire positions and how they would deal with (assault) that position. They wanted to hold the high ground with snipers to ensure their men on the ground and their helicopters did not come under heavy enemy fire. They had to work out the location of the enemy armories and how to prevent any al-Qaida from gaining immediate access to the weapon systems inside the armory.

They had to work out the details of how they would breach the armories to gain entry. Once they had secured the site, they had to move quickly into a plan to empty the armories of the tons of weaponry. Later on, other intelligence experts would study these weapons to gather further intelligence about the weapons operational systems and capability.

These U.S. Army Rangers were war gaming a tactical assault into America's heart land! On the conference room wall was a large computer screen showing a large satellite blow up of the Colorado Rocky Mountains so several different attack plans could be laid out in detail on the computer screen. They were working out the best plan to safely and rapidly secure the targets they would assault as different plans of attack were proposed. Paths of entry for the helicopters were carefully considered. This computer image of the site west of Highway 24 by Twin Lakes was so detailed one could easily identify individual trees - - even the type of tree! Certainly it was not the trees they were interested in—they were going into combat. They were planning this tactical assault in the most professional manner they were capable of. For these men would soon be hitting a terrorists command, supply and armories in the most devastating silent tactical assault they were capable of! They were using every bit of all their training, experience and skill to plan a totally silent tactical assault that they would carry out!

If everything went like clockwork, not a missile would be fired; not a single 20 mm M61 Vulcan cannon capable of firing 6,000 rounds a minute aboard the helicopters would have to engage the enemy. But the cannons and missiles would be there on site should the Operational Commander order them to engage the enemy! Never would he allow the al-Qaida to get a single aircraft airborne. The Operational Commander emphasized to all his men that he required complete silence, for a total surprise, so not a shot would be heard!

They laid out the fields of fire, the tactical targets they must secure, and the sequence of their attack. Moonlight was considered. The terrain offered cover, should cover be needed from effective live fire. They were to secure the targets, both visible to the human eye, and more importantly, the sites not visible to human eyes, that the strategic national defense satellites had pinpointed! Over a thousand pieces of data were considered as the Airborne Rangers planned the tactical assault. The Operational Commanding Officer then took a look at each of two dozen plans and incorporated the elements from each plan that he liked best into the final Tactical Operational Plan. This was then taken by him to Washington, D.C. to get the authorization required for him to engage the terrorists and prevent the terrorists attack.

★★★★

In a five-sided building located near the Potomac River a meeting was going on with the "Combat Applications Group" concerning a Tactical Operation Plan. There were eleven men in the room; some held the rank of general or major general. It was within their power and ability to stop the next major al-Qaida attack upon the United States; or do nothing by referring the matter for further study and analysis. The U. S. Army officer laid out his case to preempt the Terrorist's attack upon the United States and hit the terrorists before they could launch their surprise attack. Once the terrorists were moving it would have been close to impossible to prevent the loss of many thousands of American lives.

When the ten officers listened to the officer's presentation, they knew that they had three decisions to make: they could authorize an assault, or not authorize the assault and refer the matter for further study and analysis (it is called passing the buck). In the latter case they did not want to know what happened, as they did not want to get involved in a risky career shattering operation. For at the very least should the operation fail, the repercussions would be the abrupt end of all their careers. The third decision required was whether this was the Operational / Commanding Officer they wanted their country to rely upon to do his utmost in stopping the terrorists.

Had it been possible for an outsider to look into one of the most secure conference rooms in the United States and read the thoughts of the men involved in protecting the people of the United States, they might have been surprised that not one man there was positioning himself for political advantage or to cover his ass. Everyone there realized the necessity of stopping the impending terrorists attack. It was vital to stop the terrorists prior to allowing al-Qaida to initiate their attack. For once the terrorists initiated the attacks they would be moving in aircraft at 150-300 miles per hour and stopping them would be nearly impossible.

Yet you might be surprised that the final decision actually rested not on the Operation Plan for the tactical assault, though they were all impressed with the Operational Plan for the Tactical Assault, as it clearly was well thought out. Nor did their decision rest on the repercussions if failure occurred. The real decision actually rested upon the officer making the presentation and who would lead the assault. To a man; to the men in comprising the "Combat Applications Group;" whose oath was "to protect and defend the United States against all enemies both foreign and domestic;" the decision to go or not to go came down to the military record of the officer giving the presentation and leading the attack.

The officer had many times put his life on the line, successfully protecting the United States in operations overseas. He projected that confidence and competence that the men who had the authority to authorize the operation against the terrorists needed to enable them to feel totally confident that he could quietly and effectively eliminate all the terrorists. The ten men in the "Combat Applications Group" granted the eleventh man's request: they approved his Operational Plan and gave him the authorization to proceed against al-Qaida.

★★★★

The snipers and spotters were dressed in camouflage clothing; their faces were blacked out as they left the black unmarked helicopters. They carried silenced weapons and full battle packs as they secured the high ground. For now they were observing the mountains and valleys near Twin Lakes. Anyone entering the target area below would not leave the al-Qaida operational center nor its armories alive unless the men on the high ground allowed them egress. For now they would just observe the valley and any activity. These men were prepositioned for what was to come.

★★★★

The four-man team was not dressed in black with camouflage on their face, but instead all four men wore nice business suits when they walked into the bank. They asked to see the bank president and were shown into his office. After introducing themselves, they produced a National Security Letter requesting to see all the financial records of a specific person. Once they obtained a copy of the bank records they then requested to be let into the bank vault. The bank manager accompanied them and watched. They opened one locked safety deposit box. They photographed its contents then returned everything intact back into the safety deposit box which was then relocked. The four men had obtained what they wanted.

★★★★

The four men entered the office building at 6 p.m., after everyone had left for the day. Two men dressed in business suits looked like attorneys as they casually talked about their last fishing trip. These two men were the lookouts. A second pair of lookouts were parked a block away in a black van monitoring electronic communication. Two additional vehicles were positioned several blocks away to assist if needed. Another two men, also dressed in nice suits and carrying computer cases, entered the office after picking the lock. One man promptly searched the office while the second man hooked his computer up to the office computers and promptly, deleted one security program. He then replaced the original deleted security program with one with the same name. This security program functioned slightly different than the original program. In every way it was like the original manufacturer's program, except it was designed to overlook one spyware program. Then the computer programmer installed another program which enabled him to monitor all computer activity. Finally, he downloaded all the material on the hard drives. When they finished, they left the office as neat as they had arrived, locking the door behind them. They had come to the office to steal all the computer files.

And steal them they did.

★★★★

The phones had been giving them problems all day so they called the phone company to send out a repair man to fix the lines. Unlike most phone repair men, these men came promptly, were courteous, and quickly fixed the problem. The customer was happy with the service he received. He might not have been so happy if he knew that he had never had any phone problems until it was created by the telephone repair men who had just fixed his phone service. When the repair men left the customer's office, they had emplaced four electronic bugs! Two were active and were subject to possible detection if the unsuspecting customer had known he needed to sweep his office for bugs. Two bugs were passive unless they were later activated by an electronic signal. The latter two bugs could not be detected had the office been swept for bugs.

★★★★

The men at Fort Benning, Georgia, were loading the eighteen wheel flat beds with front end loaders and a bull dozer. Then following an experienced routine, the construction equipment was chained down for the long trip ahead. After the highway traffic had thinned out late at night, the eighteen wheelers and five ton trucks moved out on the empty highways headed west towards the Rocky Mountains. They looked like any other construction crew in the United States moving heavy equipment from one job site to another, except for the men and women with loaded M16's rifles riding shotgun in the dark green hummers traveling alongside the trucks.

Their time table was broken when an eighteen wheeler jackknifed, blocking the highway west of Kansas City. All westbound traffic was stopped until the interstate could be cleared. For 45 minutes the convoy was held up until a sergeant drove his Hummer up to a Kansas Highway Patrol car.

The Sergeant told the State Police officer, "Get me your commanding officer. Now!"

Twelve minutes later, a second Highway Patrol car arrived and the Commanding Officer of the state police walked over to talk with the Sergeant standing by the Hummer.

When the two men were out of earshot of everyone around, the Sergeant told the Kansas Highway Patrol officer that he had a schedule to keep and he was already an hour behind.

He told the police officer, "You know what happened on 9/11. Well, you know we are just a typical army construction crew," as he removed a

M16 from his Hummer, "and you know we do not go armed," removing the magazine from his weapon, he showed the police officer it was fully loaded. "Well you have my word that the men under my command and I are going into combat. If we do not make our appointment with al-Qaida you will see it on TV like 9/11 all over again. And if we don't get your help it will happen all over again."

The police officer asked what the sergeant needed and he was told, "Close the east-bound highway until the next exit and give it to me, for my military convoy. We can cross the interstate here and at the next exit we can get back in the westbound lane. We have to make up one hour of time we have lost."

Two state police cars spun out in their haste to close the eastbound traffic. Minutes later the U.S. Army convoy pulled out running 65 mph heading west in the eastbound lanes of the interstate highway. At the next exit they crossed back over to the west bound lanes. One state police car stayed with them until they reached the Colorado state line. He kept the high speed passing lane clear for the United States Army convoy.

At the Colorado line the Highway patrol car pulled over on the shoulder of the interstate as the U.S. Army convoy sped by. One Hummer pulled over for a minute and the sergeant thanked the police officer for his help. The police officer handed him his business card. The sergeant stuck the card in his wallet and jumped into his Hummer and was gone in his haste to regain the convoy. Fort Carson, Colorado was the staging grounds where all the U. S. Army units would assemble in preparation, prior to moving against the terrorists.

★★★★

During the day men were double-checking the weapon loads on the helicopters. Mini-guns, which could fire thousands of rounds of effective fire down range at a target, were armed and loaded. Hell-fire missiles were placed aboard some of the helicopters. They were going hunting and they intended to go prepared! The attack force was packing there rucksacks for the night ahead. Every man could tell you where each item they carried was located in their packs. Later on they would be putting on their bullet proof vests and putting rounds in their silenced NP5Ns. The U. S. Army Rangers would be hunting al-Qaida terrorists!

At two in the morning, the eight specially-built silent helicopters dropped out of the night sky and began their final tactical assault—of the largest terrorists operation on U.S. soil—the attack was a complete surprise. The Operational Commander was the first man off the black unmarked helicopters that night. With a Heckler and Koch NP5N in his right hand, he led the assault. This commanding officer believed in leading by being in front of his men. He had a throat mic to direct the operation from the ground and on his back, over top his bullet proof vest, was a full battle pack. He had come to fight.

As it was a black, star-lit, cold, fall night as the tactical assault began, the Operational Commander was wearing the latest fourth generation night vision goggles as were all the Rangers. Rapidly, the soldiers left the Black Hawk helicopters to deploy as they had rehearsed in their dry runs so the actual attack would go flawlessly. Tonight they would not ask for quarter, nor would they give any. They were taking down the largest terror network on U. S. soil!

Eight Black Hawk helicopters carried out the assault. Six Helicopters came in over the mountain tops and descended into the valley below. Two helicopters were deployed to take out the al-Qaida command and control center. Another two helicopters were assigned to secure each of the weapon armories. The fifth Black Hawk helicopter deployed eight men to secure the four Sm-92 Finist aircraft. The sixth Black hawk helicopter deployed another eight men to secure the two Hind helicopter gunships. The seventh and eight Black Hawk helicopters did not descend into the valley; they circled high above and were held in reserve for any emergency which might arise.

As the first two helicopter skids touched ground, out jumped eight Rangers from each aircraft. The Operational Commander was the first man out, leading the way to the terrorist's Command and Control Center, as he led the first team. The second team of eight men secured the possible escape routes out of the al-Qaida Command and Control Center. They had to stay out of the free-fire zones of the men entering the building, but still be able to kill anyone going out the back door or the windows and trying to escape or reach the weapon armories. It took 120 seconds from the moment the helicopters skids touched ground until all eight men had positioned themselves in their preplanned firing positions. As soon as these men were in place they clicked their transmitters twice, as they did not want to speak a word which might possibly are overheard.

Upon hearing the two clicks, the Operation Commander took his eight-man team through the front entrance; room by room they cleared the Command and Control Center. They fought their way quickly, through the entire structure and out the back door. To ensure that they had terminated every terrorist with extreme prejudice they moved through the structure at a walk, firing their silenced 9 mm Heckler and Koch's NP5Ns. It took 120 seconds to clear the entire structure. Not a single terrorist escaped their Operational Base Camp that night! Not a single United States Airborne Ranger lost their life.

The third helicopter touched down sixty seconds after the Operational Commanders had touched down as the Black Hawks were coming in 30 seconds apart. The Operators secured the east armory in less than 60 seconds from the moment when they touched down. Eight men formed a circle with their weapons trained outward to ensure no one could approach or enter the concealed weapons armory.

The fourth helicopter secured the west weapons armory at the opposite end of the airstrip. The eight Rangers formed a circle around the concealed armory. They, too, had secured the second armory in 60 seconds.

The fifth Black Hawk secured the four SM-92 Finist aircraft. After landing beside the aircraft, the Rangers ran up to the aircraft. While one Ranger provided cover, the second Ranger looked inside to ensure no one was onboard the aircraft. Then they secured a protective circular perimeter around the aircraft with their weapons pointed outward to ensure no one gained access to the aircraft.

The sixth Black Hawk helicopter landed in close proximity to the two Hind gunships. Here, too, eight men deployed: two men first checked inside to ensure no one was aboard the helicopters then they set up a circular protective perimeter around the two Hind gunships as well.

The reserve force of the two remaining Black Hawks awaited any request for their assistance. Yet they were not needed as the battle had lasted only 240 seconds! No sound was heard except the tinkle of the spent 9mm shell casings falling on the ground.

The Rangers quickly secured the terrorist's site. With the arrival of the armed convoy of construction equipment and trucks, the task of removing the terrorist's equipment and supplies began. The construction equipment was quickly unloaded. The terrorist's armories were breached by bulldozers and front end loaders. The contents were removed and quickly loaded into five ton trucks. The signs of battle and the forced entry of the arsenals were removed. The heavy equipment was quickly loaded onto the eighteen wheelers again. As rapidly as the assault force of helicopters, aircraft, bull dozers, front end loaders, five ton cargo trucks and hummers had arrived, they disappeared just as quickly into the first light of dawn indicating the coming sunrise.

First, four U.S. Army Rangers did a preflight on the Finist Aircraft. Then the four Rangers entered the aircraft, firing up the engines. Beside two of the Rangers were their Guardian Angels, sitting on the seat to the pilot's right. The aircraft taxied out onto the runway; then the engine was brought up to full power, the brakes released, and the Airborne Rangers took flight. One after another, the Finist Aircraft roared down the runway and became airborne. But the difference one would see if you were to look closely is that two of the Rangers had an Angel as a copilot as they flew east. The second two Airborne Rangers flew in the airplane by themselves, as their Guardian Angel would have no part in getting into one of those silly flying machines, their Guardian Angels flew beside the aircraft!

Next, an army pilot from the Special Operations got aboard the Hind and fired up the engine. Beside him his Guardian Angel kicked up her feet, placing them on the instrument panel of the copilot's position. Then the Angel smiled at the pilot, as the Hind became airborne and turned to the East and gained altitude.

One by one the Black Hawk helicopters took off flying east. Many Angels flew beside the men and women that they watched over, but an equal number of Angels preferred to fly beside the Black Hawk helicopters that they were watching over that night. Two Black Hawk aircraft remained on the ground watching their Operational Commander as he walked to and boarded the Hind. For it was their belief, and it was correct, that their Operational Commander had never flown a Hind helicopter in his life. Beside the Commander, the Angel watched her charge with concern. For seven minutes he just looked at all the numerous instruments and gages in front of him. Then he fastened his seat belt. He tentatively reached for the starter and started up the jet engine. Slowly he applied power, the aircraft moved a few inches, and then he reduced power and set it back down firmly on the ground. Four times this was repeated before the operational commander noticed an Angel sitting in the copilot's seat out of the corner of his eye. Concern was showing all over the Angel's face.

The pilot told her: "Don't worry; one of us knows how to fly!"

The Angel in the copilot's seat had started to pray under her breath.

He heard the Angel say, as she cracked a smile, *"That is what I am afraid of. Only one of us knows how to fly, and I know you have never flown a Hind helicopter before!"*

He told her to say an extra prayer for him as he applied full power to the aircraft, it quickly gained altitude and he slowly turned the helicopter gunship to the east. Behind him, the two remaining Black Hawks also lifted off, following their Operational Commander into the dawning daybreak, leaving no trace of the battle which had occurred only five hours earlier!

★★★★

Had you been camping, up among the high mountain peaks of the Front Range that fall morning at day break; you might have witnessed the flight of helicopters and aircraft flying east along with the *Flight of the Angels* accompanying them. The Army Rangers whom had prevented what would have been the worst terrorists in America's history, were the men and women of- and working with the U. S. Army Rangers of Second Battalion; Seventy-fifth Infantry.

★★★★

There is a man in Kansas who was handed a unanimous letter from his wife when he got home from work. When he opened the letter he saw his business card. "Thank you for your help" was written on the back. His business card fell to the floor as the police officer picked up a spent 9 mm shell casing out of the envelope. It was from a Heckler and Kotch MP40. The police officer sat down on his couch and cried.

"Honey, what is wrong?" his wife asked.

He told her, "Nothing is wrong now; it turned out ok. It turned out ok."

As the man cried, he prayed to GOD and told Him, "Thank you for your help."

★★★★

LEST YOU FORGET, PRAYERS ALWAYS HELP. GOD ALWAYS HEARS YOUR PRAYERS.

Sometimes one sees an individual wearing a cross; they often wear one to remind them of God and hold him close to their thoughts. Sometimes an individual might wear a spent bullet or a bullet shell casing; lest you fail to understand, that is their way of wearing a cross and holding GOD close to their heart. The object they wear may be their way of thanking GOD for the miracles in their life. Have you prayed to GOD and thanked Him for the small miracles in your life, like your good health or the car accident you narrowly avoided? Maybe you might want to thank GOD for stopping a terrorist attack and saving thousands of American lives!

★★★★

There is a quiet peaceful valley in the Rocky Mountains; it is near Twin Lakes off to the west of highway 24. It is surrounded by beautiful Ponderosa Pine, Colorado Blue Spruce, and in the fall, at the higher elevations, there are elk eating the tall grass under the golden Quaking Aspen trees. The Wind Spirits are there. The Rain Spirits often come to visit, as well. In winter, the Snow Pixies cover the mountains in beautiful white snow.

Should a tracker back-track this trail, they might see the officer in the five-sided building ordering the military spy satellites to track and analyze the targets in the valley by Twin Lakes. They might also catch the meeting of eleven men in the conference room in a five-sided building near Washington, DC. They would see the placing of wiretaps. Then came the "Black Bag" jobs to copy the hard drives of the terrorist's computers and the covert entry into the locked files and concealed wall safes and safety deposit boxes. 'Round the clock surveillance of the terrorists began and would continue until the terrorists operation would be rolled up upon the authorization, via an executive order of the President of the United States.

There were three generals who put their careers and their reputations on the line to give their approval to the Tactical Operation Plan written at Fort Benning and whom sanctioned this operation. While there are twenty-two state and federal law enforcement agencies which had jurisdiction in this case who were involved in protecting and overseeing the security of the United States, only eleven men in that five-sided building, the President of the United States and the U.S. Army Rangers, would even know what would unfold and they were not intending to share any of their secrets with the other twenty one blissfully unaware organizations!

Before the arrival of the Special Forces on the high mountain peaks; before the eight helicopters came out of the night sky; before the arrival of our Rangers which breached the terrorist's compound; before the entrance of the U.S. Army military Hummers, five ton trucks, and construction equipment; before the largest tactical assault on a terrorist base on US soil; even before all the military activity occurred, and before the terrorists were terminated with "extreme prejudice" upon the orders of President Bush, if a tracker looked carefully they might see the tracks of a Chesapeake Bay Retriever and the small tracks of a teenage girl. The teenage girl, Dancing Wind, is Arapaho; she was born on 9/11/86.

★★★★

At Fort Benning, Georgia, a Lieutenant Colonel was holding a staff meeting. Beside him was a Sergeant Major. Every man sitting at the desk was looking at the eight typed pages of inventory, which had suddenly come to be in the possession of the Rangers of the Second Battalion, seventy-fifth Infantry. The only incongruity the Sergeant Major observed as he looked around the room was the Operational Commander was missing his 1974 Special Unit Award of the Second Battalion, seventy-fifth infantry for bravery.

★★★★

Epilogue

Seasons have passed, and in reflecting upon the trail I, Dancing Wind, tracked through the Rocky Mountains, I will say this: One could say the President of the United States —for he is the Commander in Chief of the Armed Forces--did it right. The ten men who gave the eleventh man permission to engage the terrorists prior to the terrorists' attacks upon the people of our country saved our country from tremendous grief and human fatalities. The eight pilots of the Black Hawk helicopters did an excellent job. The members of the United States Army Rangers enable us to feel safe and sleep at night—even when they don't. We should be proud of them. One could thank an Arapaho girl for setting it all into motion.

Or have I really failed in my analysis?

Have I really overlooked what actually went down that night?

When I look back upon my Life Lessons, I talk about Dignity, Honor, Integrity, Loyalty, and Trust. Did not everyone rise up to the highest standards man and woman can strive to attain? Certainly, you should be proud of the men and women protecting the United States. You should be very proud of the man who led the attack and stopped these terrorists and thank GOD we have men of his caliber protecting our country. As I view it, these terrorists had No Dignity, No Honor,

nor any sense of Integrity; they had just come here to do "not very nice things" to whomever they chose to hurt. And so through a long and round-about chain of events, or you might call them "coincidences," the Angels were able to prevent the not-very-nice people from hurting a lot of innocent people.

Yet, as I reflect back upon my life lessons, there was one lesson I did not mention: Karma! Here, too, Karma came into play. Some not-very-nice men planned to hurt us very badly; many times more severe than the 9/11 attack. But instead of hurting us, as they had carefully planned, they got what was planned for us. Like the saying in the Bible, they literally reaped what they sowed.

Some may think it impossible for a teenage Arapaho girl to track a trail as I have described. Some people don't believe in Angels. But maybe our vision is too limited, for it has crossed my mind and my thoughts that maybe the Angels have been with us all the time from the inception of the idea of the tracking of the trail, which led into the terrorist's encampment, to accompanying me (Dancing Wind) on my escape through the mountains. I feel that the Angels rode the helicopters into the terrorist camp that night when not a single American soldier lost their life. I even think it is possible that Angels were working, doing their very best, when a little Arapaho girl was born on 9/11. And should you have any doubts if the story is as true and as accurate as the Angels will allow me to tell it, in my jacket pocket, over my heart, I carry my Medal of Bravery, given to me by the Operation Commander who led the tactical assault.

SUA-Special Unit Award - - - SPONTE- (Latin) Of Ones Free Will

I have done my best to accurately describe what occurred; but if you are to believe my story, you would have to believe in Angels. Certainly I do, or the Angel sitting to my right might hit me with one of her feathers and knock me on my a _ _! If I can make of you one request: as you go to bed, take the time to thank GOD for the Guardian Angels interacting in our lives. They are truly a blessing from GOD. Have you thanked your Guardian Angel recently for all the guidance and help you have been receiving?

-- Dancing Wind

www.ingramcontent.com/pod-product-compliance
Lightning Source LLC
Chambersburg PA
CBHW060250100426
42742CB00011B/1702